DROPS OF INCLUSIVITY

SUNY series, Afro-Latinx Futures
———————
Vanessa K. Valdés, editor

DROPS OF INCLUSIVITY

RACIAL FORMATIONS AND MEANINGS IN PUERTO RICAN SOCIETY, 1898–1965

MILAGROS DENIS-ROSARIO

Cover: *De la Central a Loíza* by Ramón Bulerín, mixed media, 2020

Published by State University of New York Press, Albany

For information, contact State University of New York Press, Albany, NY
www.sunypress.edu

Library of Congress Cataloging-in-Publication Data

Name: Denis-Rosario, Milagros, author.
Title: Drops of inclusivity : racial formations and meanings in Puerto Rican society,
  1898–1965 / Milagros Denis-Rosario.
Description: Albany : State University of New York Press, [2022] | Series:
  SUNY series, Afro-Latinx Futures | Includes bibliographical references and index.
Identifiers: ISBN 9781438488691 (hardcover : alk. paper) | ISBN 9781438488707
  (ebook) | ISBN 9781438488684 (pbk. : alk. paper)
Further information is available at the Library of Congress.

10 9 8 7 6 5 4 3 2 1

For El-Shaddai, the God Almighty.

∼

*For my niece Camila and her son Nicolás,
and my nephew Félix Juan.*

Contents

List of Illustrations   ix

Acknowledgments   xi

Introduction: The Illusion of Living in a Non-Racist Racist Society   1

Chapter 1   A Revised Account of the New "Colored" Possession: 1898–1920   15

Chapter 2   Reshaping Education, Race, and Citizenship: 1920–1930   39

Chapter 3   The Twisted Evolution of National Identity: 1930–1940   57

Chapter 4   Intersecting Race and Modernization: 1940–1950   83

Chapter 5   Strategizing Modernity: 1950–1965   97

Chapter 6   The Liga Opened Pandora's "Black" Box: 1950–1965   125

Epilogue: Drop by Drop   147

Appendixes   151

Notes   157

Bibliography   193

Index   217

Illustrations

Table I.1   Selected Figures from the U.S. Census of Puerto Rico,
            1899–2010   12

Figure 3.1 Former logo of Partido Popular Democrático (PPD)   78

Figure 5.1 The Puerto Rican singer Ruth Fernández on stage
            at the Caborrojeño Social Club in New York City,
            October 17, 1956.   101

Figure 5.2 "Escudo del ICP" (Emblem of the Institute of
            Puerto Rican Culture.) Lorenzo Homar. 1955,
            linoleum.   110

Figure 5.3 Cecilia Orta's art consultant business logo from a
            piece of her stationary.   111

Figure 5.4 Letter from Cecilia Orta to Luis Muñoz Marín,
            August 2, 1964.   117

Acknowledgments

I want to thank my God, the Almighty, Protector, and Deliverer, for giving me focus, motivation, and physical and spiritual strength while writing this book. This journey was not an easy one. Without Him, this book project would not have become a reality. The original idea for the manuscript was part of my doctoral thesis, which underwent many revisions. I am indebted to my dissertation committee members at Howard University: Dr. Selwyn H.H. Carrington (RIP), Dr. Franklin W. Knight, Dr. Vincent C. Peloso, and Dr. Jeanne M. Toungara. All of them were very supportive and encouraged me to continue to explore my topic. I am also very grateful to the then Chairs of the History Department, Dr. Ibrahim K. Sundiata and Dr. Emory Tolbert. It was there at Howard that I met Elaine Viterose Vanhuis. Her friendship and optimism were pivotal during those years.

This book would not be possible without the constant support of Dr. Rebecca Colesworthy, the SUNY Press acquisition editor, and Dr. Vanessa Valdés, the editor of the series Afro-Latinx Futures. They have been incredibly patient and encouraging. They identified the right reviewers, to whom I am grateful for their constructive feedback. Thanks to the developmental editor, Kirstin Fritz, who proposed a more dynamic format for the book that would connect the title and topics while introducing the stories of the Afro-Puerto Ricans featured as examples of "drops of inclusivity."

The book's cover is a mixed-media piece titled *De La Central a Loíza* by the Afro-Puerto Rican artist Ramón Bulerín. When I shared the theme of my book with the artist, he sent me several images of his recent pieces. I was captivated by the *De la Central a Loíza*. The work depicts the known and unknown people in transit from his hometown of Canóvanas to the town of Loíza. Canóvanas was the site of the sugar mill, Central Canóvanas/Loiza, which operated from 1880 until 1965. In 1910,

Canóvanas separated from Loíza and was recognized as a municipality in 1970. The dynamics of race, class, gender, and political power are part of the municipality and Central Canóvanas' history.

Canóvanas calls itself the "Indian municipality" because it was part of a Taino *cacicato* or chiefdom. However, its history illustrates a constant tension among Spanish, Black, and indigenous identity. During the Fiestas de Loíza, people from Canóvanas made a pilgrimage from a town that was gradually distancing itself from its African identity to another, Loíza, which represented blackness and Africanness. Loíza is considered a quintessential Afro-Puerto Rican town. For me, *De la Central a Loíza* connects deeply with the arguments in this book, which counters the mainstream efforts to silence and exclude people of African ancestry by telling the stories of individuals and towns to ensure that the reality of their experiences cannot be erased. The faces in this art piece could represent the men and women I refer to in my book and the many other Afro-Puerto Ricans whose lives and stories need to be rescued in future projects.

I am also indebted to my parents, Juan and Alejandrina, who are resting with the Lord. I recognize them for bringing me to this world. Despite their difficult circumstances, my parents managed to raise a family of three children (two girls and a boy) during the mid-1960s and 1970s. To take care of my sister Yvonne, my brother Juan, and me while they were working, my parents relied on immediate and extended family, including my maternal grandmother Doña Fela and aunt Titi Camby. That Afro-Puerto Rican working-class environment instilled in me the principles of family nurturing, friendship, and Black Puerto Rican identity. My close and extended family and my faith are the foundation of my life. In the early 1970s we moved from a low-income housing building to *urbanización*—a housing development. I recall we were one of just three Afro-Puerto Rican families on our street in Carolina. We were not the perfect family. As an adult, I expanded my support circle, which today includes good friends known from my school years, such as Adriana Rodríguez and her family, who have provided me with moral support through the years. There are others I met in my University of Puerto Rico days, such as Gloria Rivera and her family. During that time, I worked several part-time jobs to pay my tuition. During those difficult days, I had the privilege of knowing Neida Arroyo. She has been very supportive and has sent me newspaper articles from Puerto Rico on the island's culture and racial topics. She and her brother Víctor also helped me to fill out applications to graduate schools in the United States. Another brother, Edwin, and his wife, Annette, sent me a box with essentials for my first winter in Ithaca. While I pursued a master's degree at Cornell, I was blessed to meet another set of friends: Dr. Ayele Bekerie, Mwalimu Abdul Nanji, Margaret Mbwana, and Sylvia Nyana. Sylvia, a librarian at the John Henrik Clarke Africana Library, was instrumental in providing me with sources about Puerto Rico.

After I finished my doctorate at Howard University, I got a job at Rutgers University in the Department of Latino and Caribbean Studies. I want to thank Dr. Aldo Lauria Santiago for giving me that opportunity. The experience there gave me a better sense of the Puerto Rican, Caribbean, and Latino Studies fields. At Rutgers, I met Drs. Ana Yolanda Ramos, Carlos Decena, Edgar Rivera Colón, and many others, but it was also with them that I shared my research project. In one way or another, they have each supported my academic growth. When I moved to the Bronx from New Jersey, I met Dr. Carlos Vázquez, who had just begun his academic journey. We became good friends in addition to being neighbors. He critically read one of the versions of my manuscript. Additionally, I met Dahlma Llanos-Figueroa and her husband Jonathan, who also provided moral support.

I am delighted to acknowledge the intellectual support of many. The Department of Africana, Puerto Rican, and Latino Studies at Hunter College is where I expanded my pedagogical and research skills and met new colleagues. Many thanks, especially, to current colleagues who supported me at Hunter College, including Professor Joanne Edey-Rhodes, Dr. Ehiedu Iweriebor, Dr. Luis Álvarez-López, and Ms. Barbara Saunders the Department Administrative assistant, who have all been instrumental in keeping me focused on my research. And thanks to Dr. Arlene Torres and Dr. Anthony Browne for the creation of seminars titled "Race and Ethnic Inequality in the 'Post Racial' America" that helped me to share my work in a peer academic setting. At the Center for Puerto Rican Studies at Hunter College, I had the privilege of meeting Dr. Carlos Vargas-Ramos, who is the Director for Public Policy, as well as Jorge Matos Valdejulli, Félix Rivera, and Pedro Juan Hernández who were at the library and archives. Hunter College Library holds a manuscript collection from which I have benefited as well. Then-director Julio Hernández Delgado was instrumental in pointing out some of the collections that became source material for my articles. While this manuscript was taking shape, the different editing rounds and reviews of the manuscript were funded by two grants I received from my institution, Hunter College.

During a combination of personal and research trips to Puerto Rico, I visited the National Archives, the Biblioteca José M. Lázaro/Colección

Puertorriqueña, and the Centro de Investigaciones Históricas at the University of Puerto Rico Río Piedras campus. While updating some of my chapters, I visited the Archivo y Centro de Investigación Histórica de Carolina, Puerto Rican Planning Board and the library of the Centro de Estudios y Avanzados de Puerto Rico y del Caribe in Old San Juan and the Instituto de Cultura Puertorriqueña. At the Instituto, Ms. Laura Quiñones was essential in expediting the copyright authorization for one image used in the book. I also used the collections at the Fundación Luis Muñoz Marín, where the head of the archives, Dr. Julio Quirós Alcalá, provided me with key sources, some even after I had returned to New York. Throughout these trips to Puerto Rico, I benefited from many bookstores in Río Piedras and Old San Juan where I found a treasure trove of sources. Sections of this book appeared previously in *Hispanófila. Ensayos de literature*, no. 189 (June 2020): 17–32 and *Latino Studies* 18, no. 1 (Spring 2020): 45–65.

Finally, I want to thank the colleagues who, like me, are writing on the topic of race and racial discrimination. In many ways, they also inspired me to continue my work with this fascinating, complex, and important area of study.

Introduction

The Illusion of Living
in a Non-Racist Racist Society

There is a saying in Puerto Rico, "gota a gota, se llena el vaso" (drop by drop, you fill the glass). In other words, one day at a time, little by little, things can be changed. In the United States, the "one drop rule" declared that a person with as little as 1/32 of African blood qualified as Black. It was how African Americans were socially othered and legally excluded. Along with the history of racial phenomena in twentieth-century Puerto Rico, you will find stories that are "drops of inclusivity." These stories are some of the rare instances in which Afro-Puerto Ricans were included in the dialogue about race and the creation of the Puerto Rican national identity. Many of the stories have been left from history books. By documenting the instances where Black Puerto Ricans broke through racial hierarchies, where they were acknowledged as part of the national identity and history, we piece together the larger story of Afro-Puerto Rican perseverance but also acknowledge the slow march of incremental change. Collecting these "drops" gives us a fuller understanding of how far Afro-Puerto Ricans have come and inspires us to continue to work for racial inclusivity.

Questioning Racial Myths

Over the last sixty-plus years, researchers have conducted sociological studies on race and racism in Puerto Rico. Although most of the research

1

tends to primarily address sociological issues, historical analysis of this time period has been sparse. Therefore, this book is an attempt to analyze the phenomenon of race from a sociohistorical and political standpoint. Examining the case of Puerto Rico provides methods to identify fluid racial discourse and practices that are not identifiable by other means.

Some of the scholarship has suggested that Puerto Rico has never been the setting of racial struggles and has never had deeply rooted collective prejudice from one race against the other. Instead, they posit that Puerto Rico has offered to the world an admirable example of social/racial harmony, where all men contribute in their effort to the development of the country. The problem with these assumptions is that they both deny the history of racism in Puerto Rican society and limit the ways Black Puerto Ricans can challenge the various forms of racial exclusion pervasive on the island.

This study assesses several changing racial formations and meanings in Puerto Rico from 1898 to 1965, with a focus on Afro-Puerto Ricans and their struggle to achieve the right of self-determination during the first half of the twentieth century. In this context, self-determination is the effort of a group that seeks validation within the current of an elaborate "cultural identity," which encompasses a sense of belongingness based on certain commonalities, including nationality, ethnicity, and other cultural traits. In this sense, Puerto Rican cultural identity has gathered some of the components of its ethnic heritage, but selectively. For instance, the island triad known as the three roots (Taino-Indian, Spanish, and African), in constructing the Puerto Rican cultural and national identity, was exclusionary because the African component was left out or silenced. According to Chilean economist Jorge Larrain, in the process of modernization, "certain classes, institutions or groups" were excluded.[1] In sum, Afro-Puerto Ricans were excluded from the nation-building and modernization process, and their struggle for self-definition and inclusion is a result of that exclusion. In the Puerto Rican context, anti-Black racism is characterized and defined as a phenomenon of non-racist racism. But how can racism be non-racist? In Puerto Rican society racism is both covert and denied. This has debilitating consequences for Puerto Ricans of African descent in terms of their inclusion during the island's national identity.

The perception of race is also examined within the national discourse that evolved in Puerto Rican society during the first half of the twentieth century. Theories describing racial formation processes attempt to explain the evolution of racial consciousness in given societies. Such methods are used in this book to identify analytical structures that would be challenging to discover through other means.

In 1898, the United States invaded the island. United States' colonial regime added another level to the colonial system and reinforced the island's political and intellectual elites' racial narrative.[2] In this regard, *Drops of Inclusivity: Racial Formations and Meanings in Puerto Rican Society* examines whether Puerto Rican society, regardless of its exposure to American racial policies, subscribed to its own brand of racial narrative. This racial narrative is defined as the social construction of the Puerto Rican nation as raceless or where racial dialogue is "silenced," while at the same time Black Puerto Ricans are erased from the national identity formulation. Furthermore, the racial formula invented by the elites rearticulates the Puerto Rican society in such a way that the Afro-Puerto Ricans are racialized by the absence of whiteness in their blood as perceived in the colonial Spanish society.[3] Ironically, in Puerto Rican society race is not only biological; it is intertwined with class status and culture. On this principle, Afro-Puerto Ricans have been subjected to exclusion, disenfranchisement, marginalization, and folklorization.[4]

Disentangling Racism

In Puerto Rican scholarship, the history of slavery tends to be limited to the legal institution of slavery, failing to explore how the shadow of slavery continued to perpetuate negative stereotypes and stigmas against Black Puerto Ricans. The formulation of racial equations and discourses are linked to the island's history of enslavement. The history of slavery, as Isar Godreau and colleagues point out, is "instrumental in the reproduction of national ideologies of *mestizaje*."[5] Literary critic Arcadio Díaz Quiñones, who wrote a preeminent essay in Tomás Blanco's *El prejuicio racial in Puerto Rico*, asserts that the history of slavery led to perpetual socioeconomic disadvantages for the Afro-Puerto Rican population. Looking at the scholarship on the subject in the United States, sociologists Michael Omi and Howard Winant also observed the linkage between slavery and racialization. They contended that "racial" legacies of the past—slavery and bigotry—continue to shape the present.[6] For the purpose of this study, these three approaches are our starting point for recognizing the connections between slavery and Blackness, racialization and social exclusion.

Studies on race and racial exclusion cannot be conducted without assessing the economic strategies used by the government and non-government institutions. Pivotal to this study is assessing the modernization of the island, which was a priority for the Partido Popular and Governor Muñoz Marín's administration (1949–1965). I contend that the economic model adopted in Puerto Rico by the Muñoz Marín administration carries with it a racial equation and practices (social and institutional). What makes the case of Puerto Rico noteworthy is precisely its political and economic relations with the United States (geopolitical status), and how the neocolonial rule has re-formed Puerto Ricans' racial identity. Focusing on the process of modernization and industrialization brings a different angle to the developmental theory, which tends to overemphasize economic achievements and overlook the intersections between race and class. Omi and Winant discussed the relevance of a "nation-based" paradigm to understand the legacy of colonialism. It entails the idea of nation-building and modernity by aggressively creating economic programs, social/cultural narratives in which individual or groups that are not of European ancestry or whites are commonly perceived as a threat to the nation-building project. They are either absorbed by the nation-building propaganda or simply left out from the equation. Therefore, I apply this paradigm to U.S.-Puerto Rican relations in order to delve deeper into the symbiotic combination of colonial structure and a supposed raceless society.

These strategies are related to the process of racialization or the attribution of a racial/biological characteristic to an individual of a group, which turns out to be problematic when whiteness becomes a synonym for privilege and power, while blackness is marked for exclusion. But to what kind of historical interpretations should one refer that can be useful for public policymaking or to understand the dynamics in a society that every day is turning more and more white while blackness is suppressed and rejected? In the case of Puerto Rico, the idea of a non-racist and raceless society implies operating as a nation with one focus, that is, "Puerto Ricanness" while historically and institutionally excluding Black Puerto Ricans.

Exporting Racial Hierarchies

When Europeans (in this case, the Iberians) came to the Americas, they already had experience with other ethnic groups, specifically Muslims and

Jews. As clearly discussed by James Sweet's seminal study on race relations in the Iberian Peninsula, the Spanish had developed a racial hierarchy that could serve as a reference point to the racial model they exported to the Americas. One may assume the co-existence between Iberians with Muslims and Jews gave the Spanish some degree of tolerance. However, after the expulsion of the Moors, and the forced conversion of the Jews, Spain became more intolerant against non-Catholic ethnicities.[7] Amidst this situation, people of "olive-skinned" complexion became targets of ethnic hostilities, reinforcing ethnic divides.

Racial intolerance and racists practices were further hastened by the massive enslavement of Africans and their relocation in the Iberian cities and exportation to the Americas. In the Americas, the population of Africans and indigenous people outnumbered the Spanish, creating fears among the new settlers. Consequently, in their quest to legitimize their right to the land, the Spanish created a culture in which individuals sought to validate their ethnic/racial status and Christianity through "pureza de sangre," or purity of blood. Sociologists Michael Omi and Howard Winant added that once in the Americas, the "native" people challenged the Europeans' preconceptions of the human species. This affected the enterprise of the conquest. This realization of the "other" was a key element in the colonial society built by Iberians in the Americas.

Throughout history, racism has changed and evolved, both in its form and content, yet it has remained a dominant and pervasive force in virtually every society. The slave trade, introduced to the island in the sixteenth century, greatly influenced the dynamics of racial constructs in the society. In Puerto Rico, Spaniards created an enduring pyramidal society based on class and race hierarchies in which Spanish and Creoles (colonials of Spanish descent) held all positions of power and control. Castes that included racial mixtures among Taínos and Spaniards, or Spanish and Africans (free and enslaved), occupied a lower level. Enslaved persons were placed at the bottom of that system. That caste category classified people of color using descriptive nouns such as "mulatos," "pardos," "negros," and "morenos." Puerto Rican society has embraced these classifications which, at their core, all mean Black. Spaniards and Creoles could derive privileges from the system, meaning officials from the military, educated people, and planters belonged in this social class. Colored people who enjoyed freedom due to certain circumstances had to take whatever opportunities the system granted them.

In the eighteenth century, historical accounts showed that the island was a mixed society. In 1788, Fray Iñigo Abbad y Lasierra published a report about the island of Puerto Rico. In it, he describes the Black population of the island as follows:

> The mulattos, who comprised the majority of the island's population, are the offspring of a white man and a Black woman. Their skin color is dark and unpleasant, the color of their eyes is muddy, they are tall and well built, stronger and used to work more than the white Creoles who treat them with disdain.[8]

The Abbad y Lasierra account was one of the first reports regarding the civil and racial status of the island. In addition to testifying that racial prejudice against people of African descent was quite evident, he seems to suggest that white Creoles were lazy. In other words, for Abbad y Lasierra, the Creoles were an inferior caste and Blacks were subhuman. His construction of Creole and Black character was based on their dynamics among themselves. Or as Arcadio Díaz Quiñones put it, Abbad's account suggests Puerto Rican society was transforming through conflicts with racial and social hierarchies.[9]

Race relations were tense and contentious on the island in the nineteenth century. The Haitian Revolution and the Spanish Wars for Independence contributed to the environment of tension, harassment, and persecution against Blacks (free and enslaved). For instance, under Governor Juan de Prim (1823–1837), a civil code known as *bando contra la raza africana* (edict against the African race) banned free Blacks from gathering or socializing in the city of San Juan and banned slaves from crossing from plantation to plantation. Although Blacks made up the majority of the population by the first decades of the nineteenth century, the phantom of Haiti was still a reminder to the planter-class that a similar situation could be repeated in Puerto Rico.[10]

In the 1810s, Spain's political reorganization triggered the drafting of a Spanish constitution known as the Constitution of Cádiz. Liberal Creoles in the colonies proposed that racial representation should be organized based on demographic proportions, creating a conflict because the population of Spanish America was proportionately bigger than Spain's. As a result of the concern of being outnumbered, by using the constitution as a legal weapon, indigenous people and people of African descent were excluded from political participation. For instance, Article 18 of the Cádiz Constitution established and declared Spanish citizenship to all men born in Spain and its territories who could trace their lineage back to Spain.[11] Furthermore, Article 22 stipulated that peoples of African descent were considered Spanish citizens as long as they were conceived within a legitimate marriage, if they served the country, and stood out as respectable citizens.[12] The Constitution of Cádiz is a clear example of how the Spanish colonial system used a legal document for the benefit of its white citizens. This constitution was perhaps the first attempt of the Spanish colonial government to disenfranchise Blacks and the indigenous population and to prevent them from political participation, disguising racism under the moral and religious principle of "legitimate union." Under this criterion, it would have been challenging for many Black Puerto Ricans who were the product of nonconsensual relationships between a Creole and an enslaved person or a domestic worker to gain citizenship. Similar ordeals existed for a Black Puerto Rican couple who did not have the money to pay the fees for a wedding ceremony in the Catholic Church.[13]

Economic and political environments in some of the Spanish colonies in the Americas led some liberal planters to advocate for the abolition of slavery without confronting those who still saw this practice as a reputable business, whereas others argued that the island was dependent on free labor. In this instance, the colonial government reached an agreement that would implement the gradual emancipation of the slaves with the commitment, to some degree, to compensate the planters for their "loss."

Finally, on March 22, 1873, slavery was abolished. However, these freed men and women suffered more obstacles when they attempted to integrate into free society. Leading scholarship has demonstrated freed people of color faced difficulty when they sought to be recognized as free laborers. They lacked access to land, and more importantly, their status of *libertos* or freed men and women created another layer of stigmatization. Although they were technically free, the society was not ready for them and the system did not welcome them.[14] The *libertos* found themselves competing for work with free white laborers who were under the *libreta* system, which was a laboring code stating laborers must carry a notebook where employers logged in their working hours. Comprehensive studies on the post-emancipation period describe the economic and social abandonment suffered by the Afro-Puerto Rican segment of the population.

The previous historical analysis provides insight into how racial ideology and racial prejudice evolved in Puerto Rican society before 1898. These accounts of anti-Black attitudes, strict racial hierarchies, and codified exclusion across the centuries of Spanish occupation illustrate that the dynamics of race and racialization were embedded in the Puerto Rican society prior to the arrival of the Americans.

Using "Slippery" Language

Discussions about cultural identity and ethnicity are the means through which race and racism issues among Puerto Ricans are directly addressed. These issues have been complex, enigmatic, and often disguised by denial and silence. This book uses the term "race," which according to Omi and Winant, "signifies and symbolizes social conflicts and interests by referring to different types of human bodies." They also pointed out that even though the concept of race implies the classification of people based on skin color and genealogy, they cautioned "for the purposes of racial signification is always and necessarily a social and historical process." Racism is employed as an ideology of hierarchical power based on race. Racial discrimination and racial prejudice constitute racism in action. Racialization refers to the assignment of a racial meaning to a population group or an individual. Racial formation is used in the context of designating a particular sociohistorical process where categories are "created, inhabited, transformed and destroyed."[15]

Anthropologist Isar Godreau in her 2008 article *Slippery Semantics* studied the different examples of how Puerto Ricans express racial classifications. She defined "slippery semantics" as "a recurrent linguistic inconsistency in racial identification process that takes place when people use different systems of logical grids of racial classification during a single conversation."[16] Godreau's study helped to conceptualize the instances in which Puerto Ricans engage in "racial" conversations without identifying themselves as "racist" or being subjected to "racial discrimination." This inconsistency is challenging, especially when one aims to examine the instances where racism took place.

In this book, the term "Black" is used to identify Puerto Ricans of African ancestry. It is used interchangeably with the terms Afro-Puerto Rican or Afro-Boricua. Ironically, in Puerto Rico, the social devaluation of blackness is itself a form of denial through distancing. This practice is rampant in Puerto Rican popular and elite culture, historical narratives, political discourses, various social practices, and everyday speech.[17] Traditionally, the elite's folkloric and paternalistic sense of Black "inclusion" has been accompanied by the silence and exclusion of Blacks from the narratives of Puerto Rican history and culture.[18] In that sense "drops of inclusivity" is similar to the "exception to the rule" situation in which certain Black Puerto Ricans are allowed to "make it" and then used as the yardstick by which to measure all the other Black Puerto Ricans who "do not make it," implying that they are lacking rather than acknowledging that systemic racism prevents them from making it.

Furthermore, in this book, the use of the term "blackness" will also reflect the degree of contestation to define and redefine one's identity, as argued in Goudreau's 2015 study. She deconstructs the folkloric imaginary (scripts of blackness) of Afro-Puerto Rican culture and establishes how these scripts of blackness are historically intersected with class, gender, and personal/community perceptions of racial identity and national ideologies.

Unwrapping Racial Tolerance

Puerto Rico's racial complexity has two main historical roots. First, throughout the nineteenth century, the political elite rejected the idea of an absolutist colonial society, claiming the presence of a national or local culture devoid of racial divides. It constructed the notion of the *la gran familia puertorriqueña*, or great Puerto Rican family. The notion of the great Puerto Rican family, originating in the late nineteenth century, is part of the island's social discourse. It became further solidified as members of the Creole elite sought to establish their Puerto Rican identity in opposition to the new colonial power, the United States. In fact, Hilda Lloréns's study *Imagining the Great Puerto Rican Family* (2014) provides an excellent analysis of ideological construction of the racial tolerance and its ramifications. The study offers excellent examples of the state institutions' role in fostering the image of Puerto Rican society as racially inclusive.

Second, the United States' acquisition of the island added another layer to the colonial rule, one based on racial narratives and hierarchy, which were readily embraced by a segment of the Puerto Rican middle and upper classes, namely the elites.[19]

The United States undermined the elite's national grand design, thereby triggering an identity crisis, which was openly manifested from the political and literary points of view. The United States' form of racism, which is based on a rigid black or white paradigm, combined with little or no knowledge of the island's racial reality (the cultural dominance of a mixed-race population), disrupted the social imaginary of "racial harmony." During this period, the elite were forced to create another social structure by twisting and romanticizing Puerto Rican identity into a Hispanic one. However, the "new Puerto Rican" did not include the indigenous peoples and Puerto Ricans of African ancestry. In fact, a national identity was forged by narrowly emphasizing what is labeled as *el jíbaro* (white peasant).

Re-Tracing the Racial Debate

Literature on racism, racial discrimination, and racial classification in the Caribbean, Latin America, and the United States is quite significant. There is a bewildering array of approaches to the idea of "race" and classification pursued by the governments and peoples of these geographical areas.[20] There are two opposing arguments regarding race across disciplines. On the one hand are arguments showing the presence of racial prejudice.[21] On the other hand are those that contend that racism does not exist in Puerto Rico.[22]

The idea that there is no racism in Puerto Rico is disputable. Sociologist and educator Samuel Betances dismantles this belief when he exposes that several factors account for the mistaken belief that no race prejudice exists on the island: (1) the notion that Iberian slave laws were more liberal and humane than slave laws of other nations; (2) the belief that the absence of excessive violence and cruelty in the history of Puerto Rican race relations also indicates an absence of racism in Puerto Rico; (3) the belief that racial factors are not significant in determining the social and class patterns of discrimination; (4) the belief that race discrimination and race tolerance cannot exist simultaneously in the same family or culture, thus, the citing of mixed marriages in Puerto Rico as evidence of the absence of race prejudice; (5) the effort of American writers to find in Puerto Rico an example of a place where the problems between the races have been solved; and (6) the fact that constant comparison of race relations in Puerto Rico with race in the United States has led to misleading conclusions.[23]

Proving racial discrimination in a society that claims the contrary represents an intellectual challenge. Among the academic community, there are a variety of measures to document the presence and effects of racism and racial discrimination. For this research, both quantitative and qualitative methods are used. In addition, social scientific literature; news resources; reports from the local government; international, public, and private sources; judicial decisions; biographies; and media accounts are consulted. Revisiting the process of modernization from a more comprehensive perspective has uncovered racist practices that could be mistakenly passed as normal or simply as cultural practices.

Even those who recognize that there is discrimination based on color believe claims cannot be prosecuted because there are no effective mechanisms to investigate it, neither in the private sector nor in government institutions. Marcos A. Rivera Ortíz, a prominent Black Puerto Rican attorney and activist, argues that despite the attempts of many people to denounce being victims of racism, the judicial system in Puerto Rico rarely has ruled or sentenced anyone for this crime. Rivera Ortíz's work shows that racism is hard to prosecute because Puerto Rican society has internalized that its citizens are not racist. Supporting Rivera Ortíz's claims, the legal scholar Tanya K. Hernández finds that in Puerto Rico, despite the existence of a legal framework for addressing racial discrimination cases, very few such cases were filed in the period from the 1940s to 2001.

Another fact to consider is the trend of "whitening" that the census shows among the Puerto Rican population. The island did not gather racial data, including in the census, from the years 1960 until 2000. However, there was already a pattern of decrease among the Afro-Puerto Rican population in the census of 1899. By not having racial data for fifty years, the figure of the 2000 census suggests that the Puerto Rican white population is an overwhelming majority. Although the 2010 census shows a slight increase among the Black Puerto Rican population, they are still in the "minority." For instance, the census of 2000 shows that 80.5 percent of the population considers itself white, while 8 percent of the population classifies itself as Black/African American. Curiously, in the 2010 census, 75.8 percent of the population identified itself as white and 12.4 percent as Black/African American, an increase of 50 percent from the census figures of 2000. The numbers could suggest that Puerto Ricans of African ancestry are more comfortable with declaring their race. However, the numbers still do not translate into inclusion and acceptance.

Table I.1. Selected Figures from the U.S. Census of Puerto Rico, 1899–2010

Year	Category	Number of persons	Percentage
1899	Total	**953,423**	
	White	589,426	61.8
	Colored	363,817	38.2
1910	**Total**	**1,118,012**	
	White	732,555	65.5
	Colored	385,457	34.5
1920	**Total**	**1,299,809**	
	White	948,709	73.0
	Colored	351,100	27.0
1930	**Total**	**1,543,913**	
	White	1,146,719	74.3
	Colored	411,038	23.8
1940	**Total**	**1,869,255**	76.2
	White	1,430,744	76.5
	Nonwhite	438,511	32.5
1950	**Total**	**2,211,000**	
	White	1,762,411	79.7
	Negro	446,948	20.5
	Other races	1,344	0.1
1960	**Total**	**2,349,421**	
2000	**Total**	**3,650,195**	80.5
	White	3,064,862	8.0
	Black/African American	302,933	20.2
	Other	440,815	11.5
2010	**Total**	**3,725,798**	
	White	2,825,100	75.8
	Black/African American	461,498	12.4
	Indian/Alaska	19,839	.53
	Asian	6.83	0.2
	Native Hawaiian	379	0.1
	Some other race	289,905	7.8
	Two or more races	122,246	3.3

From 1960–2000, the US censuses taken in Puerto Rico did not include demographic information based on race. Table adapted and updated from Jorge Duany, *The Puerto Rican Nation on the Move: Identities on the Island and in the United States* (Chapel Hill: The University of North Carolina Press, 2002), 247. All data from US Department of Commerce, United States Census Bureau, 1899–2010.

Outlining Racial Exclusion and Drops of Inclusivity

The opening chapter, "A Revised Account of the New 'Colored' Possession," describes the historical setting of the Spanish-American War and its consequences for Puerto Rican society. It analyzes the American perception of Puerto Ricans by focusing on the process of the creation of the "Other." It uses contemporary documents of the period such as *Report on the Island of Porto Rico* by Henry K. Carroll (1899) and scholarship on the period to argue that the project of Americanization was a clear illustration of the racialization of Puerto Ricans.[24] It discusses the example of a Black Puerto Rican named Simón Mejil, who was the first Black islander to receive an official title by the Americans. Simón Mejil serves as an example of what may appear to be a progressive act in a society of marked racial hierarchies.

Chapter 2, "Reshaping Education, Race, and Citizenship," focuses on the role of education as part of the socioeconomic strategies of the insular administration to improve the socioeconomic conditions of Puerto Ricans and the push for an Americanization project. Amid such a racial environment, Black Puerto Ricans took advantage of the opportunities to improve their social status by attending either segregated or racially integrated institutions of higher learning. For them, getting a degree in the United States translated to more than just socioeconomic status but also to having a voice in national politics.

The third chapter, "The Twisted Evolution of National Identity," examines the evolution of national identity as it was reformulated by the intellectual class as well as the two main political leaders: Pedro Albizu Campos (head of the Nationalist Party) and Luis Muñoz Marín (founder of the Democratic Popular Party). It investigates the methods developed through political ideologies, such as populism and nationalism, that influenced the exclusionary discourse of race in society, which excluded Black Puerto Ricans. In the midst of this discourse, the Black-Puerto Rican organization *Liga para Promover el Progreso de los Negros en Puerto Rico* (League to Promote the Advancement of Blacks in Puerto Rico) became the leading voice in denouncing racism in Puerto Rican society.

Chapter 4, "Intersecting Race and Modernization," focuses on dismantling the myth of racial harmony. It examines social contradictions through two court cases that ended with a landmark ruling. The discussions surrounding the cases illustrate that in Puerto Rican society, due to a long history of miscegenation, racial harmony indeed is a myth. The chapter also looks at the role of educational and cultural institutions in constructing and reinforcing the myth of racial harmony.

Chapter 5, "The Voices of Modernity," concentrates on the modernization of Puerto Rican society and economy. The island's role in the fight over communism served to contextualize the lives of Ruth Fernández and Cecilia Orta. Both Black women used their careers—a singer and art teacher/artist, respectively—as vehicles to navigate the nuances of being Black women. The chapter provides a rare discussion of the 1962 visit of Dr. Martin Luther King, Jr. to Puerto Rico. The analysis focuses on the impact of his visit for Puerto Rico and how the intellectual class embraced his message of reconciliation and inclusion while practicing the opposite.

Chapter 6, "The Liga Opened Pandora's "Black" Box," revisits the League to Promote the Advancement of Blacks in Puerto Rico and their role in exposing racial bias in the government. The pivotal moment of the chapter is the analysis of the Senate hearings about racial discrimination in financial institutions against Black Puerto Ricans. Witnesses' declarations reveal the different stand on race from the people affected by it and the offenders. The chapter also situates the issue by integrating foreigners' views on the island's racial discrimination and how local intellectuals reacted to it.

Discussing and documenting Puerto Ricans' narrative of being either racially tolerant or raceless represents an intellectual challenge. When one looks at the island's colonial history, it is evident that race and racism are a constant issue. What makes it fascinating to address these issues is how the element of comparison between the island and the United States' racism has served to deny racism and deviate the attention to the island's discrimination against Afro-Puerto Ricans. Despite attempts to exclude Black Puerto Ricans from the national identity and modernization of the island, as a Puerto Rican saying goes, "ellos no se quedaron da'o,": they stroke back. In this book I hope to provide a different perspective of Afro-Puerto Ricans' contestation and negotiation toward systemic racism. Each one of the stories included in the book demonstrates their resilience and ingenuity.

Chapter 1

A Revised Account of the New "Colored" Possession

1898–1920

The defeat of the Spanish fleet in Santiago de Cuba on July 3, 1898, along with the destruction of the Spanish fleet in the Pacific Ocean and the takeover of the port of Guánica on July 25, 1898, ended the Spanish-Cuban-American War. On December 10, 1898, the United States and Spain signed the Treaty of Paris, which represented the end of the Spanish Empire in America and the consolidation of the United States as a new empire. For the inhabitants of the new possessions—Cuba, Puerto Rico, Guam, and the Philippines—the Treaty of Paris dictated that the U.S. Congress would determine their civil rights and their political conditions.[1]

Landing Puerto Rico

When the Americans invaded Puerto Rico on July 25, 1898, the population of the island was already in despair. The Spanish-Cuban War that began five years previously drew all of Spain's attention to Cuba while neglecting the Puerto Rican population.[2] Spain used Puerto Rico as the center of military operations, and a considerable number of the local troops were deployed in Cuba. The conflict between Spain and Cuba altered the distribution of foodstuffs. Planters and food distributors took advantage of the scarcity of staples and overpriced these items. Hunger and desperation increased because the population had no jobs and no money to buy food.[3] In the political arena, the ideological divisions among the elite (liberals vs. orthodox), specifically people who supported the island's self-determination or supported the Spanish colonial apparatus, added another layer of tension and dissatisfaction.

When the Americans landed in the Bay of Guánica, which in those days was a coastal village under the jurisdiction of Yauco, they did not encounter major problems getting off the gunboat *Gloucester*, rowing to the beach and raising the American flag. According to the log of the USS *Gloucester*, Lieutenant H.P. Huse and his crew confirmed there was no fortification in the town. The log of the *Gloucester* also describes that local people were moving around the lighthouse. Once the Americans entered the village, they fired one shot as a signal, which provoked people to run in different directions. The marines fired a second shot toward the staff of the Spanish flag, which was not hauled down. They then lowered it and raised the American flag.[4] According to Lieutenant Huse, raising the flag attracted the attention of the local militia and triggered a gunfire exchange. The American troops continued the expedition. Meanwhile, remaining residents apparently escaped to surrounding areas. Part of the Americans' plan was to gain the support of the population to avoid confrontations and obtain information on the whereabouts of the Spanish army.[5] The American expedition advanced through Guánica and later to other towns with soldiers from the fleet of war ships that included the USS *Massachusetts*, USS *Dixie*, USS *Wasp*, and USS *Yale*. A Spanish man named José María Morciglio volunteered to pilot the *Wasp*.[6]

The chronicles of Puerto Rican soldier Captain Angel Rivero's document that while the Americans advanced to the center of the town, they came across a Black man named Simón Mejil López, also known as "maestro Simón," whose livelihood was making barrels. He "was the only one in town who did not run away when the American invaded."[7] Rivero continued, saying that Simón Mejil was appointed chief of police, and three other men—Pascual Elena, Salvador Muñoz, and Cornelio Serrano—were placed under Mejil's authority. Following Rivero's account of the events, Brigadier General Garretson met with the ward commissioner, a Spaniard named Agustín Barrenechea, and asked him to remain in his position. Others in the town with specific functions under the old regime, such as lighthouse attendant Robustiano Rivera who was Puerto Rican, remained in their jobs.[8] It is unclear who appointed Simón as chief of police, but it was likely Garretson, as he was the one who arranged for Barrenechea to retain his position.

Rivero's account focused on the historic relevance of the creation of the "first police after the American invasion," stating that some locals, including the war commissioner, did not oppose the Americans. Rivero went on to add that five men (two Puerto Ricans, including Simón Mejil, and three Spaniards) "welcomed the new flag" (*se acogieron a la nueva bandera*).[9] As part of a series of actions representing the American control over the island, one may suggest that the fact that Americans appointed a Black Puerto Rican as chief of police implies a shift in the island's social structure. It also suggests a "breaking" with the racial hierarchies as established by the Spanish colonial apparatus. As was the norm of the Spanish colonial system, any person of African or Indian ancestry seeking to enlist in the militia or to hold any political position was required to prove his *limpieza de sangre*, or purity of blood.[10] Yet one should not be misled by the novelty of Mejil's nomination because, as the historical account reveals, everybody except Mejil and three others, whose races are not disclosed, ran away. It is possible that the Americans had no other choice. American soldiers followed standard protocol, asking who was in charge and then allowing that person to remain as Guánica's ward commissioner. In a particular way, the status quo of the social and racial hierarchy continued. For Simón Mejil, however, the appointment was historical and an exception to the social order.

A Drop of Authority

At the time, Simón Mejil's race did not appear to be an obstacle for his appointment to a position as important as chief of police, with three men under his charge. Rivero highlights only Mejil's race and does not provide the race of the other three. Evidently, Mejil was the only Black person there. Rivero did specify that Barrenechea was a Spaniard from Vizcaya, whom we can assume was white.[11] Besides Rivero's account, little information is available on Mejil. His death certificate indicates that he was born in Mayagüez. His parents, Rafael and Albertina, have conflicting origins. The census of 1910 indicates that Rafael was born in Venezuela and Albertina in a Caribbean Dutch colony and that they both lived in Mayagüez.[12] Another curiosity is that Mejil was born around 1823 before the abolition of slavery (1873); therefore, if his parents were migrants from Venezuela, and arrived as free people, Simón was also a free afro-descendant.

In another document it appears that Simón Mejil remarried in September 1887 to María Balbina Cabó Bertú, a "mulata" natural of Maracaibo, Venezuela. The marriage took place in Yauco and they lived in Guánica; the name of their street was July 25. Furthermore, if the information of the census of 1910 is correct, Simón Mejil was bilingual. The same document shows him still working as a barrel maker in the sugar mill and indicates that his wife, María, was a midwife. In the census of 1920, Mejil was still living with María; he was approximately ninety years old and knew how to read and write. Mejil's wife María passed away in 1920, and on December 12, 1923, Simón Mejil López died. He was ninety-five years old and died of natural causes. The person who reported Mejil's death was his brother-in-law, Epifanio Rodríguez, brother of his first wife, Lorenza.[13] A daughter, Nieves, born to Lorenza, had died.

Without underestimating the historical situation, it must be taken into consideration that when Mejil was appointed as chief of police, he was close to seventy years old. Finally, Rivero's recollection of the war and the specificities related to immediate changes that took place with the arrival of the Americans, such as the appointment of a Black Puerto Rican as chief of police, are a passionate criticism against the break-up with colonial Spanish social hierarchies.

Since it appears that an American military man of high rank appointed Simón Mejil, an apparent different type of hierarchy or social order was established with this appointment. It sparked a chain of events and individual reactions. Rivero was part of the Spanish army, and his point of view might be interpreted as a criticism of the American system, or perhaps his account was merely an objective documentation of the event. Again, as the census and Mejil's death certificate show, whatever the purpose behind the appointment of a Black person as the head of the police, the appointment was indeed significant. As mentioned earlier, such an appointment was not common practice under the Spanish colonial system, nor in the United States—at least not in the segregated states. It could have also been a convenient strategy for the Americans that, for the purpose of the discussion of this book, symbolically marked a new historical period and the shaking up of racial relations. While for some people, the American invasion brought chaos and destruction, for others—perhaps for Simón Mejil—it symbolized a new era of prosperity and the integration of Puerto Rico into the American community.

Intriguingly, the appointment of Simón Mejil could have triggered suspicion regarding the apparent liberalism of the American soldiers. The death certificate of Simón Mejil does not state that he was chief of the police or associated with the police. It said he was a barrel maker. This could be explained by suggesting that American soldiers thinking they could make such decision in defiance of the way things operated in the area, appointed Mejil and realized that things operated differently there. The other reason could be that Mejil, who was an old man in that period, was not interested; there was too much turmoil. Guánica became independent from Yauco on March 20, 1914. One of the streets in the center of Guánica is named after Simón Mejil (see appendix A). It crosses from west to east, including July 25 Street, which is the central street. The city hall is located there.[14] There are inconsistencies in the spelling of Simón Mejil's last name in the census and Google maps. Sometimes it is spelled "Mejías," which is more common than Mejil. While the Censuses of 1990 and 2000 have the surname Mejil, the Census of 2010 has it as "Mejías." On this subject, one may conclude that the variations in the spelling are due to a lack of proper verification. In any case, Simón Mejil was a historical figure in Guánica, and island wide. He deserves a permanent place in the memory of the Guánica residents and all Puerto Ricans.

Justifying Colonization

In Puerto Rico, the American army used English language to proclaim peace and liberation, thus positioning English as the juxtaposed alternative to the language of the oppressors (Spanish). In Ponce, General Nelson A. Miles, Commander-General of the U.S. Army, proclaimed that "the chief object of the American military forces will be to overthrow the armed authority of Spain . . ."[15] Miles went on to state that "We have not come to make war upon the people of a country that for centuries has been oppressed, but, on the contrary, to bring you protection, not only to yourselves, but to your property; to promote your prosperity, and bestow upon you the immunities and blessings of the liberal institutions of our government." This proclamation became the "social contract" with the fine print omitted that Americans offered to Puerto Ricans. The fact that Miles's famous proclamation was given in English symbolically represented the new change. The renowned political scientist Benedict Anderson (1983) noted that even across different historical periods, countries that emerged as dominant powers employed lexicons to introduce themselves as liberators and ultimately promoted nationalism among conquered groups. Rhetoric such as Miles's speech was an important tool to promote the ideals of egalitarianism, liberation, and inclusion.

Written language also played an important role in the shaping of events. For example, the mayor of Yauco, Francisco Mejía, read a proclamation in Spanish in which he encouraged his *cuidadanos* (fellow citizens) to support the American troops. He enthusiastically decreed, "Because of God's amazing intervention we were returned to the bosom of America in whose waters we were placed by Nature."[16] This propaganda and the official support of the mayor of Yauco reflects the atmosphere of liberation and change that Americans represented for many Puerto Ricans. The mayor's highlighting of the "divine" nature of the American presence was perhaps the first example of constructing a social imaginary among Puerto Ricans—about the importance of United States as the new colonizers.

Perceiving the Other

From the times of the Spanish colonization, the sense of superiority is informed by the social imaginary or construction of "the other" as inferior, barbaric, and primitive. In the case of European nations in Africa, the Americas, Asia, and the Caribbean, the construction of "the other" as inferior in relation to Western social values was a common denominator. Spanish conquistadores and colonizers since 1492 took a similarly skeptical approach to the inhabitants of its colonies and looked with curiosity at what they considered different and inferior.

Similar attitudes define the relationship between the United States and the new territories they occupied in 1898, including Puerto Rico. José de Oliveras, who served in the Spanish War as a United States Navy reservist, visited Puerto Rico after U.S. troops took control of the island at the end of the 1898 war. Oliveras was born in California and grew up during the Mexican American War. His upbringing, son of a "Californio" father and an American mother, provided him with a bilingual education and a fervor to further the expansionist ideals in America. These facts, along with his deployment in the Navy, made him the ideal candidate to evaluate the newly acquired U.S. territories. Oliveras, equipped with a pen and a camera, described the United States' latest endeavor, the takeover of Spain's last colonies in the Americas. He wrote on the takeover of San Juan:

The future of San Juan, from a progressive standpoint, is prob-
lematical. Under the new rule, the city will doubtless experience
some changes, a few improvements—as modern tendencies
imply, but the customs and traditions of her community are
too deeply rooted to be susceptible of any marked alteration,
and while the populace hail with unassimilated pleasure the
ingress of their brothers of the North, it is questionable if the
peace-making propensities of the latter will be viewed with
any degree of enthusiasm much less adopted.[17]

Oliveras's assessment of Puerto Rico and its people exemplified the trend
of dominant nations sending envoys to evaluate the lands and native populations of the new territories, resulting in published journals, accounts,
and reports.[18] In this case, Oliveras's "Our Islands and Their Peoples"
became the United States' ultimate reference on Puerto Rico, fueling
mythical notions about the people of the tropics. In addition to the social
imaginary or how people, in this case, the Western society, imagined
their social reality of what was considered "the other," these writings
helped the imperial power elaborate a plan intended to restructure the
social, political, and economic systems of the newly conquered territories.
Finally, prophesizing well before the long and bitter battle for the granting
of American citizenship to Puerto Ricans, Oliveras's statement suggests
the benefits Puerto Ricans could gain from their association with "their
brothers of the North."

An important note within this literature is its paternalistic views and
airs of curious superiority. More importantly, the literature of war correspondent's literature became intrinsic to the colonial discourse.[19] Prominent
Canadian philosopher Charles Taylor critiques the definition of the social
imaginary as a product of "intellectual schemes" to maintain control or
perpetuate their ideology. Taylor argues that the social imaginary refers
to the way doctrines are accepted collectively. Nonetheless, in most of the
enterprises of conquest and colonization there is a dynamic in which the
"dominant/hegemonic" group, regardless of their demographic, perceived
itself as superior/different from the "dominated/minor" group.[20] Similar
attitudes define the relationship between the United States and the new
territories they occupied in 1898, including Puerto Rico.

The history and trend of dehumanization, racialization, and construction of "the other" repeats itself again in Puerto Rico with the Spanish
American War. In this way, both Spain and the United States (albeit four

hundred years later) imposed a colonial system on the island and turned the course of its history for the "better" or for "good"—according to the conqueror. In both instances, the imperial rhetoric concurred that the core differences between the Western and non-Western cultures, including race, were determinant factors in the successful development of a state, a nation or a society. The American narrative about the takeover of Puerto Rico provides an interesting example of the construction of "the other."[21]

War historian David Trask reported that American soldiers involved in the invasion did not have a good impression of Puerto Ricans.[22] Americans considered Puerto Ricans an inferior race, and this paternalist/racist attitude was one of the motivations of the U.S. invasion of the island. Sociologist Juan Hernández Cruz evaluated aspects of American soldiers' racist attitudes toward the Puerto Rican population. He analyzed documents about the troops as well as individual accounts of some of the soldiers. He concluded that the American soldiers looked at Puerto Ricans with disdain.[23] This sentiment was based on the racial background of the islanders. Interestingly, most of the soldiers participating in the invasion came from the American south. The same study also uncovered that interactions between the soldiers and the local population indicated that the American soldiers saw Puerto Ricans as inferior and of a "lower caste." A noteworthy example was one soldier, Lannon, who wrote that it would take a long time before Puerto Ricans could improve themselves and become citizens of the United States.[24] Scholars Lanny Thompson, Jorge Duany, and Kelvin Santiago-Valles, among others, who analyzed photographs, reports, and narratives by Americans following the occupation, pointed out that Americans perceived Puerto Ricans as "naïve," "ignorant," and "childish."[25] The negative perception of Puerto Ricans was part of the Americans' racist discourse. By rendering Puerto Ricans "the other," they justified their imperialistic agenda.

Differing Perceptions of the Invasion

Puerto Ricans perceptions of the *cambio de soberanía* (transfer of power) varied greatly, particularly between social classes. Historical records identify members of the elite as important collaborators in the invasion. Roberto H. Todd and Julio H. Henna belonged to the Puerto Rican political elite that strongly opposed Spanish rule and viewed the United States as a good model of democracy and modernity. A writer and journalist, Todd was born in Saint Thomas and was co-founder of the Puerto Rican Republican Party. Under American rule, he became the mayor of San Juan (1903–1923). Henna, a medical doctor with a degree from Columbia University, based his political activities in New York City. Both Todd and Henna traveled to Washington, DC, and met with Henry Cabot Lodge, an influential Congressman for Massachusetts. In this meeting, Henna and Todd proposed the benefits of a U.S. invasion of Puerto Rico. They also provided information on the military garrisons, forts, and maps.[26] During that visit, Congressman Lodge suggested that Henna and Todd visit Theodore Roosevelt, then the Under Secretary of the Navy. Todd and Henna were too late to actually influence the decision; by then, the United States had decided to intervene in Cuba, so the invasion of Puerto Rico would be a consequence of the Spanish-Cuban conflict.[27]

Another segment of the Puerto Rican elite supported the invasion because they were inspired by United States' achievements in technology, economy, democracy, and intellectual life.[28] During the conflict, the United States imposed an economic blockade on Spain, so Puerto Rican businessmen and planters were losing money. It is possible that the elite supported the Americans in hopes of securing material income. Other members of the elite believed that the presence of the United States would be brief and they would regain the short-lived political autonomy given by Spain through the Autonomous Charter of 1897.[29]

Historian Gervasio García made an important assessment of the dilemma between the Puerto Rican political and intellectual elite in relation to the U.S. invasion of the island. He noted that historian Salvador Brau, to a certain degree, became an advocate for the American cause on the island by highlighting their "civilizing virtues."[30] Indeed, Brau, who began an early career as a writer under the Spanish regime, gradually positioned himself as a key figure in the political and literary arena. When Americans took over, Brau spent the last years of his life as the official historian of Puerto Rico under the payroll of the new colonial regime. García added that this story reflects the evolution of the trend to "legitimize" the American presence on the island, while at the same time they were establishing alliances with the "new conqueror" and distancing themselves from the proletarian/working class. This class divide, which has nuances of racial hierarchies, would become more evident with the transformation of the economy from agrarian to industrial.

The American presence in Puerto Rico also prompted several reactions among the working class. During the Spanish administration, workers were under constant scrutiny and harassment and were not allowed to organize labor unions.[31] Puerto Rican workers knew that workers in the United States were well organized. They hoped that the American presence on the island would allow them to use labor unions as a tool to demand better working conditions and help their status quo. There was an expectation that Americans would bring prosperity, equality, and social justice.[32] As mentioned earlier, with little confrontation on the part of Puerto Ricans, the Americans rewarded locals, members from the working class, with positions in the municipalities and on the police force, such as Simón Mejil.[33] Thus, when the Americans arrived in San Juan on October 18,1898, the capital surrendered to them. President McKinley placed the island under military rule.

Living under a New Colonial Order

The invasion of Puerto Rico and Cuba was part of the expansionist and imperialist campaign of the United States. The American imperialist fever began in the mid-1840s with the expansion to the West. Once they reached the border of the Pacific Ocean, they decided to extend their power overseas. The timing of the Cuban-Spanish conflict fed the momentum of the expansionist debate in the U.S. Congress. With the ideological support of Manifest Destiny, the United States fancied itself the "police of the Caribbean."

Between October 18, 1898 (the takeover of San Juan), and May 12, 1900, Puerto Rico was ruled by three American generals who reported to the Secretary of War.[34] The political and economic transformations made by the American generals are key to understanding the discontent and confusion among some segments of the population. For example, General John R. Brooke (October 18—December 9, 1898), dissolved the local assembly and the provincial deputation. He changed the spelling of the island from Puerto Rico to "Porto Rico" and established a new Supreme Court. In addition, he ordered the military court to address the situation of the *partidas*, or mobs. Moreover, Brooke established English as part of the school curriculum. Apparently, many of the changes upset Puerto Rico's liberal and autonomist sectors because they stripped political control from the elite. Luis Muñoz Rivera chronicled the discontent of the elite in a series of editorials in his newspaper, *La Democracia*.[35] Muñoz Rivera became the first Commissioner Resident of Puerto Rico, a position created under the new government. He relocated to Washington, DC, and interacted with U.S. Congress members, but the Commissioner did not have voting rights in the Congress.

On December 6, 1898, General Guy V. Henry took Brooke's place. His administration lasted until May 9, 1899. During his administration, there was a confrontation with the members of the *Junta Autonómica* (Autonomist Council) that was created by Spain due to the demands of the Creole class. The dissolution of the Junta led to controversy over their rights and powers. The clash resulted in the dissolution of the Council and the *criollos* loss of power. Immediately following this dispute, General Henry appointed American civilians and militia as heads of key departments and agencies,[36] a measure that did not differ from the Spanish system. Under the Spanish, the country was working under a similar hierarchy where Spanish, or *peninsulares* (Spanish born in the colonies), held positions of authority while the *criollos* or offspring of Spanish born in the colonial territories had limited power.

Under the administration of General Henry, three drastic measures resulted in severe repercussions in the Puerto Rican society—the separation of church and state, the Americanization of the island, the prohibition of cockfighting, the lottery, and consumption of alcohol.[37] These measures symbolize the clash between two cultures, influenced by the Americans' Anglo-Saxon-Protestant notions of temperance and animal cruelty. Immediately after the enactment of these laws, a segment of the Puerto Rican elite denounced Americans' abuse of power. More importantly, the protesters demanded the resignation of General Henry, the termination of military rule, and governance of the island by Puerto Ricans,[38] but Washington ignored these claims.

Decisions made by both the United States and Spain drove Puerto Rico into extreme poverty and hunger. When the United States placed a blockade against Spain, they triggered even greater scarcity. The American occupation plunged Puerto Rico into a state of chaos. A series of disturbances broke out in the haciendas owned by the Spanish. In Puerto Rican historiography, these acts of property destruction are known as *partidas sediciosas*, or mobs.[39] The *partidas* were groups of poor people—bandits or thieves—dedicated to destroying Spanish properties. The mobs killed cattle and took the meat to eat. In many cases the planters were killed. One interpretation given to the behavior of these civilians is that they were channeling their frustrations against the oppressor, in this case, the Spanish, and took advantage of the chaos associated with the war to attack private property. Other interpretations of the mobs refuted their timing, suggesting that the mobs were already taking place during the blockade, and that a segment of the population was expressing its anger toward the Spanish long before the arrival of the Americans.[40]

The American colonial administration, also referred as insular government, was uncomfortable with the methods that the elite used to proclaim their disapproval. They used newspapers such as *La Democracia* (f. 1890) and *La Metralla* (f. 1898) to articulate their views, but the colonial government in many cases censored the media.[41] The names of the newspapers, "democracy" and "the machine gun," suggest a symbolic representation of Puerto Ricans anticolonial discourse. Naming newspapers with catchy and suggestive titles was a tradition established by the Creoles to oppose Spanish rule. In that tradition, these newspaper titles ironically hint at inequality and oppression. Both the names of these newspapers and the articles published in them addressed issues pertaining to colonialism and disenfranchisement. It also shows how language—in this case, Spanish—was used as a tool of resistance against colonialism, be it a decadent Spanish rule or an incoming American regime.

In Washington, the articles prompted rumors that General Henry was not handling the "Porto Ricans" well. They considered the elite's attitudes an example of why Puerto Ricans were not fit to govern their own country.[42] General Henry resigned, and on May 9, 1899, General George W. Davis took over as governor of Puerto Rico.

Davis's administration was an attempt to complete the centralization of the government. He identified the differences between the liberals (who promoted independence) and *anexionistas* (supporters of the annexation of the island to the United States) and tried to bridge the gap between the two groups by selecting representatives of each party as members of his cabinet. Davis limited the right to vote to literate, taxpaying males over twenty years of age.[43] To avoid more violence, General Davis ordered the creation of the Insular Police and deployed garrisons to the specific regions affected by the turbulences. Originally, the Insular Police consisted of four hundred "natives" under the leadership of an American official. This law enforcement body was tasked with the restoration of order and apprehension of individuals behind the *partidas* by incentivating people with cash rewards for anyone who offered information that could lead to the arrest of the rebels. [44] The need for Americans to create the Insular

Police presents a paradox. While the Americans occupied Puerto Rico with the purpose of bringing "justice and liberty" previously denied to Puerto Ricans by the Spanish, they ended up protecting the Spanish from the Puerto Ricans.[45] The Insular Police became the vehicle through which the colonial government harassed workers during strikes and cracked down on other civil challenges that emerged in Puerto Rico. According to historian Negrón Portillo, the Americans also held speedy trials.[46] Negrón Portillo states that American's measures to end the mobs were a military-political move to end a situation that could put in jeopardy the image of political and social stability that they wanted to maintain.[47]

Moving toward Americanization

With its occupation of Puerto Rico, the United States determined how Puerto Ricans, at the dawn of the twentieth century, were oppressed and denied full political participation. This restructuring made Americans the upper layer of the social status of the island. In 1899, the United States' Department of War conducted a census in Puerto Rico. President McKinley appointed Commissioner Henry K. Carroll to write a special report on the island's civil government and social conditions.[48] This census would become an integral document because it provided an assessment of the natural resources and the people of the "new possession."

A complete report on the population of Puerto Rico and its natural resources was crucial for the Americans' effort to put into action the colonial government and the project of Americanization. In a comprehensive study about the process of Americanization in Puerto Rico, humanist and political scientist Aida Negrón de Montilla defines Americanization as the process in which foreign-born peoples adopt American values and customs (assimilation).[49] For the purpose of her study, Negrón assumed that the process of Americanization in Puerto Rico began with the American invasion and the occupation of the island.[50] Indeed, the census of 1899, also known as the "Report of Porto Rico," provided Americans with the "blueprint" to facilitate this project. In this regard, Commissioner Carroll became the agent of the government's Americanization agenda. Dr. Henry K. Carroll was a minister from a section of the Methodist Church, which posited that Protestantism functioned as a "civilizing religion." This approach took expansionist political goals even further, stating that the United States' mission was to evangelize and civilize the Western Hemisphere.[51]

According to the ideology of Manifest Destiny, the United States was chosen by God to protect the inhabitants of the Spanish colonies from the tyranny and corruption of the Catholic Church. Most Americans believed that the dominance of the Catholic religion was not compatible with the liberal democracy of the United States.[52]

The data gathered in the census provided Americans with a more detailed profile of the customs and traditions of the Puerto Ricans. In his report to President McKinley, Carroll openly condemned the high rate of illegitimate births, gambling, cockfighting, and poverty in "Porto Rico."[53] These findings corroborated the American assumption that the Spanish colonial system was strongly influenced by the Catholic Church. They regarded the backwardness and miserable conditions of Puerto Rico as a natural consequence of the Catholic Church and the Spanish government.[54] The Americanization of the island could correct the "vices" and "evils" rooted in Puerto Rican society pointed out by Carroll in the report. Measures to implement the Americanization of Puerto Rico included General Henry's imposition of the separation between church and state and the elimination of religious teaching in public schools. Pointedly, when the Americans began appointing Protestant clerics as heads of the Education Department and using Protestant missionaries to run the public school system, they did not seem concerned with the possible conflict between church and state. As pointed out by historian Samuel Silva-Gotay, the new government's Protestant missionaries became the solution to the high rate of illiteracy on the island.[55] Within Carroll's descriptions of Puerto Rico's social, cultural, and economic structures, he writes a list of "recommendations" that reflect much of what the Foraker Act of 1900 outlines for Puerto Rico's new infrastructure.

In his report, Commissioner Carroll pointed out that education was the key to the success of the project of Americanization. It is not a coincidence, then, that Commissioner Carroll emphasized the restructuring of the educational system, particularly in the rural areas, where the majority of the Spanish missions had been established.[56] It is obvious that in Carroll's primary role to evaluate the socioeconomic conditions of the "new possession," the public educational program—albeit using Protestant-sponsored schools—turned out to be one of the most colonial projects that the United States implemented on the island. More importantly, he supported the idea that Puerto Rican children would be taught education in the English language.[57]

The correlation between Carroll's report and the Foraker Act is important because it shows the elaborate nature of the new system, which was
characterized by a series of political, demographic, and economic maneuvers
that in many instances had already been used against Native Americans,
African Americans, and people from other occupied territories. Moreover,
in the case of Puerto Rico, some of these strategies—specifically with citizenship—were unique due to the specific circumstances that surrounded
the takeover of the island. Carroll's recommendations, which included
extending American citizenship to Puerto Ricans, voting rights, and the
election of their own delegates among others, made it clear that the United
States considered Puerto Rico a colony.

Two other documents became crucial to the implementation of the
Americanization/civilizing project: the Foraker Act (1900) and the Jones
Act (1917). The Foraker Act ended the military regime and established a
civilian government, and the Jones Act reorganized the government into
three branches and extended American citizenship to Puerto Ricans. These
two pieces of legislation, which were preceded by the "Report on Porto
Rico," which consisted of a census and a report to the President (1899)
by Carroll, paved the way for the establishment of a new colonial order
on the island. The Foraker Act, enacted in 1900, changed the name of
the island from Puerto Rico to Porto Rico and established English as the
official language of the judicial system, the school (until 6th grade), and
the government. The Foraker Act dictates in Section 7, "That all inhabitants continuing to reside wherein who were Spanish subjects . . . shall
be deemed and held to be citizens of Porto Rico, and as such entitled to
the protection of the United States."[58]

The difference between the recommendations made by Carroll in
1899 and the Foraker Act in 1900 enabled the United States to flourish as
an empire without being obliged to incorporate its new territory into the
Union. Both documents suggest that the United States had no intention
of making Puerto Rico a state. Instead, it was deemed to be "protected"
by the Constitution without being given the rights of a state. Sociologist
César J. Ayala and historian Rafael Bernabe argue that despite resistance
from the labor and middle classes in Puerto Rico, the colonial policies set
up by the Foraker Act were instituted in Puerto Rico, leading to an influx
of American businesses and corporations on the island. "These middle-class
and labor groups saw the imperial urge as another manifestation of the
voracity of the corporations they had for years denounced at home."[59]

Further, the Foraker Act established the creation of a civilian government. Differences between the United States' desire for colonial rule and Puerto Ricans' demands for their fair inclusion in the "benefits" associated with their new relationship with the United States led to dissatisfaction on both sides, mainly when it came to the open trade between their economies.

It is clear that Puerto Rico came into United States' possession as a new sort of colony, not as a prospective state. Although in neither document (Foraker Act or Report on Porto Rico) is Puerto Rico referred to as a colony of the United States, that is the implication of both documents. Between institutionalizing English as the island's primary language for the government and primary education, as well as appointing a governor and expanding the U.S. laws to the island, Carroll's recommendations to President McKinley in 1899 outline a process for the colonization of the island. Although the Foraker Act could be interpreted as the establishment of a "partnership," the exact wording indicates otherwise. In Ayala and Bernabe's words: "The acquisition of Puerto Rico was followed by a series of actions that grimly evidenced the U.S. hegemony over the Caribbean and Central America. . . ."[60] For the United States, its involvement in the Spanish-American War was more than a civilizing mission—it was part of its project to expand its empire. For many Puerto Ricans, the Americans' presence was perceived as hopeful and an alternative to improve the island's economic and political status.

Outlining the Color Spectrum

According to the 1899 census, the population of Puerto Rico stood at 953,243. Of this number, 589,426 citizens were classified as white and the other 363,742 were counted as black. Some studies have pointed out that the division of the people into two categories does not seem logical because of the amount of mixed-race people who already existed on the island. Under the Spanish system, racial classification was much more comprehensive and based on the racial characteristics of the population. For example, the Spanish census classified the population as *blancos, mulatos, pardos, morenos libres,* and *esclavos* (whites, mullatoes, free blacks, and slaves).[61] This racial classification system contrasts with the form used in the United States. The American classification suggests an imposition of their own racial codes informed by their own standards of black or white.

The racial characteristics of the Puerto Rican population played a central role during the debates on citizenship. Critical studies on the subject contend that racism was a key aspect of American ideology during the expansionist and imperialist campaigns.[62] In fact, the major territories acquired by the United States in 1898 (Cuba, the Philippines, Guam, Hawaii, and Puerto Rico) became the laboratory in which the racialization of the people of the newly occupied territories would be evaluated to determine whether they "deserved" to become "Americans."

In his essay "Fulfilling the Manifest Destiny," Constitutional Law Professor Juan F. Perea discusses how the case of Puerto Rico parallels the conquest of Mexico. He noted that the Treaty of Hidalgo and the Treaty of Paris were drafted with the purpose of stripping the inhabitants of the conquered territories of their citizenship and leaving their fates to the U.S. Congress.[63] Perea focused specifically on the role of the Supreme Court as an institution that supported the white supremacist view of American citizenship. For example, in 1848, after the Mexican-American War when New Mexico was annexed to the Union, the status of the inhabitants changed from Mexican citizens to subjects of Congress. An amendment to the Treaty of Guadalupe Hidalgo granted U.S. citizenship to Mexicans, but with restrictions controlled by Congress. According to Perea, Mexicans were at a disadvantage because they were racially mixed in comparison to whites.[64] Regarding Puerto Ricans, the Treaty of Paris distinguishes between "Spanish subjects, native of the Iberian Peninsula" and "native inhabitants of the territories." Consequently, the "native inhabitants" lost their Spanish citizenship and became "subjects to the will of the U.S Congress." Chief Justice Tanay argued that the authors of the Constitution had this perception of Blacks: "They had more than a century before been regarded as beings of inferior order, and altogether unfit to associate with the white race, either in social and political relations; and so far inferior, that they had no rights which the white man was bound to respect; and that the negro might justly and lawfully be reduced to slavery for his benefit."[65] The Dred Scott decision (1857), in which a former slave was denied citizenship by the Constitution, is a prime example of the court's white supremacist policies.

The Dred Scott Court decision was reversed by the Fourteenth Amendment, which created birthright citizenship for all persons born in the United States. However, the Supreme Court continued supporting Jim Crow after Reconstruction. Perea assessed: "The Court's deference to

Congress in determining citizenship on the basis of race, and to the states in allowing racial segregation, allowed a majority racism to control the outcomes and determinations of citizenship and participation in social and political life."[66]

Rubin Francis Weston, an American historian, agrees that there was a racial dimension to American citizenship. In his comparative study of the United States' imperialist policies on the territories of Cuba, Puerto Rico, Hawaii, Hispaniola, and the Philippines, the author argues that U.S. extension of the Constitution and citizenship to the inhabitants of these places revolved around the question of race. Through an analysis of congressional records and court opinions, the study demonstrated that, in Puerto Rico, the Republican administration delayed granting citizenship to Puerto Ricans because they were of "doubtful quality."[67] However, President Taft was willing to give his support to the cause of citizenship without the "concomitant hope of statehood."[68]

According to Weston, the Democratic administration was also reluctant to grant American citizenship to Puerto Ricans. A quotation from Joseph G. Cannon, Representative for Illinois, illustrates this point: "Considering all the conditions with Haiti, Santo Domingo, Central America and elsewhere . . . Puerto Ricans do not understand, as we understand it, government of the people, and by the people . . ." because of their language and culture, meaning non-Anglo-Saxon. He continued: "75 or 80 percent of those people are of mixed blood in part and are not the equal to full-blooded Spaniard and not equal, in my judgment, to the unmixed African, and yet they were to be made citizens of the United States."[69] This statement suggests that racial mixture was not acceptable.

Representative James L. Slayden of Texas, who also opposed the bill, expressed racial concerns. Slayden gave the example of Black Americans as one of the causes of not having achieved a "moderate success" in the government. He went on to use the example of Haiti as a completely Black Republic unable to govern itself successfully.[70] In other words, there was a consensus among some members of the United States Congress that racially mixed and Black races were not capable of self-governance. Consequently, citizenship was out of the question.

Since a military regime was established in Puerto Rico, American generals were asked to report on the behavior of the "Porto Ricans." In a brief to Congress, General Davis reported that Puerto Ricans were not qualified for self-governance. He also observed that mixed-raced Puerto Ricans considered themselves white, a notion that contrasted with strict dualistic notions of black and white in the United States.[71] Even before General Davis's report, the Committee on Pacific Islands and Puerto Rico expressed concerns regarding the racial classification of the islanders. The Committee reported racial prejudice in Puerto Rico and a tendency of the mulatto to deny the existence of Black blood in his veins.

According to Weston, "one of the first fruits of American occupation was to bring to Puerto Rico a disdain for Negro blood."[72] However, the census showed that the Black population was in decline before the 1899 census. The practice of denying Black blood was one continued from the times of Spanish colonial rule. We can forget the Spanish colonial use of the *pureza de sangre* (purity of blood) as a way to promote "whitening." The United States' occupation reinforced racial discrimination already embedded in Puerto Rican society. Instead of a social concept, the Americans introduced the island to a biological interpretation of race.

The decision to turn Puerto Rico into a territory was supported by Commissioner Carroll. In his recommendations to President McKinley, Carroll wrote "that the Constitution and laws of the United States be extended to Porto Rico," and, "a territorial form of government, similar to that established in Oklahoma, be provided for Porto Rico. . . ."[73] In this sense, the Census of 1899 turned out to be a double-edged sword. On the one hand, it was an important document for the study of Puerto Rico and its peoples at the dawn of the twentieth century. On the other, it became the evidence, or "smoking gun," that Americans needed to justify the invasion and subjugation of Puerto Ricans to another colonial government. Some local people took advantage of the new colonial apparatus to introduce an anti-Black Puerto Rican agenda.

A Drop of Leadership

Labor leader Ramón Romero Rosa (1863–1907), born in San Juan on August 30, 1863, overcame social and racial barriers, including limited access to formal education, and took every opportunity to improve his life. Historian Amílcar Tirado Avilés observed that through Romero Rosa's work as a typographer—which he began as an apprentice at the age of fourteen—he not only made a living but also educated himself by reading the texts that passed through his workshop. It was in that workshop, according to Tirado Avilés, that Romero Rosa was introduced to the labor movement. He became more militant in the labor struggle, attending meetings and then using the press as a vehicle to educate the working class about their rights as laborers and political subjects.[74] Romero Rosa participated in the creation of *Federación Libre de Trabajadores* (1897) and then the American Federation of Labor (AFL), recognizing in a public statement that the establishment of an AFL chapter in Puerto Rico was key to finding support for Puerto Rican laborers and expressing solidarity with a wider labor community toward the United States.[75]

In the immediate post-invasion period, concerns about the United States' impact on the political and economic situation of the workers were widely discussed in the labor union press. As a writer and, later, a legislator, Romero Rosa took a leading role in exposing racist statements against Black Puerto Ricans. In a letter published in Puerto Rico's labor union newspaper, *La Miseria*, on March 29, 1904, Romero Rosa addressed "all Black Puerto Ricans" and "comrades in the struggle," informing them of some tragic facts of Puerto Rican history.[76] Romero Rosa alerted Black Puerto Ricans to a proposal presented by Ramón De Castro Rivera, the Commissioner of Immigration under Governor Charles H. Allen (1900–1901). The proposal placed limits on the number of white Puerto Ricans leaving for the United States while encouraging the relocation of the Black population overseas. The petition went on to suggest that any whites coming to Puerto Rico from the United States would be more than welcome but there were already enough Black people on the island. In his study on race among the working class in the late nineteenth century, historian Ileana Rodríguez-Silva declared, "It is difficult to know whether De Castro's letter had a significant impact on colonial policy, but this petition reflects a more general concern regarding blackness and immigration on the island."[77]

To understand Romero Rosa's letter, it is important to evaluate the period of Puerto Rican history in which he was active. First, the island was under American rule. American sugar corporations were recruiting Puerto Ricans to work in locales as far-flung as Hawaii as well as locations in Latin America because they had agricultural experience in a tropical setting.[78] Second, American businessmen and even government officials—such as Governor Allen—acted as negotiators between American companies and the colonial regime to facilitate the recruitment and exportation of Puerto Rican workers. The mobilization of Puerto Ricans as laborers for the mainland fostered the establishment of Puerto Rican communities in the United States.

De Castro Rivera's proposal suggested to the American colonial government that Puerto Ricans recruited by American companies to work overseas should consist of "two thirds blacks and mulattoes" and "one third whites." To Romero Rosa, who was Black, the petition—which included the opinion that "Black Puerto Ricans were good-for-nothing, and they should be sent to Ecuador because there were too many of them in Puerto Rico"—was a "racist" action and an "aberration."[79] Romero Rosa denounced the xenophobic nature of the petition, highlighting the historical role of Black Puerto Ricans. He described De Castro Rivera's bias as pervasive among the "white exploiters from Boriquén," who became wealthy at the expense of the hard work of Blacks.[80]

It is significant to note that Romero Rosa's language implies a forthright sense of racial consciousness. This was 1901, three years after the American occupation, and it was still notable for a Black Puerto Rican to be critical of race and color. Romero Rosa represents an unsung group of late nineteenth-and early twentieth-century Black Puerto Ricans who entered into the contemporary discussion equating race with class.[81] This demonstration of outrage provides clues to understanding the issue of race in the Puerto Rican labor movement. We should keep in mind that Romero Rosa—and many other labor leaders and activists—made race and class synonymous, taking a stand against economic exploitation as well as racial discrimination.

Romero Rosa's letter reaffirms that Africans were the foundation of the Puerto Rican working class. Nonetheless, labor leaders' embrace of the Taíno people, who were the original inhabitants of Puerto Rico, suggests they used the indigenous element as a symbolic reference in their struggle against socioeconomic oppression. This shows that a segment of the Puerto Rican population was proposing a dual identity, combining African and Taíno heritage. Puerto Rico was segmented into four identities: Taíno, African, Spanish—meaning European—and *jíbaro*. In this context, the working class's response to the discriminatory mainstream racial discourse can suggest assimilationist rhetoric, accommodationist posture, or simply internalized racism. In addition to highlighting the role of enslaved Africans, Romero Rosa recognized Puerto Ricans' Taíno heritage. He articulated a new racial discourse through his use of the noun *borinqueño*, meaning native of Borinquén, and the Arawak name for Puerto Rico. His statement also outlined the racial differences among Europeans, Africans, and Taínos.[82]

However, there is another possible interpretation of Romero Rosa's uses of the term *Boriquén* instead of Puerto Rico. In 1804, when Haiti became independent, Haitian leaders reasserted their own Taíno past, restoring the island's name from Saint Domingue to Hayti (Haiti). This maneuver, according to historian David P. Geggus, reflects the Haitian leadership's desire to break with its colonial past and reaffirm the country's history prior to the arrival of the French.[83] The example of Haiti may have served as an inspiration for a Black Puerto Rican's allusion to the island of Puerto Rico as *Boriquén*. Like the Haitians, who proudly claimed their island's indigenous past, Romero Rosa's reference to Puerto Rico as *Boriquén* is a reaction against American colonial oppression.

For this labor leader, the *borinqueño* discourse was a response to the mainstream discourse romanticizing the *jíbaro* (white peasant). Romero Rosa disparaged Black Puerto Ricans through a language of disapproval and self-denial by referring to what Blacks endured during the Spanish colonial system: racism and racial oppression. The rhetoric of a Boricua nation imagines a Puerto Rico free of colonialism.[84] However, Romero Rosa's rhetoric contained a level of contradiction. He was articulate in his condemnation of racism in Puerto Rico, but his language reflected a level of internalized negative stereotypes associated with Blacks. For example, his letter referred to Blacks as members of an "unfortunate/unhappy race." In another segment, while criticizing the atrocities committed by the Spanish in Puerto Rico, he used the phrase "que si bien mostraban la blancura en el rostro, llevaban ennegrecidas la entrañas y el corazón" (although they showed their whiteness in their faces, their insides and hearts were black). This clearly illustrates how even a sociopolitical activist such as Romero Rosa assimilated the dominant racial discourse.

Since the Americans' arrival to the island, assimilation was an interesting aspect of the Puerto Rican brand of racism. Literary critic Isabelo Zenón Cruz, following post-colonialist theorists such as Frantz Fanon and Albert Memmi, concluded that due to colonialism and oppression Black Puerto Ricans denied racism by turning the dominant racist discourse against themselves. In doing so, they perpetuated a negative stereotype about the African race and blackness created by whites.[85] Therefore when Romero Rosa used the phrase "their insides and hearts were black," he attributed an undesirable attribute to the "good" whites. The Spanish tainted their positive attributes through their colonization and abuse of the indigenous people, and so their souls became black/dark, meaning evil.

Drops of Participation

Revisiting this historical period reveals how Black Puerto Ricans in their different capacities reacted to the new colonial situation. In the field of literature, the playwright, actor, and researcher Roberto Ramos-Perea, in his groundbreaking anthology on Black Puerto Ricans writers during the nineteenth century, showed that parallel to the so-called intellectual elite, who were mostly whites, there was a group of prominent Black Puerto Rican counterparts who participated in the discussion about the island's situation after the arrival of the Americans. Among them were Ramón Morel Campos (brother of the composer Juan Morel Campos), who founded the organized labor newspaper, *Revista Obrera* in 1893, Eleuterio Derkes, Luis Dessus, José Elías Levis Bernard, José Celso Barbosa, José Ramos y Brans, and Eduardo Conde, to name just a few.[86] These individuals found little acceptance in the intellectual circles because of their race. However, determined to voice their position before the Spanish and then the American ruling class, they used literature as a vehicle to participate in the cultural conversation.

Ramos-Perea contends that many of these writers in the early twentieth century, in addition to their "racial struggle," were questioned pointedly about their political views, as was the case with Dr. Barbosa, who took a stand in favor of the Americans. Novelist and journalist José Elias Levis Bernard (1871–1942) used his column in *El País* to clarify the assumptions that all Black Puerto Ricans favored the Americans. In it, he responded to an earlier publication that denounced "black Puerto Ricans [as] sympathizers of the Yankees," suggesting that Blacks were traitors. José Elías Levis Bernard responded that there were few colored Puerto Ricans supporting the "enemy" (the United States), and he challenged the Union Party activist and politician Mariano Abril to provide their names. He went on to say that in Puerto Rican society, Black Puerto Ricans were taken into consideration only for carnivals and amusement, and then were stabbed in the back or simply labeled as "traitors to Spain."[87] This exchange, generated in response to the American invasion, revealed the ideological divides existing within the different sectors of the population.

Based on this example and new evidence uncovered by scholars such as Roberto Ramos-Perea, we can see the role of Black Puerto Ricans in the island's politics was publicly contentious. Puerto Rican scholarship has tended to attribute the leading role to the white elite, excluding the contributions of Puerto Ricans of African ancestry on this pivotal issue. In contrast, Levis Bernard challenged the white hegemony. He publicly denounced Mariano Abril, who along with Luis Muñoz Rivera and other autonomists represented the "patriotic" front. This, in the Spanish language of the period, was *una afrenta* (an affront). It was a challenge to the system, an intellectual confrontation. Further, for a Black Puerto Rican writer, having the chance to publish in one of the main newspapers was a rarity. In this regard, Ramos-Perea pointed out that eventually, it was more "tolerated" to allow the "inclusion" of writers who were obviously colored in the "reformist social circles."[88] In this way, Afro-Puerto Ricans took advantage of the fissures that existed in the system to participate, from a racially conscious point of view, in the island's politics and intellectual endeavors.

Chapter 2

Reshaping Education, Race, and Citizenship

1920–1930

The establishment of a colonial system that subjugated the residents of the "colonized" territories required a meticulous apparatus in which new values were imposed on society. It would be impossible for the United States to sell the Puerto Rican elite and new professional class on the advantages of being part of America—even in a substandard way—without using pivotal institutions to create and promote the new social values and social order. At the turn of the twentieth century, having a formal education became an important path to improve economic conditions aside from working in agriculture.

During the period of American military rule (1898–1900), the United States seized control of the school system.[1] Aida Negron's study describes how the United States used education to indoctrinate Puerto Ricans into the principles and values of American culture. This included bombarding Puerto Ricans with the supposed "superiority" of American culture, religion, and liberal democracy through textbooks, patriotic songs, and the celebration of American holidays.[2] The United States also began appointing Anglo-Saxon Protestant males to key positions in the Department of Education. Even Dr. Juan José Osuna, the first Puerto Rican appointed as Commissioner of the Department of Education, was a Protestant. This pattern of appointing religious individuals to oversee the educational system used evangelism to pave the way for Americanization. The indoctrination of American religious and moral values was intended to prepare Puerto Ricans for the changes that would be brought about by political and economic orders.[3]

The Americans realized the educational infrastructure of the island was in bad shape. There were few qualified teachers because many teachers had relocated to Spain. The remaining teachers were not well trained, and school buildings were unsuitable for the large school-aged population. The Census figures of 1899 show that of 322,393 school-aged children, only 29,172 (9 percent) were attending school regularly. To remedy this situation, the United States arranged to send teachers and students to America to receive training and enrich their academic experience. In his long volume on Puerto Rico's history of education, Osuna noted that by 1901 Puerto Rican teachers were being recruited from public schools to attend preparatory schools in New York, Vermont, New Hampshire, and Minnesota. According to Osuna, sending Puerto Rican students to vocational schools in the States was less fruitful. He believed that "mistakes had been made in selecting some of the schools."[4] The climate, language, and customs of Puerto Rican students likely factored into their nonadaptation to the American school system.

When English was established as the official language of public education on the island in 1900, licensed Puerto Rican English teachers became an important item in the agenda of the Commissioner of Education. English teachers first from the United States and then native Puerto Ricans were essential for the implementation of the Americanization plan. In his 1907 report, Commissioner Roland P. Falkner (1908–1911) proudly declared the achievement of training licensed English teachers and the increase of Puerto Rican English teachers in 1906 from 44 to 113 in 1907.[5] This success could be attributed at least in part to the $10 increase in salary for Puerto Rican professors who had adequate documentation of their proficiency in the English language.[6] In her research about the role of the school system during this period, historian Solsiree del Moral analyzed documents related to the recruitment of teachers and their participation in the implementation of Americanization. Her research shows the different political positions these teachers represented in the formulation of a new Puerto Rican nation. Career teachers used educational opportunities to advance within the new colonial structure and used their teacher's union to engage in political strategies. This made them, to some degree, responsible for spreading the curriculum imposed by the Americans that implied that Puerto Ricans must become more "suitable" to be granted American citizenship so the island could ultimately become a state of the Union.

Del Moral's sources show that the newly established Department of Education, from its commissioner to the instructional staff, re-created or "re-imagined" the Puerto Rican national identity using an Hispanic-centered discourse, which they thought would place Puerto Ricans in an advantageous position, in front of the United States. In doing so, embracing the Latin race became the only option for the Puerto Rican elite and other important political figures to cope with the American establishment's rejection of them.[7] The colonial administrators and political elites created contradictory and ambivalent racial and class classification policies. They generated a situation in which individuals representing the oppressed segment of the social/racial hierarchies took advantage of these ambivalences and navigated through them by taking advantage of the new imposition. Some of them made careers as teachers who at the same time advanced through the socioeconomic ladder while facilitating the American educational agenda. In this regard, the U.S. colonial system of education, like the former Spanish system, was not really committed to preparing future intellectuals; rather, they pushed for a more skilled labor force. This might also explain why vocational education became so popular among Black and non-Black Puerto Ricans.[8]

A Drop of Education

Andrés Tirado Sánchez, a native of Coamo, was born on February 7, 1887, to Juan Tirado Bonilla and Lorenza Sánchez. Juan Tirado worked as an artisan and shoemaker. Andrés had two siblings, Emilio and María. Depending on the year of the census consulted, Tirado Sánchez was listed either as mulatto or white.[9] In a personal interview, Tirado Sánchez's grandson, the historian Dr. Amílcar Tirado, claimed that his grandfather was a short man with light skin and straight hair who could pass as an Indian. According to the U.S. Census of 1910, in the municipality of Coamo mulattoes made up 46.6 percent of the total population (17,129).[10] The Tirado Sánchez family was part of this figure. It would appear that racial/color difference did not impede Andrés from marrying a white native of Coamo.

On March 22, 1918, Andrés Tirado married Librada Santiago, who was from a wealthy white family. His grandson, Amilcar Tirado, said that the family of Librada did not accept Andrés because he was a mulatto. The fact that Tirado Sánchez was a professional could have softened the attitude of the Santiago family against him, as was the custom in small towns. Apparently, Andrés's in-laws thought his race was more important than his profession as a bilingual teacher. Librada was disinherited because of her marriage to Tirado Sánchez.[11] Interestingly, in the 1920s census the Tirado-Santiago family is counted as white.

In their study of whitening in the 1920 census, sociologists Mara Loveman and Jerónimo Muñiz argue that part of the explanation for the surplus of whites in the census was that enumerators were sensitive to interracial marriages and would arbitrarily count the mulatto spouse as white. A similar pattern was applied to a racially mixed educated household. If the parents were educated, the offspring would be counted as white.[12] Indeed, the offspring of Andrés and Librada in the census of 1920 and 1930 were counted as whites. The couple had three children: Andrés, Rizalina (aka Rosalina), and Amílcar.[13] After the death of his wife, Librada, in 1926, Tirado Sánchez was forced to raise his children on his own, perhaps with the help of his mother, Lorenza, who was still alive. Although Librada Santiago passed away in 1926, the household was once again listed as white in 1930. Andrés Tirado's grandson was the key to elucidating the apparent contradictions found in the censuses, where he appeared labeled as two races. Tragedy impacted the family again in 1938 when Tirado Sánchez's first-born, Andrés, passed away from tuberculosis. By the early 1940s, Tirado Sánchez traveled to San Juan with his son Amílcar and left him under the care of his godparents; he then returned to Coamo and remained there until he retired from his teaching job.[14]

Andrés was one of the recipients of the scholarship program sponsored by the Insular Government to study at the Tuskegee Normal and Industrial Institute (hereafter Tuskegee or Tuskegee Institute) in Alabama. He, along with other candidates, traveled to Alabama, where they registered in a two-year vocational degree program. Two young men, including Andrés, represented the District of Coamo. Andrés wanted to become an English teacher. According to Tuskegee records, the second person did not finish the program. The Tuskegee catalog from the academic years 1905–1907 records Andrés,[15] who was listed in the catalog with only one family name (Tirado). A petition letter from July 18, 1906, written in English and directed to Booker T. Washington, refers to a group of students—among them Andrés Tirado—allowed to have twenty-five cents extra for expenses. The letter stipulates that the money was credited to the Tuskegee treasury because the "Porto Rican" government had deposited the funds. The seven petitioners signed the letter.[16]

Andrés Tirado also appears in the Report of the Commissioner of Education for the fiscal year 1906. It accounts that following Council Bill

12, ten young men, including Tirado, and ten young women received grants to "receive education in industrial arts and trades."[17] Dr. Amílcar Tirado shared that his grandfather was bullied by other Tuskegee students because they did not believe he was Black. Upon his return to Puerto Rico from Tuskegee around 1907 or 1908, his grandfather worked as a rural English teacher in his hometown of Coamo.[18] Dr. Tirado also said that his grandfather was proud of his American education. Tirado Sánchez was affiliated with the Republican Party because of the party's "liberal tradition." Because of his political advocacy, Tirado Sánchez ran for office when Dr. Celso Barbosa, a Black Puerto Rican with a medical degree from Michigan, led the Republican Party.

Andrés Tirado Sánchez was part of that new generation of Puerto Rican English teachers. However, since he was a rural teacher, his salary was less than it would have been if he worked in the urban center. His endeavors and success were not typical for the average person in Puerto Rico under American rule. According to his grandson, Tirado Sánchez was also involved in the effort to organize the teacher's union in the district, which later merged with the *Asociación de Maestros de Puerto Rico*, a nationwide teachers association. In the *Porto Rican School Review*, which was a publication of the Department of Education and included matters about the Asociación, Andrés Tirado Sánchez is listed as the president of the Coamo chapter.[19]

The Asociación was founded in 1911 in the municipality of Ponce. Its leadership was comprised of active and retired public-school teachers from San Juan and Mayagüez. According to historian Solsiree del Moral, this organization was crucial for the new generation of teachers, like Tirado Sánchez, to be represented in the colonial establishment. She went further, stating that the Asociación "became the venue through which teachers channeled their goals, professional demands as well as ideological visions for schools and children."[20] In fact, the Asociación became the major entity to challenge the colonial agenda and improve their status as educators. However, according to historian Aixa Merino Falú, the leadership of the Asociacion consisted of mostly white and middle-class people who blocked the participation of Black Puerto Rican teachers, particularly Black women.[21]

At that time, the political atmosphere was undergoing profound changes. In 1938, a new political party was created under the leadership of Luis Muñoz Marín (see chapters 3 and 4). In the 1940 census, Andrés Tirado was not working as a teacher but as a "Coffee Inspector" under the program Puerto Rico Reconstruction Administration, commonly known as the PRRA. The PRRA, implemented under the administration of

President Roosevelt, aimed to improve the island's infrastructure, including island-wide electrification, and to assist farmers, including coffee growers, to organize their business. All these new changes were pivotal toward the industrialization of the island.[22] The same census documents that Tirado Sánchez was unemployed as a teacher for at least two years, at precisely the same time that his first-born Andrés died of tuberculosis. Being a single parent and taking care of his family as well as teaching in the rural area probably was too demanding for Tirado Sánchez, or perhaps he needed a change. Although he was not working as an educator, one can suggest that his education contributed to his attaining a supervising position in PRRA, which could be translated to a reasonable income. Tirado Sánchez used his education to build political networks. He moved to old San Juan in the late 1940s. In San Juan, with his oratory skills, Tirado Sánchez offered his services writing eulogies for funerals. Thanks to his education and bilingual skills, he also worked as a juror in the District Court, a position that validated him as a respectable gentleman.

Racializing Education

The public school system was also used to reinforce American racial standards. Historian José Navarro observed that the effort of Americans to encourage public education for all Puerto Ricans, regardless of race or class, contradicted their own practices in the continental United States. The best example of this was the implementation of Jim Crow laws that segregated African Americans from whites in public schools, while campaigning for free education for all Puerto Ricans.[23] Navarro further states that the recruitment of Puerto Ricans and Cubans for segregated vocational institutions such as the Hampton Normal and Agricultural Institute in Virginia, the Carlisle Indian School in Pennsylvania, and the Tuskegee Institute in Alabama was an attempt to use these institutions as an educational model for the inhabitants of the new territories.[24]

An analysis of the documents from the Commission of Insular Affairs, the Carroll Report, and the Report of the Commissioner of Education convinced Navarro of the racial aspect of this practice. He found that of forty-five Puerto Rican students sent to the United States, twenty-one ended up at manual and training schools, with the majority attending the Tuskegee Institute.[25] The United States encouraged the enrollment of Puerto Rican students mainly for "manual training." This practice was common in states with large numbers of African American and Native American populations. Instead of providing an infrastructure where minoritized people could obtain a regular college degree, they were funneled into "short-term" careers that would translate to lesser salaries, slowing their opportunities to climb the social ladder.

Despite these shortcomings, Tuskegee was one of the only educational opportunities available to a fortunate few. According to data from the 1910 Census on Puerto Rico, there were very few schools in rural areas, as well as prevalent poverty and high illiteracy rates. According to the Census, the population of Puerto Rico was 1,118,012. Based on the 1910 Census, from the age of ten and older, illiteracy was much lower in the urban population than in the rural population—39.7 percent compared to 74.2 percent. It was lower for males than for females, both in the urban and in the rural population. Among mulattoes, the urban percentage was 51.61, the rural 80.5; among Blacks, the rates were 57.3 and 79.5 percent.[26]

Letters to Booker T. Washington requesting Tuskegee course catalogs and recommendations suggest that Black and non-Black Puerto Ricans were keen on the idea of getting a vocational degree. [27] A letter from Lino Padrón-Rivera[28] explains, "After having heard of your good method of Instruction, as regarding education . . . I would like to know if it will be possible for me to enter into your school as a student."[29] At first glance, Padrón-Rivera's example suggests that the establishment of the American education system was gaining popularity among some members of the poor class. His letter refers to his misery due to "being poor," a condition suffered by 80 percent of the island's population. Lino does not mention his race. Unlike Tirado Sánchez, who was a mulatto, Lino Padrón-Rivera's parents were migrants from the Canary Islands.[30] Since racial segregation as known in the United States was not a part of Puerto Rican culture, were these students aware that they were being sent to racially segregated schools? Regardless, the fact that Padrón-Rivera and many other Puerto Rican youth were persuaded to apply only to a traditionally Black institution implicates the process of racialization to which Puerto Ricans were subjected.[31]

In contrast to Padrón-Rivera, many of the Afro-Cuban inquiry letters in Tuskegee's archival collection were more explicit and acknowledged their blackness. Those who were not overt created a problem for all the parties involved. For instance, in a letter addressed to Booker T. Washington, Joseph Forney Johnston (the governor of Alabama), mentioned a complaint filed by a white Cuban family. The letter reveals that the Cuban's parents did not know that Tuskegee was a school for the education of "colored youth." Apparently, they were enthusiastic about sending their children to Tuskegee until they discovered Tuskegee was a school for Blacks. They complained to the state of Alabama, claiming this information was "intentionally suppressed."[32] Cubans were particularly race conscious. Their history, including the racially motivated Ten Years War (1868–1878), placed them at the forefront of the issue of race relations in the Caribbean.

Using Cuba as a departing point to address race in the Caribbean region—particularly in the former Spanish colonies—experts in the field argue that class and race are integral to understanding relations in the Caribbean rather than race by itself.[33] Therefore, attending Tuskegee became a source of "upward mobility" for African descendants not only in the United States but also in Cuba. Historian Frank A. Guridy concluded in his study on Afro-Cuban students at Tuskegee that, "Rather than wage in as counteroffensive to imperialism, the Tuskegee-Cuban connection shows how many Afro-diasporic subjects in Cuba and the United States attempted to take advantage of the opportunities created by the emerging imperial structure."[34]

A Drop of Advocacy

In the early decades of the twentieth century, the connection between the labor movement and the issue of race was evolving in Puerto Rican intellectual and political discourse. The Puerto Rican situation was no different from that in many countries in Latin America, where the word "race" was sometimes interchanged with the word "class" or "social condition" (implying poverty). This made it even more challenging to prove the presence of racialization. Even language employed by social advocates often subordinated race to class. An advocate for the working class, Dr. José Celso Barbosa explored the intersections of race and class.

Dr. José Celso Barbosa was a Black Puerto Rican and founder of the Puerto Rican Republican Party. Born in 1857, Barbosa—as he preferred to be called—graduated from a Jesuit seminary and furthered his studies in the United States. He earned a medical degree at the University of Michigan at Ann Arbor in 1880.[35] Before arriving at Michigan, Barbosa had lived in New York City and received a scholarship to study English at Fort Edwards High School. During his time at Michigan, Barbosa mingled with intellectuals and eventually became involved with labor and socialist activities generated by the influx of German, Irish, and Dutch immigrants.[36]

When Barbosa lived there, the state of Michigan was the center of the Grange movement. Led by farmers, the movement waged a significant challenge against the two-party system in the United States and was a catalyst for the Populist Movement.[37] There is no doubt—as suggested by historian Miriam Jiménez-Román—that Barbosa's experience in Michigan influenced his political beliefs regarding the plight of the "Black masses."[38] During the nineteenth century, Blacks in Michigan comprised about 2 percent of the total population. Although that figure may seem small, this population consisted of many highly educated and successful African Americans. Despite their successes, however, they experienced segregation in many ways. Just before Barbosa's arrival in the United States, Michigan became an abolitionist state and a stronghold of the Republican Party.

At the end of 1880, Barbosa returned to Puerto Rico. He began to practice medicine, but not without obstacles. Antonio S. Pedreira, Barbosa's biographer, wrote that in 1881 the Spanish colonial administration refused to recognize Barbosa's degree, so he turned to the U.S. consulate for assistance in obtaining accreditation. The American consul contacted the Spanish Governor, General Eulogio Despujols, who notified Dr. Barbosa that he could work as a medical doctor.[39] Pedreira provides an intriguing description of Barbosa's dealings with the Spanish medical bar. He stated that some people, including Spanish and Creoles, were skeptical, as well as jealous, because Barbosa had obtained a medical degree in the United States. They were jealous also, perhaps, because Barbosa was first "un hijo del pueblo," (a son of the people) and the workers had never reached so far—plus, Barbosa was the first Black surgeon.[40] Pedreira was a Hispanophile, and in the 1920s he was the founding director of the Department of Hispanic Studies at the University of Puerto Rico. His depiction is a rare example of a member of the elite illustrating that Barbosa was subjected to racism and prejudice as a result of his race and humble origins. Able to resume his medical profession, Barbosa earned the respect of his community when he successfully controlled the spread of smallpox in the late 1880s and gained a reputation for assisting poor patients without charging them. Under the Spanish regime he was part of the Sociedad de Socorros Mutuos.[41] Once the Americans were established, Barbosa joined the Red Cross.

While practicing medicine, Barbosa became more involved in political activities. He joined the Partido Ortodoxo, which advocated for greater political autonomy for Puerto Ricans, with an emphasis on popular democracy and social equality. He also became a member of a prestigious Estrella de Luquillo Masonic Lodge (1885) and founded a credit union. He co-founded and was a stockholder in the Banco Popular, the first Puerto Rican bank, which is still in operation.[42] This was a noteworthy achievement for an Afro-descendant at that time. In the political arena, Barbosa became an advocate of American Republican ideals and had ideological differences with other political parties that advocated for autonomism. In 1900, Barbosa founded the *Partido Republicano* of Puerto Rico, which aimed to annex Puerto Rico into the United States.

Barbosa's charm and integrity attracted people from diverse backgrounds. In this sense, he became not only "*un hombre del pueblo*" (a man of the people), but a populist leader as well. Barbosa never accepted the presidency of his party but, as Jiménez-Román notes, Barbosa "kept a pattern of control of it behind the scenes" through his writings in *El Tiempo*, the party's newspaper.[43] Under U.S. rule, Barbosa met with Commissioner Carroll in 1898 and supported the idea of gradually introducing English hoping, which he thought would contribute to create a new generation of English speakers envisioning that territory would transition eventually to statehood.[44] Barbosa became a member of President McKinley's Executive Advisory Committee on Puerto Rican affairs in 1900. In 1901, he traveled to Washington, DC, and met with President McKinley to propose the creation of the jury system on the island. He also asked the president to create grants for "Puerto Rican colored students" to attend schools in the United States, believing that education could help combat racial discrimination.[45] President McKinley's successors renewed Barbosa's appointment as part of the Executive Advisory Committee. Dr. Barbosa remained in the position until 1917. When the U.S. Congress granted citizenship to all Puerto Ricans, Barbosa was elected senator to the Insular Senate. He remained in public office until his death in 1921.[46]

Examining the Color Problem

Barbosa and his ideas were the targets of much criticism. His political enemies raised questions regarding his seemingly contradictory beliefs. Some interpretations suggest that Barbosa's support for the annexation of Puerto Rico to the United States was illogical because of the United States' tradition of racism against Blacks. Barbosa responded to these accusations in a series of writings titled "El problema del color en Puerto Rico" (The

Color Problem in Puerto Rico) and "El problema de razas en los Estados Unidos" (The Race Problem in the United States).[47] These articles were originally published in the newspapers *El País* and *El Tiempo* (the first Puerto Rican bilingual newspaper) from 1896 to 1920.

"El problema de color en Puerto Rico," which is divided into two parts, is the most controversial of Barbosa's essays. In the first part, Barbosa discussed the issue of race and color in Puerto Rico stating, "There is no color problem on the island."[48] In the same essay, however, Barbosa stated that Black Puerto Ricans must be vigilant and that political parties must not establish divisions on lines of race or color. Regarding Barbosa's stand on the nonexistence of a color problem, Samuel Betances in his essay "The Prejudice of Having no Prejudice in Puerto Rico" commented on Barbosa's writings. The sociologist argued that Barbosa contradicted himself by first denying the race issue on the island, and then providing a class-based solution to it.[49]

Barbosa insisted that the color problem would not go away "if the colored race try to avoid by all means possible racial confrontations, neither demanding their rights on racial basis, nor considering a favor the actions of justice done to colored men."[50] He was convinced that Black Puerto Ricans could obtain political participation, and then lobby for the enactment of laws impeding the institutionalization of racism as it existed in the United States. He did not deny that there was a color and race problem but believed that racism was not institutionalized in Puerto Rico as it was in the United States.

In the second part of the essay, "El problema de raza en los Estados Unidos," Barbosa analyzed the racial situation in the United States. He highlighted the struggles and achievement of African Americans, viewing them as role models for Black Puerto Ricans. However, critics of Barbosa's essay have ignored his advocacy for similar achievements for all Blacks while proposing assimilation. His statement speaks for itself:

> The black race had the opportunity to demonstrate its conditions
> to adapt to the current civilization in the United States, in the
> countries of South America, in the Antilles, and even in Europe,
> people of black blood have won high distinction, both political
> and civic, and have shone in the arts and literature. But they
> have moved in an environment of tolerance that has accepted
> them as equals, and once they have risen, they have ceased
> being exponents of the African race and gone on to occupy

a position of high distinction in the proclaiming of the great
Latin culture, confusing themselves within the heterogeneity
that is called Latin civilization. Transforming their descendency
through amalgamation, through crossing, they have succeeded
in being classified as of the white race, and in thus they cannot
be presented as exponents of the advancements and progress
of the African race.[51]

Barbosa's statement acknowledges the presence of an African diaspora
community throughout the world. He implies that Blacks have been
assimilated. He also reveals contradictions in his beliefs as to what was
best for Puerto Ricans, and particularly for working-class and educated
Black Puerto Ricans to be more proactive in avoiding discrimination.
Barbosa's writings reflect what Pilar Barbosa termed "su posición ante la
historia" (his position in history).[52]

In the introduction to the 1984 edition of "El problema del color
en Puerto Rico," Dr. Pilar Barbosa defended her father's apparent contradictions. She argued that Barbosa was reacting to the pervasive racism
in Puerto Rico. In the group of articles that comprised "El problema de
color en Puerto Rico," particularly "Negrofobia," Barbosa reacted to racist
slurs made by members of the Creole elite and noted that superiority is
not manifested by race but by individual intellectual capacity.[53] The essays
"Negrofobia" and "En nuestro terreno" were written during the granting of
U.S. citizenship to Puerto Ricans. These essays make it clear that Barbosa
was responding to the U.S. Congress' debate of Puerto Ricans' "capability"
for self-government due to their racial background.

In his essay "No está en lo cierto," Barbosa compared the U.S. brand
of racism to the Spanish colonial variety. According to his daughter, Barbosa "demuestra que los prejuicios raciales y de castas también existían
en nuestra isla antes del cambio de soberanía" (shows [in the essay] that
racial prejudice and castes existed in our island before the change of ruling
[from Spain to the United States]).[54] Barbosa's most powerful examples
were his personal experiences both before and after his time in the United
States. In both instances, he was humiliated by Spanish authorities—first
during his attendance at the Jesuit seminary, and then in his attempt to
practice medicine. These incidents help explain why a Black Puerto Rican
might favor the annexation of Puerto Rico to the United States. Based on
what Barbosa saw in Michigan, the U.S. system appeared more progressive
than that of Puerto Rico.

Barbosa became an icon for the Black Puerto Rican population, which largely followed his example, and became, first, Republican and, later, an *estadista* (pro-statehood or annexation). According to historian Gervasio García and sociologist Angel Quintero, "pro-annexation [sentiment] among workers was not simply a desire of Americanization, but rather an instrument in their social struggle against the Spanish system."[55] Historian Fernando Picó concurs that "el racismo en Puerto Rico durante el periodo colonial español eran tan crudo que por eso negros puertorriqueños se afiliaron al Partido Republicano dirigido por Barbosa" (due to the crudeness of racism during the Spanish colonial period, Black Puerto Ricans affiliated with the Republican Party led by Barbosa).[56]

Deciphering the Question of Citizenship

The question of whether to offer U.S. citizenship to Puerto Ricans first came up in Commissioner Henry K. Carroll's 1899 "Report on Porto Rico," written for President McKinley. Commissioner Carroll's first recommendation reads "that the Constitution and laws of the United States be extended to Porto Rico; that all citizens of that province who do not, under the terms of the Treaty of Paris, announce their intention to maintain their allegiance to Spain be declared citizens of the United States."[57] At a glance, Carroll's proposal could have fast-tracked the path to citizenship. The type of territorial status Carroll proposed was that applied to newly incorporated territories such as Oklahoma, which was an "Indian territory." Oklahoma was annexed to the Union in 1907, and maintained first as a jurisdiction and then as a territory from 1890 until 1907. In his book entitled *Almost Citizens*, Sam Erman observes that, essentially, the United States applied their previous experiences with Indian territories to Puerto Rico. Erman added that the status of "jurisdiction" justified the exclusion of Native Americans from American citizenship.[58] It took the inhabitants of Oklahoma more than a decade to obtain state status along with citizenship. Puerto Rico went through a similarly political process that took several years. The enactment of the Foraker Act in 1900 solidified the island's status as a U.S. territory. The document ostracized hopes for annexation and citizenship.

Both the Foraker Act of 1900 and the Jones-Shafroth Act of 1917 suggest that the United States had no intention of making Puerto Rico a state. Instead, it was deemed to be "protected" by the Constitution, without being given the rights of a state. Sociologist César J. Ayala and historian Rafael Bernabe argue that despite resistance from the labor and middle classes in Puerto Rico, the colonial policies set up by the Foraker Act were instituted in Puerto Rico, leading to an influx of American businesses and corporations on the island. "These middle-class and labor groups saw the imperial urge as another manifestation of the voracity of the corporations they had for years denounced at home."[59] Further, the Foraker Act established the creation of a civilian government. Differences between the United States' desire for colonial rule and Puerto Ricans' demands for a fair inclusion in the "benefits" associated with their new relationship with the United States fell short, mainly when it came to open trade between their economies.

As early as General Davis's administration (1899–1900), members of the Puerto Rican ruling class expressed frustration and disillusionment because of the slow pace of American changes on the island. In 1900, as part of the Foraker Act, English was imposed as the official language, and many Puerto Ricans thought this could be the first step toward citizenship and annexation to the United States. The discussion of whether or not to grant Puerto Ricans U.S. citizenship sparked another debate among members of the Congress. There was some concern that, if granted U.S. citizenship, Puerto Ricans would demand to become part of the Union. Some members of the House introduced a bill in 1900 to grant citizenship to Puerto Ricans. However, it was not until sixteen years later that the subject received serious consideration. Wisconsin Representatives Henry Cooper and Elmer Morse observed that, in Puerto Rico, slavery was abolished voluntarily, and the government compensated the planters. This was considered a sign of a civilized society. The Congressmen also contended that the "Negro population was no larger than in the great state of South Carolina."[60] In other words, Puerto Rico was no different from some of the southern states of the United States. Although Weston observed that the quality of American citizenship of Blacks in the south was not as high as it should be—meaning a substandard category—the Congressman still recommended that U.S. citizenship should be granted to Puerto Ricans.[61]

When President Woodrow Wilson was re-elected in 1916, Puerto Ricans thought that a Democratic president would bring badly needed changes to their island. Citizenship came up for discussion again. In the House, the debate centered on the suitability of Puerto Ricans for self-government. Puerto Rican Resident Commissioner Luis Muñoz Rivera was an advocate for self-government and defended the political attributes of his people:

> My countrymen . . . refuse to accept a citizenship of an inferior order, a citizenship of a second class, which does not permit them to dispose of their own resources nor to live their own lives nor to send to this capital their proportional represen-tation. . . . Give us statehood and your glorious citizenship will be welcomed to us and to our children. If you deny us statehood, we decline your citizenship, frankly, proudly, as benefits a people who can be deprived of their civil liberties, will preserve their conception of honor.[62]

It is obvious that Muñoz Rivera was aware of the cultural and racial prej-udices that existed between Americans and Puerto Ricans.

Representative Cannon addressed the question of race:

> When you talk about a people for self-government, certain things are to be taken into consideration. One is the racial question. Puerto Rico is populated by a mixed race. I was informed by the army officers when I was down there that when the census was taken every man that was pure African was listed and counted as such, but that there was 75 to 80 per cent of the population that was pure African or had an African strain in their blood . . . Will anybody say that I am abusing the African. I am not any more than I am abusing the Filipino or the Moros; and I am certainly not abusing the African in the United States . . . But the Commissioner from Porto Rico said that this bill is not as liberal as he wanted it, and he hoped more and more would be given, and as I listened to his remarks, I thought he was referring to statehood. God forbid that in his time or my time, there should be statehood for Porto Rico as one of the United States.[63]

In response to the Congressman, Muñoz Rivera argued that despite their "Latin blood," Puerto Ricans never rebelled against the law. Accord-ing to Muñoz Rivera, it was difficult to comprehend why Americans were reluctant to grant citizenship to Puerto Ricans on the grounds of their "race." He even tried to compare the percentage of people of African descent in Puerto Rico to that in the southern United States. For Muñoz Rivera, the racial mixture of the island made it difficult to categorize race. What he did not understand is that in Puerto Rico a trace of Spanish or Latin blood makes a person white, whereas for Americans one drop of "black blood" makes a person Black.[64] The Commissioner Muñoz Rivera died in November of 1916. His successors were also opposed to citizenship without full citizenship rights.

After 1916 the debate about U.S. citizenship, possible annexation, and independence sparked controversy and frustration among the different sectors of the Puerto Rican classes. The political elite used the topic of granting American citizenship to demand greater political recognition while debating the question of Puerto Rican identity. Another segment of the Puerto Rican elite argued against U.S. citizenship for the Puerto Ricans. They insisted that U.S. citizenship would become an obstacle for the island's independence.[65]

World War I led the United States to redefine its policies with its insular territories. The United States was in a constant state of anticipation of a direct attack by Germany. The United States also feared that the invasion of Holland and Denmark by Germany could result in the presence of Germany in the Caribbean.[66] The Wilson Administration developed a plan that forged the continuation of its control of the Caribbean. Meanwhile, the discontent of the Filipinos and Puerto Ricans regarding citizenship alerted the Wilson Administration to the need to act since the national security of the United States would be in jeopardy if the Caribbean were not under its control. The imminent threat of war, the territorial expansion of the United States, the demand for labor, and the urgency to enroll U.S. citizens in the war effort could all be factors in the U.S. Congress' timely decision to grant U.S. citizenship to Puerto Ricans, effective March 2, 1917. The Jones-Shafroth Law (effective March 2, 1917), gave all Puerto Ricans U.S. citizenship and separated the executive, judicial, and legislative branches of the Puerto Rican government.[67]

The dilemma of and opposition to the Jones-Shafroth Act of 1917 rested on whether Puerto Ricans would be considered protected citizens of the United States. The Act granted those abiding by the U.S. laws all rights and privileges that come with a limited citizenship. Under the Act, Puerto Ricans residing on the island did not have the right to vote in presidential elections. Also, the island would not have representation in Congress, only a Commissioner Resident with no voting powers. American citizenship would propel the exodus of Puerto Rican migrant workers to the U.S. mainland and create the Puerto Rican Diaspora. This discrepancy is what makes the United States' relationship with Puerto Rico so distinctive. It allows the United States to flourish as an empire without being obliged to incorporate its new territory into the Union.

Chapter 3

The Twisted Evolution of National Identity

1930–1940

In response to the suffering and apprehension caused by U.S. colonialism and discrimination, the Puerto Rican elite reimagined the history of the island and its people, shaping a new national identity. They challenged what was perceived as Puerto Rican national identity, informed by two major influences: Hispanicization and Americanization. Intellectuals leaned more toward Hispanicization than Americanization. Americanization consisted of establishing English as the language of the public schools, the courts, and the insular government. This drive encountered both resistance and acceptance, depending on the political affiliation of those involved. Republicans or pro-annexationists who were supportive of the island's annexation to the United States considered Americanization one step closer to statehood. Nationalist and *Partido Popular Democrático* (PPD) sympathizers embarked to reject the measure.

The process of molding this new national identity was captured in the publications of a group of intellectuals known as the *Generación del Treinta*. This group, active in the 1930s, sought solutions to the island's identity crisis. Their work reflected the ongoing crisis of racial legitimacy faced by the Puerto Rican elite. Some of the main exponents of the movement were María Teresa Babín, Emilio S. Belaval, Tomás Blanco, Luis Palés Matos, Concha Meléndez, and Antonio S. Pedreira. Pedreira and Blanco stood out among these intellectuals, taking a similar approach in articulating Puerto Rico's national identity. One part of the discussion consisted of criticizing the racial composition of the island, while the other essentialized the Spanish heritage and European ethnicity through the allegory of the rural man known as the *jíbaro*.

In 1934, Antonio S. Pedreira (1899–1939), a writer and a literary critic considered the leading figure of the 1930s movement, wrote the essay *Insularismo*.[1] In this work, Pedreira created a metaphor for the Puerto Rican citizen, comparing them to a vessel. This vessel, shaped by colonialism, struggles to find its path (i.e., is adrift). Pedreira's essay seeks to answer the question, what constitutes the character of the Puerto Rican people? Pedreira examined the three-sided racial makeup of the Puerto Rican people: Taíno, African, and European. In other words, Puerto Ricans have a tri-part biological identity. He noted that the indigenous component was essentially eliminated because the weakness and biological deficiencies of the native Taínos led to their extinction. Pedreira described Africans as physically strong but intellectually weak. The discourse attributed so-called Puerto Rican docility to the island's Taíno past, which led to the extinction of the Taínos. Further, Pedreira characterized the African and European elements as opposite forces in constant conflict.

Pedreira gave primordial role to the Spanish heritage and ethnicity. He argued that the Spanish brought balance to chaos to the race of the Tainos and Africans. His views are significant because as a key leading voice in the intellectual class, his piece resonated among many of his contemporaries. He even argued that by 1880 the Creole class had developed a more liberal approach to the island's colonial status when they demonstrated intellectual capacity to negotiate with Spain over better conditions for the island, which politically yielded in 1897 with the creation of the *Junta Autonómica*. For the first time, this gave Puerto Ricans the opportunity to be in a political position of power. But their autonomy was truncated by the U.S. invasion, which hindered the prospect of an independent Puerto Rico. According to Pedreira's metaphor, the vessel sank. However, he proposed a solution for the situation that was affecting the island, referring to the population's mulatto nature and the island's colonial status. Puerto Ricans had become weak, but Pedreira proposed that a celebration of Spanish language and Hispanic heritage—what he considered the positive aspects of Puerto Rican culture—could empower the population. In other words, Pedreira's solution to colonial backwardness was the adoption of a Hispanic-centered approach.

The problem with Pedreira's solution is that it censured African and Taíno components of Puerto Rican heritage to erasure. His proposal was anthropological and pseudoscientific racist rhetoric embedded in a sense of denial and exclusion. In his essay "Del Hispanismo al racismo," sociologist Juan Flores pointed out that *Insularismo* exemplifies similar intellectual movements, such as posivitism, *indigenismo* that evolved in Latin America during the reformulation of nation-building discourse. In it, non-European ethnicity was characterized as naïve and passive to justify their exclusion from the nation-building process.[2] In the case of Puerto Rican society, Pedreira's presumptions reinforced ideas on the so-called inherent inferiority of the indigenous and African races in comparison to the Spaniards.[3]

Pedreira's work also illustrates the pessimistic attitude about the racial make-up of the island generally held among the elite. They channeled their frustrations with the American colonial apparatus into the glorification of their Spanish heritage. This maneuver resembled Benedict Anderson's idea of "official nationalism," or strategies of dominant groups that feel threatened, excluded, and displaced in the face of the emergence of a new dominant group.[4] Similarly, Chilean economist Jorge Larraín asserted that in the process of modernity, the idea of national identity "is normally constructed around the interests and worldviews of dominant classes and groups . . . and the criteria to define it are always narrower and more selective than the increasingly complex and diversified cultural habits and practice of the people."[5] In this way the Puerto Rican elite of the 1930s protected their culture against the American colonial apparatus by constructing an "official" national identity that excluded African and indigenous people.

Pedreira's essays generated a series of reactions from the intellectual community. One of these intellectuals was the poet Luis Palés Matos (1898–1959). In response to the evident exclusion of the African element from Puerto Rican culture, Palés Matos wrote a series of poems in 1937 compiled in a book titled *Tuntún de pasa y grifería*. This collection, whose title translates to "the drumbeat of wooly-hair people and mulatto things," examines Puerto Rican culture by highlighting the island's African heritage in celebratory language. Moreover, it precedes the writings of Alejo Carpentier and Nicolás Guillén in Cuba.[6] Literary critics consider Palés Matos's work a good example of the negritude movement, whose celebration of African identity spanned the Caribbean and Atlantic world and included such renowned writers as Langston Hughes. In his poems, Palés Matos idealized the role of African culture in Puerto Rico. In poems such as "Danza Negra" (Black Dance), "Pueblo Negro" (Black Country), "Mulata Antilla" (Mulatto Caribbean), and "Majestad Negra" (Black Majesty), Palés

Matos characterized Puerto Rican cultural identity as "Africana, negra y antillana" (African, Black, and Antillean). The titles of his poems are reaffirmations of the African character of Puerto Rico, as Palés Matos scholar Mercedes López-Baralt observed. The discourse of the *Generación del Treinta*, as Palés Matos shows, on the one hand acknowledged the African admixture of Puerto Rican society, which provided a distinctively Caribbean character. On the other hand, other members of the *Generación* viewed the mixed racial nature of Puerto Rican society as the cause of the passivity that doomed Puerto Ricans to colonial oppression. The nature of the social exclusion and discrimination of the *Generación del Treinta* is evidenced by Blanco and Pedreira's exaltation of the political trajectory of the Creole class. For them, the *jíbaro*, or white peasant, embodied the essence of Puerto Rican national identity.

Palés Matos's writing was a reaction to a discussion that began five years prior to the publication of *Tuntún de pasa y grifería*. In 1932, the politician and writer José De Diego declared that "negritude poetry" as intellectual craft had been imported to Puerto Rico. In response, Puerto Rico's main newspaper *El Mundo* published an article in the fall of 1932 criticizing negritude and declaring it of foreign origin. Palés Matos himself was interviewed in the newspaper, and he declared that this literary movement, within which he worked, was indeed a tribute to the African race. Skeptical on this point, literary critic and Black Puerto Rican advocate Isabelo Zenón Cruz questioned Palés Matos's stand. Zenón Cruz noted that even Palés Matos's apparent defense of the African culture was discriminatory against Black Puerto Ricans because, although his poems were celebratory, at the same time they undermined and folklorized African culture in Puerto Rico.[7] Zenón Cruz used Palés Matos's 1932 interview to rebuke the writer's claims and added the following commentary:

> Palés has separated the Black man from us; he did it when he stated that the black race is intermixed with us. Palés Matos has denied Blacks their Puerto Rican identity when he stated that they "live spiritually and physically with us." However, the "us"—referring to Puerto Rican-ness—does not belong exclusively to Palés Matos, neither as a *blanco* nor as a Puerto Rican, and much less as an Antillean . . . Palés not only flunks in denying Puerto Rican-ness to Black people on the island, an attribute that also belongs to them as to whites, but also by perceiving blacks as of "primitive nature," a perception that is

the result of the ideological construct of the white exploiter. There is no such thing as primitive nature, which is not essential but the result of the viral exploitation and shameful systematic isolation that the European and the *criollo blanco* [white creole] imposed on black people.[8]

Although the *El Mundo* interview took place several years before the publication of *Tuntún de pasa y grifería*, Zenón Cruz deemed the dual tone of Palés Matos's interview patronizing and exclusivist. He provocatively denounced the elite's appropriation of the *patria*-nation discourse and brought to light the discriminatory rhetoric disguised in it. So, despite the avant-garde or liberal quality of his work, Palés Matos's poetry ultimately echoes the pervasive generational trend of diminishing and silencing blackness.

The discussion of race and racism against people of African ancestry in Puerto Rico became the focus of writer and literary critic Tomás Blanco's *El prejuicio racial en Puerto Rico*, published in 1938. He compared the U.S. brand of racism to that of Puerto Rico, concluding that Puerto Rican racism was mild. Blanco's most quoted phrase is, "In Puerto Rico we don't know what racial prejudice is."[9] Literary critic Arcadio Díaz Quiñones, in his in-depth preliminary study of Blanco's work, argued that Blanco created a moral barrier by twisting Puerto Rico's history and reemphasizing the Creole planters' good will to abolish slavery. For Blanco, this was done to avoid further racial conflicts and cleared a path for a harmonious society, or what he called the great Puerto Rican family.

In his article titled "The Jíbaro Masquerade," historian Francisco Scarano discussed the Creole elite quest for self-definition in the early nineteenth century. Scarano added that the Creole class used the *jíbaro* as an identity trope. Some members of the proto-nationalist Creole elite went as far as to impersonate *jíbaros* in the local press and in literature to protest what they considered Spanish oppression.[10] Scarano concluded that "the impersonations reveal much about the way that certain people, who evidently occupied subordinate positions, laid claim to a new political order in which, after much discreet struggle and patience, they would finally enjoy coveted forms of power."[11] Impersonation was strategic for a subordinated elite, but the class (i.e., the *jíbaros*) paradoxically adapted the culture of another subordinated group (i.e., Black Puerto Ricans), the *jíbaros*, to confront Spanish colonialism. One may note the recurring theme of the quest for a national identity, and indeed it seems the new elite of the 1930s played "the *jíbaro* card" to defend their culture against the threat of the American colonial establishment. What the emerging Creole elite of the early nineteenth-century shared with their twentieth-century counterparts was that, in both instances, the group's counterattack originated from a subaltern position. Further, both groups excluded the colored population in their quests to affirm a national identity. By giving the role of protagonist to the *jíbaro*, meaning whites, the *Generación del Treinta* perpetuates the hegemony of the elite.

The local media saw continuous debate about Black Puerto Ricans and their reaction to the American colonial apparatus. Historian Solsiree del Moral mentions some of these self-identified Blacks, such as Manuel Gaetán Barbosa (1875–1938), who was appointed judge of the San Juan District Court in 1913. In 1920, he ran for a Senate post under the Republican Party but lost to Celestino Iriarte Miró from the Union Party.[12] Enrique Lefebre (1880–1942) advocated for the rights of Black Puerto Ricans. Lefebre, an attorney, journalist, and literary critic, published a pamphlet in which he proposed the creation of a race-based group to advance the cause of the colored class.[13] The reactions of Manuel Gaetán Barbosa and other Black Puerto Ricans echoed the struggles of African diasporic people in other societies, such as Arturo Schomburg in the United States.

A Drop of Organization

Juan Falú Zarzuela was born in 1900 in the town of San Mateo de Cangrejos, also known as Santurce. This town was founded in the late eighteenth century by self-emancipated Africans coming from non-Spanish territories who found refuge in Puerto Rico. Santurce is also the home of many families and individuals who were pushed out of the colonial center or voluntarily relocated at the outskirts of San Juan.

According to his daughter, Dr. Georgina Falú, Falú Zarzuela was a civil rights activist, educator, and politician. Falú Zarzuela navigated the waters of racial segregation and disjunctive political ideologies that were pervasive in Puerto Rico at the turn of the century. A fervent follower of José Celso Barbosa, in 1932 he was an elected official for the Puerto Rican Republican Party, representing Santurce as its *comisario* or county executive. His biography points out that Falú Zarzuela was the first Black Puerto Rican to occupy a political post in an historically Black district.[14] Falú Zarzuela founded a race-based organization named *Liga para Pro-*

mover el Progreso de los Negros en Puerto Rico (League to Promote the Advancement of Blacks in Puerto Rico) in 1937. The naming of the *Liga* suggests it was created after the principle of the National Association for the Advancement of Colored People (NAACP).[15]

The creation of the *Liga* indicates that Black Puerto Ricans were actively engaged in a discussion about national identity parallel to the arguments of the 1930s generation. The group's nine founding members included a woman, Dolores Luzunaris, who was appointed vice president of the organization. The group was registered as an "association for not pecuniary profit" on July 20, 1939, at the Offices of the Executive Secretary (today the State Department).[16] Dr. Pedro C. Timothee and Benito Alonso Paniagua, outspoken members of the Black Puerto Rican community, also joined the organization.[17] The group met at 30 Isern Street in a neighborhood of Santurce. The paperwork supporting the registration shows that the organization was created to last "indefinitely." This suggests that the founders, aware that a new kind of racist environment had begun shaping Puerto Rico's politics and national discourse, foresaw that Black Puerto Ricans would need ongoing support.[18]

Item number four of the registration documentation established the fact that the Liga sought "to strive for the cultural betterment of the Negro in our country . . . to outspread among the Negroes in Puerto Rico the knowledge of participation of Negroes in the historical development of the island and the world . . . to uplift the standard of living of the Negroes in Puerto Rico."[19] Another important goal was identifying resources to promote higher education by creating scholarship funds intended to sponsor better education within the Black Puerto Rican community. Reading between the lines of this document, one finds an implied denunciation of the exclusion of Afro-Puerto Ricans. The organization described another objective as "spreading among Black Puerto Ricans the acknowledgment of their participation on the island and global historical developments, and their contribution in sciences, arts, literature and other intellectual manifestations. . . ."[20] The *Liga* and its founders saw themselves as a racialized and oppressed community, and they decided to act against their marginalization. Falú Zarzuela and his fellow members not only had the courage to break with the silencing of Black Puerto Ricans from mainstream national discourse and history, they also positioned themselves as prominent figures in the struggle to eradicate racism and achieve social equality.

Historian Ada Ferrer's *Insurgent Cuba* employed the peculiar concept of "racelessness" in her explanation of the nuances of racial rhetoric developed by Cuban insurgents in order to find a conciliatory discourse during their war with Spain in the 1870s. Interestingly, Spain also recognized that racial difference in Cuba could be exploited to create tension surrounding conflicting views of nationhood. The rhetoric of a "raceless nation" was meant to prevent racial conflict from becoming an impediment to the new Cuba. Afro-Cubans realized that this was a travesty: "The ideology of a raceless nationality, even as it suggested that race has been transcended, gave black insurgents and citizens a powerful language with which to show that that transcendence was yet to occur."[21]

Ferrer's concept could also help explain the reaction of Black Puerto Ricans to the discourse of racelessness introduced by the white elite. Spain's efforts to divide Cubans through emphasis on racial tension were emulated by the United States in Puerto Rico. Puerto Rico was divided into several imagined communities: white intellectuals, Black intellectuals, the working class, and the insular apparatus. In her examination of political consciousness and literary production among the popular class and the elite, historian Lillian Guerra concluded that racial, class, and cultural divisions are essential to Puerto Rican identity. Guerra's analysis established a different interpretation of the social exclusion of Black Puerto Ricans from national discourse.[22] While teasing out a national identity formula, the people involved in the process idealized the Spanish identity and ethnicity and removed the African and Black race from the formula.

Despite the exclusivity embedded in the emerging Hispanophilic leanings of the 1930s writers, Black Puerto Ricans navigated the system by establishing race-based groups intended to foster self-pride and integration into society. It seems paradoxical that the system preventing them from competing equally and being treated as equals—in this case, the social hierarchies and insular government represented by the United States—nonetheless allowed them to not only create such an organization but also to officially register it with the State Department. The Liga's documents of registration were signed, stamped, and approved by an official of the insular government. For the Liga and its members, the creation of the organization in 1937 was the beginning of a series of debates and allegations of racism. Although the Liga was dissolved in 1949, Falú Zarzuela continued to make headlines into the 1950s and 1960s on behalf of the dissolved group. After participating in the drafting of the Constitution of the Commonwealth of Puerto Rico in 1952, Falú Zarzuela switched his political affiliation from the *Partido Republicano* (founded by Dr. Barbosa) to the *Partido Popular Democrático* (PPD) and continued his militancy on behalf of the Black Puerto Rican community until his death in 1977. His descendants have continued his struggle for the rights of Puerto Ricans of African ancestry.[23]

A Drop of Nationalism

Nationalism had long been a pressing issue in Puerto Rican intellectual and political circles. While local historiography reveals that the Creole class developed nationalist consciousness in the years between 1765 and 1868, other scholars, such as literary critic and historian Manuel Maldonado-Denis, have identified the period between 1898 and 1932 as the peak of nationalist activity in the island.[24] It was also an era of coalitions and alliances among the main political parties. These parties supported either independence or statehood.[25] Due to the nationalistas militancy and emphasis on independence, the party did not gain wide popular support. In fact, the Nationalist Party (NP) remained outside of the electoral process for several years. When Pedro Albizu Campos took leadership in 1929, the NP's strategies began to change.

Pedro Albizu Campos was born out of wedlock on September 21, 1891, in Ponce, Puerto Rico. His mother was a freed slave named Juliana Campos, and his father was a wealthy Basque, Alejandro Albizu y Romero. Albizu grew up in an impoverished neighborhood established in 1873 by freed slaves after the abolition of slavery.[26] His mother died when he was still a child, and an aunt raised him. Albizu struggled to get a formal education. At the time, poor children were discouraged from attending college. A highly intelligent young man, Albizu earned his high school diploma in only three years. In 1912, Albizu received a Masonic scholarship to pursue an academic degree in the United States. While studying at the University of Vermont, he was encouraged by a faculty member to transfer to Harvard University. In 1916, he received a bachelor of arts degree. In the fall of 1916, Albizu attended Harvard University Law School.[27] He also joined the ROTC and volunteered to serve in the infantry. Albizu was commissioned to the rank of First Lieutenant in 1918, just before the signing of the armistice of World War I.

Albizu returned to Harvard in the fall of 1919 to finish his law degree, which he earned two years later. At Harvard, he participated in political organizations supporting the Indian Independence Movement. It was at a lecture by Indian intellectual Rabindranath Tagore that Albizu met Laura

Meneses del Carpio, from the Peruvian elite, who later became his wife.[28] The two married in July 1922 and returned to Puerto Rico that year. Once back, Albizu joined the *Partido de Unión*. By 1924, Albizu became disenchanted with the *Partido de Unión* and its annexationist politics, so he left to join the Nationalist Party.[29] Immediately after joining the NP, Albizu was elected to be the party's vice president. He ran for election to the island's Congress on behalf of the twenty-first precinct of Ponce in 1924 but lost.

In the 1932 elections, Albizu again campaigned for a seat. He lost again but won more than 3 percent of the required votes. Pedro Albizu Campos's militant leadership inspired Puerto Ricans to be uncompromising in their resistance against American colonization. Numerous confrontations between the Insular Police, strikers, and nationalists created a sense of bitterness in the hearts of many Puerto Ricans. Clashes between the Nationalists and the Insular Police led to the persecution, incarceration, racial profiling, and killing of several members and leaders of the NP.[30] The NP supported the cause of the workers. The leadership realized that their party and the workers were both being oppressed by the United States. In Washington, there were concerns not only for public opinion, but the federal government was aware that the workers were well organized and received advice from political leaders affiliated with political organizations that were considered subversive by the United States.

A letter from Governor Robert Gore to President Franklin Delano Roosevelt evidences Americans' concern about the influence the NP might have on the workers. In the letter, Gore informed the president of the rise of Albizu Campos and his party. He also extended other concerns, writing, "I believe you should know of this trend which is secretly carried in the hearts of many of our supposed pro-American citizens." More interesting is that in this letter he openly proposed to profile Albizu Campos. Governor Gore commented:

> Because of the high organizing ability of Campos, the independence leader who is a Harvard graduate, this movement will be kept alive. He is a Negro with a race complex. This complex grew out of the refusal of the army during the war to permit him, a training [corp] officer, to officiate with the white troops. Campos is a tireless and enthusiastic organizer . . . I am sending a copy of this article to the war department for their files.[31]

In this letter, Governor Gore epitomizes the American pragmatic approach to nationalism and race. They assumed that the Puerto Rican independence movement was harmful. This attitude suggests the Americans' partial understanding about self-sovereignty and the organic agency of the native peoples in this effort. Interestingly, labeling Albizu "Negro" illustrates another dimension of the racialization of Puerto Ricans by American authorities. Governor Gore, like many Americans of that time, did not understand Puerto Ricans' problem with being treated as Blacks in the armed forces or anywhere else. For Albizu, as with many Puerto Ricans who confronted the polarized racial system in the United States, it was troublesome to be forced to be "black" when race was subordinate to nationality in your own country. The imposition of U.S. racism on the island triggered many overlapping layers of prejudice. Workers struggled against oppression by demanding better working conditions. For politicians like Albizu, striking back against the colonial establishment was the only option for the island's freedom. This linked the nationalist leader to the working class.

The NP, under Albizu, in addition to their unswerving push for independence from the United States, focused on promoting nationalist symbols of Puerto Rico. For instance, the nationalists advocated the elimination of the English language from public schools in Puerto Rico in their publication, La Nación. Although the NP campaign drew the support of several segments of the population, it was obvious that the nationalist agenda, which consisted in the independence of Puerto Rico as a Latin nation, was more pressing than the defense of the Spanish language. Paradoxically, the Spanish language, which Puerto Ricans defend emotionally, was introduced to the island by colonialism. However, the NP's anticolonial efforts do not represent a patriotic deed as the language's defense does.

In fact, the party's leadership, particularly Albizu, relentlessly promoted Hispanic traditions and the latinidad of Puerto Rican culture. Albizu regarded Hispanic culture and the Catholic religion as essential components of Puerto Rican nationhood. Some historians and Albizu scholars, particularly Luis Ángel Ferrao, argued that Catholicism was "one of the fundamental principles of the party's ideology." The party's activities often began with a Catholic mass. Many of Albizu's speeches were theologically charged. Ferrao noted, for example, a reference to the town of Lares, the location of the famous Puerto Rican insurrection, as the "holy land." Albizu's wife, Laura Meneses, wrote that Albizu sought in Catholicism the "barrier that could stop the American destructive influence."[32] Her interpretation supports Ferrao's view that Albizu used Catholicism as a countervailing force to combat U.S. imperialism.[33]

Anthony Stevens-Arroyo, another Albizu scholar, noted that Albizu's Catholicism was a manifestation of his class position. Albizu, like much of the intellectual class, channeled his frustration with the American occupation into recreating the "seigniorial past of the plantation life." [34] They intentionally evoked a glamorized version of Spanish culture in order to contrast it with the U.S. Anglo-Saxon culture. Ironically, the recreation of an aspirational "plantation life" discounted the role of slavery inherent in the plantation economy.[35]

In 1934, Albizu was invited to speak in support of a sugar workers' strike. He rallied workers in the towns of Yabucoa, Fajardo, Humacao, and Guánica to maintain their efforts. As a result of his interaction with the workers, nationalist leaders succeeded for the first time in identifying a common cause with the working class against the oppression of American corporations. However, this unifying effort was short-lived. The NP advocated for the creation of a Hispanic-centered Puerto Rican Republic. They sought to make Puerto Rico a sovereign nation by following the Latin American populist political movement that exalted Catholicism as the foundation of their independence and their republican platform. The defense of the Catholic religion was a double-edged sword because many workers were socialists and had no religious affiliation, while another sector was Protestant. Workers saw it as a contradiction to belong to a party that defended Catholicism, a religion associated with the Spanish oppressor.

Albizu's exaltation of Spanish culture can be interpreted as another example of Puerto Rican populist leaders focusing more on class or economic issues than on racial divides. On October 19, 1935, Albizu published his famous speech "Concepto de la raza" in the newspaper La Palabra in commemoration of Columbus Day, or "Dia de la Raza," as it is commonly known in Latin America. In the speech, Albizu defined raza as the Ibero-American race. He wrote:

> When the President of the Republic of La Plata, Don Hipólito Yrigoyén, institutionalized the Día de La Raza, to what race was the high-ranking Argentinean officer referring? Was he framing the concept of race to a particular group rather than to the ethnic mosaic that comprises America? The Argentinean president referred to the Iberian-American race. For us race has

nothing to do with biology, neither with complexion, nor hair texture or the shape of the eyes; for us race is the preservation of values and characteristic institutions. [36]

Albizu's conception of race was essentially Iberian. It was European at its core, rejecting the African or indigenous influence. Albizu's concept of race depended on culture. He went on, stating, "The supremacy of the Spanish race in Europe tested what a good balance between courage and sanctity can give to the world." For Albizu, race was intertwined with cultural nationalism, which generally refers to cultural practices that define a nation. One may look toward sociologists Michael Omi and Howard Winant's definition of the nation-based paradigm to explain Albizu's viewpoint.[37] Albizu employed a pigmentation-based lexicon to describe other cultures' liberation movements and national adjectives to highlight community political mobilization. For instance, Albizu talked about the "yellow people" who united in support of their Eastern civilization. He also pointed out that the "Ethiopian races reacted similarly in Africa." All these examples were used by Albizu to rally Puerto Ricans against the American political burden, by diffusing the term "race."

Furthering his cultural nationalist plea, Albizu viewed race as a cultural attribute rather than a biological one. He believed that in Latin America, contemporary races were derivatives of a true race (Iberian). Again, in his "Concepto de la raza" (Concept of Race) speech, he emphasized the cultural dimension of race, saying, "We distinguish ourselves because of our culture, bravery, nobility, and our Catholic civilizing views." In Albizu's view, the Iberian culture was the only embodiment of true spirituality, the wellspring of race, and indeed the core of Puerto Rican national identity. What emerged from Albizu's pronunciation was the elevation of Spanish culture to create universal appeal among the Puerto Rican people.[38]

In this context, one may conclude that the colonial and hegemonic dialogue triggered by the American establishment, whether in the domestic sense (e.g., U.S. references to Latin American immigrants) or in the colonial setting (i.e., Puerto Rico) present a reinterpretation of traditional articulations of racial discourse. Revisiting Albizu's views on race, sociologist Kelvin Santiago-Valles suggested that Albizu's position must be seen in a broader Atlantic context. For Santiago-Valles, Albizu "counter-attacked" denouncing U.S. capitalism and reviving the plantation lifestyle. This was Albizu's way of deconstructing the historical narrative in which Puerto Ricans were subjected and dissipating negative racialization at the hands of the American colonial oppressor. Santiago-Valles pointed out that Albizu directed his counter-attack at the elite because the elite excluded the working class from discourse on national identity in order to protect themselves from economic and identity crises.[39] In other words, Albizu realized that the political and intellectual elite were leading the island down a wrong political path. In order to redirect the "adrift ship"—as Pedreira characterized it earlier in this chapter—Albizu appealed to the working class.

Santiago-Valles added that Albizu reconstructed Puerto Rican national identity from below. In Albizu's Hispanic-centered rhetoric, race was subordinated to culture. Further, Albizu's interchangeable usage of race/culture defied American colonial racial discourse by claiming Puerto Ricans as an integral part of the "Latin Race." However, the "Latin race" was also problematic. For instance, historian Solsiree del Moral argues that in addition to becoming a "power attraction" for middle-class and intellectual Puerto Ricans at the turn of the twentieth century, the term "Latin race" was used as a "shield against accusations of blackness from the US colonial government."[40] As for Albizu and others in the period, the struggle to connect with a wider Hispanic identity spans decades and resurfaces in numerous contexts.

Perhaps the class-cultural basis of Albizu's stance on race illustrates Omi and Winant's views associated with the term race. They declare, "the effort must be made to understand race as an unstable and 'decentered' complex of social meanings constantly being transformed by political struggle."[41] Albizu's pro-Iberian argument became the racialization of the Iberian-American people. Therefore, by matching the Iberian civilization legacy with the American Anglo-Saxon civilization, Albizu sought this legacy as a viable defense against American-Anglo-Saxon imperialism. The NP's view of the motherland and their rhetoric of a *raza iberoamericana* eventually excluded the working classes and many others from the new Puerto Rican national identity.

Popularizing Racial Democracy

The 1930s also witnessed the triumphant emergence of Luis Muñoz Marín and the *Partido Popular Democrático* (PPD), which was founded in 1938.

This party would become the core of the populist movement in Puerto Rico. Silent regarding racial issues, the PPD focused on class coalition and egalitarian political participation. Muñoz drew from several Latin American populist models, including those of Venezuela, Mexico, and Peru. He believed in the myth of racial democracy formulated in the 1930s by a group of Latin American intellectuals including José Vasconcelos and Alfonso Reyes in Mexico, José Rodó in Uruguay, Rómulo Gallegos in Venezuela, and Juan B. Justo in Argentina. These intellectuals were all members of the elites of their respective countries. Positivism and Darwinism influenced their ideologies and they tended to address questions of race in one of two ways: by celebrating the racial mixture of the Americans without truly addressing discrimination or by simply denying racism. Muñoz and his political party followed the trend of disregard for questions of race, excluding Black Puerto Ricans from discourse on national identity. Instead, Muñoz linked Puerto Rican identity to an idealized image of the *jíbaro*.

Muñoz romanticized the year of his birth—1898, the same year the United States invaded Puerto Rico. He saw a kind of mystic significance in this fact, declaring, "The American regime and I arrived together in Puerto Rico." He perceived his coming of age under American tutelage and colonial rule as a dual process. He wrote: "We have grown up together, with slip-ups, seeking to learn something, trying to know more each day what it is about."[42]

While in the United States, Luis Muñoz openly denounced the excesses of United States imperialism in Puerto Rico through his writings. After moving back to Puerto Rico in 1931 at the age of thirty-three, Muñoz used his father's newspaper, *La Democracia*, to promote the concerns of the labor movement. He sought the removal of Governor Gore from office. During his term in the Puerto Rican Senate beginning in 1932, Muñoz used his Washington connections to demand the inclusion of Puerto Ricans in the Roosevelt Administration's New Deal Program.[43] The core of Muñoz Marín's program was to bring economic progress to all Puerto Ricans, particularly "the forgotten ones."[44] Muñoz saw Puerto Rico as an island divided by class rather than race.

In his view, Puerto Rican culture, while primarily Spanish, had developed under the influence of both Spain and America. He was interested in what might be possible by combining Spanish heritage with American traditions of democracy and individualism.[45] Muñoz Marín's Anglo-Saxon-Hispanic-centered approach to Puerto Rican culture was part of a broader contemporary discussion. His articulation of a project of national unity adopted a less confrontational approach to Puerto Rican racial background by simply avoiding the topic. To Muñoz, culture reflected a degree of civilization, and his argument suggests that the Spanish heritage brought civilization to Puerto Rico. When he justified the United States' presence on the island, Muñoz Marín focused on the prevalence of Latin culture, which was strongly influenced by American culture. This was undoubtedly a projection of his own experience, in which he was able to experience the best of both worlds.[46]

In contrast, writer and social critic José Luis González's group of essays, El país de cuatro pisos, used the metaphor of a four-storied country to explain Puerto Rico's historical dilemmas of power, race, and class.[47] He argued that Africans and people of African descent constituted the first "floor" in the formation of Puerto Rican society. González's Marxist-influenced point of view saw Puerto Rico as a society divided into two cultures: the dominant oppressors (people of European descent and Creoles) and the lower layers composed of artisans and militia, as well as skilled and enslaved Africans brought to the island before the abolition of slavery in 1873.[48] In establishing the contribution of Africans to Puerto Rico's sociocultural DNA, González stated:

> I am not claiming, needless to say, that these Puerto Ricans had any idea of "national homeland," for in fact no one at that time in Puerto Rico entertained, or could have entertained, such an idea. What I am claiming is that it was the blacks, the people bound mostly to the territory which they inhabited (they were after all slaves), who had the greatest difficulty in imagining any other place to live.[49]

In other words, González affirmed that enslaved and runaway Africans were the first "jíbaros." They were the first inhabitants of the mountains and the ancestors of the founders of communities such as Loíza, Caimito, and Cangrejos, as well as those further established in places like Aguadilla, Humacao, and Ponce. After emancipation, freed slaves also formed communities outside traditional areas of sugar cane activity, such as Caguas and Guayama.[50] González was correct when he wrote, "As for the white campesinos or countrymen of those early times, in other words, the first jíbaros . . . found [themselves] obligated to adopt many of the life-habits of those other poor people already living in the country, namely the slaves."[51] In this statement, González challenged the use of the *jíbaro* as the foundational basis of Puerto Rican national identity.

Muñoz made use of an interesting combination of strategies to reach out to both the elite and the poor. Successful campaign components included his use of the slogan "Pan, tierra y libertad" (bread, land and liberty) and the icon of the "pava," or straw hat, which was associated with the *jíbaro*, or rural man. In his analysis of the utilization of image and text to encourage political participation, rhetoric and media studies scholar Nathaniel I. Córdova proposed that the image and slogan both "functioned to invoke the archetypal myth of the *jíbaro*."[52] Córdova's study contextualized the implementation of the PPD's campaign strategies. The *jíbaros* represented by the man in the *pava* were already part of the social imaginary of the intellectual elite. Muñoz and his team used the identity trope to rally and unite a society divided by ideology, class, and race. Muñoz's integrationist formula bridged the gap between rich and poor. What is fascinating about his strategy is that the same symbol used to label "the other"—rural people—was also recognized and validated by the elites. The identity trope of the *jíbaro* in his *pava* reversed the negative stereotypes Muñoz's own social class had about rural people and came to form the ethnic foundation of the political party.[53]

According to Córdova, the icon of the *pava* served as the "consonant for the illiterate" and the "legible emblem . . . for the ballot recognition the party needed in order to garner voters."[54] The slogan "pan, tierra y libertad" represented a cry for social justice and a promise of a *caudillo* (political leader) to his followers. This paternal promise can be interpreted as an important example of Muñoz's populist strategy. Muñoz and his party empowered the rural people, turning them into political agents through his radio speeches, visits to rural areas, and conversations with countryman in simple language. He was careful to remind the *jíbaros* that they were the key to the Party's success.

Córdova's study dovetails nicely with Scarano's examination of the *jíbaro* masquerade trope discussed earlier. It argues that in the nineteenth century the Creole classes essentially despised the jibaros but created of them a symbol to challenge the Spanish colonial rule. In this sense, Córdova like Scarano departs from the premise that the elite appropriated symbolism for political gain. In the early nineteenth century, the Creoles had appropriated the cultural symbolism of the *jíbaro* to appeal to the Spanish colonial officials—since *jíbaros* were direct descendants of

Spanish settlers—using their language. In the twentieth century, Muñoz, representing the new elite, used the *jíbaro* as the emblem of his political party across class lines. In Córdova's words, Muñoz "opened up possibilities for identification with a myth that reverberated deeply with the island's heritage."[55]

Muñoz attributed the Popular Democratic Party's electoral victory in 1940 to the participation of people from all levels of society—including Black Puerto Ricans. In fact, many Blacks were key members of the party and gained prominent positions in it. Evaluating the socioeconomic situation of the island, Muñoz did not hold the middle class responsible for their direct or indirect involvement in the abandonment of the rural masses, a rhetoric circulating among the union workers and politicians at the time. On the contrary, he argued that the middle class was more concerned with its misfortunes and "missed from its sight the other Puerto Rico." Muñoz Marín's focus on connecting the two classes contributed to the PPD's acceptance by the poor and the rich all over the island.

In the meantime, he had the full support of the middle class. During his first rallies, Muñoz collected a considerable amount of money from the *centralistas*, or sugar mill owners. With these contributions, Muñoz placed advertisements in the PPD's newspaper, *El Batey*.[56] This newspaper became strategic in targeting the *centralistas* and in uplifting workers' spirits. *El Batey* was part of Muñoz's doctrine of "catechism para el pueblo," or catechism for the people.

The naming of the party's newspaper provides a good example of how the Popular Party's ideology of inclusion failed to envelop Puerto Ricans of African ancestry. *Batey* is an Arawak word for a yard or compound where the Taíno would congregate. However, the word *batey* has different connotations in different parts of the Spanish-speaking Caribbean. In Cuba, *batey* means mill yard. In the Dominican Republic, a *batey* is a barrack where Haitian workers live. In Puerto Rico, the rural population adopted the term *batey* to designate meeting places on sugar plantations. The choice of *batey* for the party newspaper's title is an example of Luis Muñoz Marín and his party's desire to establish an essentialist semantic connection between rural whites and Arawak-Taíno culture.

Historian Silvia Álvarez-Curbelo suggested that Muñoz took advantage of cultural and economic discourses to sell his populist program. The sugar economy, controlled by large American corporations, exploited rural workers and displaced the middle class. Muñoz identified this problem and established a common ground between the two affected classes. Furthermore, he successfully presented his party's program as a solution to Puerto Rico's disadvantageous economic situation.[57] Muñoz explained this strategy of targeting displaced agrarian families and rural workers when he wrote in his memoirs, "the work of the Popular Party was not limited to rural areas. It began in the countryside for humanitarian reasons and because it is in these areas that the less fortunate live, due to the agricultural nature of the island's economy, and the benefits that the population and urban centers receive should be rooted in the rural area."[58] He further acknowledged that there were problems in the urban centers as well and that he would reach them later in his campaign, but he stressed that the rural area was in immediate need.

Muñoz wrote that people suffered at all levels in both the rural and urban areas. Their great hope was that the PPD would alleviate their economic difficulties.[59] On this point, Nathaniel Córdova noted the ritualistic dimension of the relationship between the electorate and the Party. He observed that the word *pan*, bread, which is part of the party slogan, "was tied to the *jíbaro*" because it was associated with "needed substance for self and family, as a blessing from God for all and as a 'gold' valued possession since it can be shared with others that are less fortunate."[60] Voters came to view the Party as the only entity capable of solving their problems. At the same time, voters understood that the Party could only function with their support.

Muñoz used Catholic Christian language when referring to his teachings to his party as "catechism." This word refers to the oral teaching of Catholic doctrine. In this context, Muñoz used the trope of Christianity to reach rural people with the PPD doctrines. At the same time, he reminded the rural population to work as a community and a nation to implement social change. The *jíbaro* was appointed with the task of holding aloft the banner of the Puerto Rican nation.

Art theorist Murray Edelman—also quoted in Córdova's work—contended, "Elections are powerful symbols, myth, and rituals in several important aspects. They chiefly symbolize the will of the people and therefore sanctify the entire governmental process as democratic because they can be cited as the basic influence on it all, directly or indirectly."[61] Edelman went on to assert that when art and political campaigns are combined, their influence is "multiplied and extended."[62] Muñoz's campaign successfully captivated a community because of a strategic combination of symbols, words, and, most importantly, the mystification of the *jíbaro*. The PPD created an environment of acceptance and a sense of shared community among both the poor and the elite. Muñoz's formula worked, and it resulted in the beginning of the era of the *populares*.

Building a Raceless Nation

The PPD built a new nation mostly embodied by the white rural population. Although race was not part of the PPD's ideology, in subtle ways it continued to play an influential role in Puerto Rican society. Identifying racial exclusion in a place the word *race* does not even enter mainstream discussion, as was the case in Puerto Rico, requires the use of alternative sources and means of analysis. A sample of the PPD registration form from the municipality of Culebra in 1939 illustrates this point.[63]

The form has a narrative template stating on the member's behalf that they endorse the candidate and reaffirms, "On my behalf and other subscribers, whose petitions are included with mine, I want to reiterate that the name of the party that they represent is 'Partido Popular.'" It proceeds to describe the party icon: "The emblem of the mentioned party is the profile of typical rural man from Puerto Rico, whose straw hat is also typical to them; the profile shows the man's hat with the front straight up and the back of the wing of the hat turned down." The description continued: "The profile is surrounded by the slogan 'bread, land and freedom.'"[64] Immediately following the description is an image with the figure of *la pava*, which voters learned to identify from the PPD's campaigns. The affidavit went on to provide the names of the new candidates. The second column of the page outlines the different positions, with the candidates' names and addresses.

The application included an authentication process, which included the name of the mayor and municipality secretary and protocols for reaffirming the name and identity of the petitioner. The petitioner signed, along with the witnesses. Another space is provided for the petitioner's fingerprints. Based on the sample collected, most of the petitioners provided fingerprints along with their signatures. The six affidavits from the municipality of Culebra reveal much about the political process, the continuum of racial classification, and, ultimately, the twisted construction of national identity. For instance, from the six forms, one male is classified as "blanco," Spanish for white, and to the other five, their race is one "N" for Negro (Black), one "M" for Mulatto, and three "Trig" (trigueño) or mixed Black under the lighter hue.[65] The form shows that in addition to taking an oath, each petitioner pledged to the Party. The electorate accepted the party's ideology and demonstrated trust in the candidates and the party.

These images resonated with signers from different backgrounds. Of the three females and three males, only one male was able to sign his name. Jesús T. Piñero, who ran for Senator at Large in 1940 and in 1946 became the first Puerto Rican governor appointed by the U.S. president, signed the affidavits on behalf of the two of the female petitioners. This detail, which reflects high levels of illiteracy, bolsters Córdova's argument about the image-text value of the party's emblem and the ways in which it enhanced literacy aptitudes. He quotes Manuel Álvarez Nazario and his study about the language of rural Puerto Ricans.[66] The study examines oral communication such as sayings or proverbs and symbolisms as a way to obtain knowledge and informal education in the rural area. Córdova proved his thesis that despite Puerto Rico's high level of illiteracy (31.5%, with 36.6% in rural areas), the PPD successfully used images to communicate with the rural population. One angle not explored by Córdova is the PPD's capitalization on oral tradition in their efforts to establish a channel of communication.

The voter also had to provide information on color and birthmarks. The color question seems to have been answered in some instances by petitioners themselves and in others by clerks or officials handling the forms. Of the six petitioners, only one was classified as *blanco*, or white. The color classifications of the other five petitioners ranged from "M" for *moreno* to "T" for *trigueña* to "N" for *negra*—all classifications assigned to Black Puerto Ricans. What could have been a defining moment for the PPD in terms of the color question simply became another opportunity for the reinforcement of traditional racial constructs. Indeed, the color and birthmark questions resemble those included on forms used by the Spanish authorities to collect data about slaves after the 1870 Moret Law required an inventory of slaves to be taken.

Slaves' physical characteristics were documented and to be used to help identify potential runaways.[67] The registration of slaves represented a reinforcement of the dominant racial paradigm. Establishing a parallel between the PPD affidavit form and the Slave Register of 1870 serves as a reminder of Omi and Winant's statement regarding the colonial system's role in the formation of twentieth-century racial ideology: "Racial legacies of the past—slavery and bigotry—continue to shape the present."[68] The "color" question in the PPD affidavit reflects the fact that inquiries as to an individual's race or color, a term used interchangeably with race in Puerto Rico, were customary in Puerto Rican society.

Thus, the Popular Party's inscription and narrative, which fostered a generic colorless citizen, created a misleading discourse in which the evolution of national identity occurred within the context of a raceless nation. In fact, this iconography subtly excluded people of African ancestry from the nation-building project.

Returning to Córdova's study on images of the Popular Party, one finds a focus on the contrast between the white background of the party's flag and the red of the icon (figure 3.1). Córdova suggested that the profiled logo's depiction in bright red brings universality to image, and that the contrast between red figure and white background can be interpreted as a "neutralization of race." In support of this argument, Córdova emphasizes that it was critical that the "image fostered identification with the myth of the *jíbaro* that had been the project of the island's cultural elite."[69]

In this context, a thorough examination of the PPD's strategies to promote itself as a savior can help to shed light. Edelman's theories about art and political parties became useful, especially his statement that "the implicit incorporation of an ideological position is likely to mean that the political message and its ramifications respecting virtue and vice are both more memorably imprinted on the mind and more readily accepted."[70]

Thus, voters confirmed their new identity as one of the "popular" regardless of the color of their skin. The influences of the party emblems among the electorate fit with Edelman's views about images and their political functionality. He declared, "'rhetorical assurance' as signals of trends that contradict their surface meanings, a common function of

Figure 3.1. Former logo of *Partido Popular Democrático* with Spanish motto: "bread, land, liberty."

officially disseminated myths and other symbols. Because the reassurances are misleading, they must be repeated often as an official dogma."[71]

The *pava* did not symbolize an inclusive, colorless political party; on the contrary, it perpetuated the hegemony of rural whites and the elite. In pledging to the PPD, the electorate confirmed their acceptance of—or, at most, negotiation with—the new sociopolitical order and raceless discourse espoused by Muñoz Marín and his party. Indeed, the PPD's use of rhetoric and imagery parallels Omi and Winant's arguments.[72] The PPD's success is yet another instance of a dominant elite shaping a national discourse that failed to represent the diversity of Puerto Rican society.

The semantics of the PPD form can be interpreted as perpetuating the racial lexicon with which we have observed Puerto Ricans engaging at the institutional level of the political party. The seemingly innocent "color" question contradicts the fact that racial classification is highly considered. By 1930, Puerto Rico's colored population was decreasing. The 1930 census bulletin highlighted this fact and concluded that the decline was "a result of gradual change in the concept of race classification as an applied by the census enumerators."[73] Census options for racial classification were limited to "white" or "non-white."

There was no concession to Puerto Rico's distinctive racial scheme, with categories between "black" and "white" ranging from "*café con leche*" to "*trigueño.*" The new binary classification system reduced Puerto Ricans' options for categories with which to identify. It is not surprising that colored Puerto Ricans, under the influence of the PPD's Hispanophilic rhetoric, preferred to distance themselves from their African roots and to self-identify as whites.

In the supposedly raceless nation under construction by Puerto Rico's intellectual and political elite, it was common for those involved in gathering race-related data to describe their subjects based on phenotype. From this data, we can reconstruct only a blurry picture of the population; however, the very purpose of this section is to demonstrate the ephemeral nature of racial discourse on the island. While a new political entity, the *Partido Popular*, promoted a more inclusive fellowship of Puerto Ricans, old practices and social constructs related to race remained pivotal for membership in the party. The myth of the rural white man, or *jíbaro*, was strongly rooted in Puerto Rico in the 1930s and 1940s. In this period, Puerto Rico's socioeconomic situation forced thousands of Puerto Ricans to leave the island. Among these migrants, who settled in many U.S. cities, was Rafael Hernández (1892–1965).

A Drop of Nostalgia

Along with many other Black Puerto Ricans musicians, Hernández made New York City his home. Hernández, who wrote more than 3,000 pieces, is widely considered to be the most prolific and international Puerto Rican composer, though many of his most famous hits were written abroad. He belonged to a small group of popular musicians of African ancestry who, according to ethnomusicologist Noel Allende-Goytía, created a musical repertoire encompassing Puerto Rican society on the island and abroad.[74] Hernández's lyrics reflect his experiences in Puerto Rico, Europe, Cuba, the Dominican Republic, New York, and Mexico. The romantic, celebratory, and patriotic themes of his songs drew in an ethnically diverse group of admirers in Puerto Rico and Latin America.

Hernández, nicknamed "el Jíbarito," wrote his famous song "Preciosa" in 1937. The song, evoking Hernández's memories of the island, touched the patriotic spirit of Puerto Ricans, who considered it a second national anthem. In a two-way cultural exchange, Puerto Ricans on the island were consuming music created by diasporic Puerto Ricans while Puerto Ricans in the diaspora used the music to connect to their homeland.

"Preciosa" embodied a new national Puerto Rican sentiment, affirming the island's preciousness.

> *Yo sé de tus hembras trigueñas,*
> *y del olor de tus rosas*
> *y a esa mi tierra riqueña,*
> *por siempre la llamaré, preciosa.*

(I know of her darkly colored women/ know the smell of her roses/ for this is my rich earth/ always I will call her precious.)

In "Preciosa," Hernández captured the racial imaginary of Puerto Rico, which is commonly understood as a three-part equation: Taíno/Indian, Spanish, and African. He feminized the island, calling it by its Arawak name, *Boriquén*. Hernández placed *"hembras trigueñas,"* a euphemism for Black women, as the first, most immediate link to his memories of Puerto Rico. . . . Did *trigueña* simply work with the rhythmical nature of the composition? Or was Hernández imagining a new racial hierarchy? *Trigueña* can be used to describe a brunette, someone with olive skin, or a Black individual, but in general it implies a non-white person.

Regardless of his apparent exaltation of women of color, Hernández, reaffirmed the established social imagery when he placed the Spanish in a leading hierarchical role:

> *Y tienes la noble hidalguía*
> *de la madre España*
> *y el fiero cantillo del indio bravío*
> *lo tienes también.*

(And you have the nobility /of mother Spain/ and the fiery song of the brave Indian /that you also have.)

Hernández traced Puerto Rico's nobility to Spain and its bravery to the Indian. In this patriotic song, Spanish descent is a positive asset. He, like so many others, resorted to an affirmative construction of Puerto Rico as an Antillean and Hispanic nation.[75] In his study on the evolution of Puerto Rican music, a reflection of the social imaginary, Allende-Goytía notes that Hernández's work is part of the appropriation of a cultural discourse that is essentially patriotic, Caribbean, and politically militant.[76] However, despite the patriotism found in "Preciosa," African heritage is nonexistent as a cultural component of the *patria* in the song.

If one interprets *trigueñas* literally, then Black Puerto Ricans are subtly visible—if only from a sexualized point of view. Literary critic Mercedes López-Barat commented on Hernández's obliteration of blackness in his characterization of Puerto Rico within the intellectual context of the *negrista* movement. López-Barat pointed out that Hernández's song was inspired by a false image of the Puerto Rican nation. It hid Puerto Rico's African heritage and revived it as the Taínos.[77] One can add to López-Baralt's statement that, in this era, Puerto Rican musical and literary tradition tended to characterize Blacks as a de-civilizing force in the equation of the Puerto Rican nation, while the Spanish were glorified as members of the strongest race.

Whether in popular song or political campaign, Puerto Rican national discourse in the 1930s was plagued by a paradigm of racial exclusion. The phenomena of exclusionary language and imagery demonstrates Chilean political scientist Jorge Larrain's point those leading figures—a group in which popular entertainers and politicians fit under—"[tell] and [retell] the narrative of the nation which is presented in national histories," and how, in the process, "the discourse of a nation interpolates individuals so they identify with it," even if the message they identify with is one of exclusion.[78]

Chapter 4

Intersecting Race and Modernization

1940–1950

In the 1940s, Puerto Rico's insular government took steps to implement a formula of modernization, nation-building, and economic development. The elite took the lead in the modernity project driven by their aspirations to establish a more Westernized society. Modernization included essentially overhauling the customs around race, particularly what was considered racial inferiority. During this process, the elites struggled to demonstrate their cultural preeminence as a racially mixed and tolerant society, perpetuating the myth of racial harmony. While those embracing their Spanish heritage were growing in number, so were those wishing to embrace both Spanish heritage and U.S. citizenship. The latter were particularly outspoken about their reconciliatory political views with Americans. The beliefs of the Puerto Rican elite were marred by contradictions. Those who strongly supported economic ties to the United States believed they would result in prosperity and capital development. However, to achieve a higher degree of modernization, they had to adhere to policies aimed at controlling the population introduced in the 1930s, suppressing cultural identity, restricting labor rights (labeled *vices* and disorders by American social scientists), and continuing the research started on the island in the 1940s.

Impeding Modernization

During this period, scholarship in the social sciences was influenced by American views. For instance, in 1945, Earl S. Garver and Ernest B.

Fincher published their influential report *Puerto Rico: Unsolved Problem*, which emphasized the racial composition of the Puerto Rican population and their socioeconomic conditions. First, they compared the *jibaros*, or white peasants, with the Appalachian people in the southern United States.[1] Second, they noted that because "many 'white' Puerto Ricans have Negro blood, racial discrimination becomes virtually impossible" because of the racial intermixing.[2] Finally, they stressed the need for Puerto Rico to continue its political and economic relationship with the United States because it would lead to economic development and the eventual elimination of their social problems, meaning poverty, overpopulation, and racial mixing.[3]

Historian Alejandro de la Fuente's work traces the evolution of Cuban national identity, focusing on the efforts through which the white intellectual elite tried to create a unique formula encompassing the racial diversity of Cuban society. In that sense, the scholar notes that the white elites "were prisoners of their own ideological creation," while their efforts were focused on delegitimizing Black Cubans.[4] Although the white Puerto Rican elite did not engage in as openly contested relations with Blacks as Cuban white elites did, Puerto Ricans constantly needed to prove the modern nature of their culture by wielding institutional power to reinforce a so-called cultural supremacy. This has been demonstrated by the different approaches aimed at affirming a hegemonic discourse focused on emphasizing European ancestry. Another frequently used strategy was the manipulation of the arts and applied sciences to celebrate the island's racial mixture or heritage.

In Puerto Rico, like many other Caribbean and Latin American societies where the racial composition of the population was always a concern, the hegemonic elite addressed race through literature and mass propaganda. These discussions seemed apologetic, filled with proposals of how to fix what was perceived as "degeneration" because of Puerto Ricans' racial mixture with the African race.[5] For example, in Puerto Rico, Cuba, Venezuela, Mexico, and other countries, in their process of modernization, the elites used their ability to articulate their identity dilemma and began to highlight the cultural past by either becoming Hispanophile or *indigenista*. In other countries such as Brazil, Argentina, and Cuba, state law encouraged white migration to solve racial problems or simply ostracized peoples of African ancestry and denied their access to power.[6] De la Fuente's seminal study about racial democracy in Cuba provided an accurate definition of the period that can be widely applied to the region. He contended, "while contesting or just ignoring the idea that racial miscegenation meant degeneration, Latin American thinkers accepted the premise that ample sectors of their population were basically inferior and their human stock needed to be 'improved.'"[7] In countries where the United States had strong influences, this ideology of miscegenation as a negative social attribute was used as an alternative method for addressing a population's racial make-up.

Regardless of the level of racialization to which Puerto Ricans were subjected, violent racist practices in the United States prompted the Puerto Rican upper class to argue that, in comparison to the United States, racism in Puerto Rico was light and prejudice nonexistent.[8]

Building a Modern National Identity

During the 1940s, Puerto Rican politics experienced a dramatic change, initiated by the electoral triumph of the Popular Democratic Party (*Partido Popular Democrático* [PPD]). Party members—also known as *populares*—filled the seats of the Senate and House of Representatives. The PPD engaged in a more aggressive political campaign to address the question of national identity. For instance, during this period the government abolished the use of English as the primary language of learning in public schools, although its use continued in the courts and government. This elimination took place because Puerto Rican academic, intellectual, and political leftists promoted Hispanic pride. Key players in this period included Vicente Géigel Polanco, Luis Muñoz Marín, Jaime Benítez, and Tomás Blanco, among others.

Pivotal institutions, such as the University of Puerto Rico, led these nation-building initiatives. Founded in 1903, the University of Puerto Rico (UPR) initiated many important projects addressing a wide range of educational issues and promoting Puerto Rican culture. Many faculty members contributed research on how to improve the living conditions of the Puerto Rican people. With the establishment of the Department of Hispanic Studies in 1927, the institution became the hub for articulating and seeking an alternative solution to modernize the island infrastructure and intellectual class. UPR faculty members and academic administrators became vocal about their Hispanic-centered perspective. An example of UPR's advocacy was the creation of the 1940 Forum, intended to reconcile views about Puerto Rican society's racial/national identity. The group served as an opportunity to legitimize the University of Puerto Rico as the island's first higher education institution.

According to María E. Rodríguez's chapter about the University of Puerto Rico's Forum of the 1940s, the ideological tensions between political and intellectual leaders were central to how the PPD and university staff positioned themselves as individuals committed to the modernizing agenda throughout the reconciliation between academia and official politics.[9] PPD members revealed their cross-party ideologies when Jaime Benítez, Chancellor of UPR's Río Piedras campus, and Vicente Géigel Polanco—a former Nationalist sympathizer—crossed party lines to associate with Luis Muñoz Marín in his new ideological/populist project. These developments also highlight two approaches to the national identity ideologies (Hispanic vs. Hispanic-American) to what was considered an exclusive nationalist ideal, as formulated by the *Generación del Treinta*. The formula of *The Great Puerto Rican Family* served as the creed of the old discourse.[10] According to Rodríguez, the tensions arose in the form of *Criollismo* vs. *Hispanismo* notions that found advocates in elites on both sides through the interconnections between state and cultural institutions.

Eventually, the social science field on the island evolved to one that reflected the populist agenda combined with Western approaches. Jaime Benítez, at the time the UPR Provost, was a proponent of Western values and approaches. Commenting on these developments, sociologist Ángel Quintero points out that, in 1947, the social sciences were institutionalized, whereby researchers tended to focus on studies in support of Puerto Rico's modernization and modernity by either addressing racial identity and/or ignoring racial discrimination on the island. Through UPR, the interplay of relationships among intellectual elites of the United States, Latin America, and Puerto Rico sparked a new national identity discourse on the island. As the island's primary center of higher education, the University of Puerto Rico positioned itself as the intellectual center of the modern state.[11]

Chilean social scientist Jorge Larraín contended that, in Latin American nation-building societies from 1810 to the 1950s, national identities embodied two poles of culture and existed on two fronts. On the one hand was the public forum in which the media, intellectual, and research centers were given the task of articulating the discourse of racial harmony. On the other were the groups he calls the "social base," which became advocates and defenders of a version of their culture but "sometimes are not represented in public versions of identity."[12] This led to a struggle for dominance between these two versions and interpretations. It seems logical to concur with the first option because the state had the necessary infrastructure and—more importantly—the state's educational institutions provided the interpretation of culture that better aligned with the views of the elite and the political establishment.

The University of Puerto Rico represented the side of the intelligentsia. The state wanted its support for public policies intended to legitimize the official culture and facilitate its implementation. The Forum of 1940 epitomized, as Rodríguez points out, "the national integration of the defense of democracy and culture."[13] The state institution of higher education took the leading role in producing a new breed of professionals whose mission was the modernization of society. At the same time, these scholars and professionals were supportive of modern cultural ideals. Thus, UPR needed to inject their curricula with new courses and visits by prominent scholars aligned with the said visions. This socio-intellectual attitude would be authenticated with the series of UPR visiting scholars who represented the establishment's philosophical ideals.

Advocating for a Small Nation

Among the distinguished thinkers sponsored by the UPR was Venezuelan historian and diplomat Mariano Picón-Salas who served as the keynote speaker at UPR's forty-second commencement in 1946. His lecture, "Defense of the Small Nation," was a critique against those powerful nations that—because of their geographical size and military power—feel entitled to dominate the world. The speech was just the beginning of a series of remarks in which Picón-Salas alerted Puerto Ricans that, even though small in size, the island could achieve big accomplishments as a nation. He encouraged Puerto Ricans to take the first step by using natural resources, embarking on the path to industrialization.[14] The scholar provided inspiring examples of small nations such as Greece and Crete: the cradle of great civilizations and conquest enterprise.[15] He thus urged Puerto Ricans not to feel intimidated by the fanfare of the military supremacy of certain neighboring countries, clearly referring to the United States.

Indeed, Picón-Salas was acting as an advocate on behalf of Puerto Rico. He also acknowledged the economic conditions that forced thousands of Puerto Ricans to migrate to the United States. He talked about the struggle of the Puerto Rican diaspora, whose hearts, despite being in a land of cold weather, burned with love for their island and resisted assimilation.[16] He continued saying that the island (society) "already began with its first cultural task, which is domesticating the land and put it to the service to the peoples and overcome fears associated with living in isolation."[17]

For the University of Puerto Rico, it would have been influential to have a visiting scholar and diplomat the caliber of Picón-Salas. One may imagine the audience that day from the university president, the chancellor, important members of the faculty, and then the students—all of them listening to this brilliant man who was enamored of the island, its people, and the university campus. Picón-Salas was proud to be from the small province of Merida. He was a close friend and cabinet member of Rómulo Gallegos, the president of Venezuela. He spent many years as an ambassador to Venezuela as well. Picón-Salas was uniquely qualified to provide an assessment of the challenges Puerto Ricans were facing.

Using metaphoric language of praise when describing Puerto Rico, Picón-Salas referred to it as a Hispanic nation while criticizing the current political situation on the island. He aimed to convey that societies like Puerto Rico trigger a constant demand among their people to showcase their modernity and capability, a demand that was channeled into the new infrastructure projects supported by the United States but keeping their own characteristics as a Hispanic society. Picón-Salas's magisterial speech shed light on the new tensions between the intellectual and political elites during the period. He was instrumental not only in his pedagogical capacity but as the precursor of such ideals. His speech served as a validation for all the students who attended the ceremony.

Marketing Puerto Ricanness

In the mid-1940s to prepare for the forthcoming American capitalist and tourist industries, local authorities collaborated with the American Empire builders by engaging in a massive social transformation of the island. UPR representatives joined members of the Hotel Association and the Office of the Governor to propose a documentary film about the people of Puerto Rico. Correspondence from April 25 and July 31 of 1947 among high-ranking UPR officials, special aides to Governor Piñero, and Teodoro Moscoso, president of the Industrial Development Company (better known as *Fomento*), defined a plan to film a documentary based on two of Enrique Laguerre's classic literary novels: *La llamarada* (1935) and *Solar Montoya* (1941).[18] Both works dealt with the life of Puerto Rican workers in the cane fields and featured protagonists that represented the *jíbaros*, or white peasants. Interestingly, Laguerre was of African ancestry, but his work reflected the Hispanic-centered ideology of the era.[19]

The negotiation for the film project directly involved the president of Twentieth Century Fox Studios, Spyros Skouras, who also visited the United States' Virgin Islands to carry out a similar project there. In fact, René Marqués, another contemporary Puerto Rican writer, sent a letter to Governor Piñero supporting the documentary. According to Marqués, it was an excellent opportunity to promote a positive image of the island. He added, "*La llamarada* embodies the ideal of social justice achieved under the current government."[20]

This film project was a preliminary test for large-scale initiatives produced by the *División de Educación a la Comunidad* (DIVEDCO). DIVEDCO was created by the government in May 1949 and charged with implementing a massive educational program for the rural and lower classes. Inspired by the New Deal's Works Progress Administration (1935–1943), DIVEDCO recognized that writers, artists, social scientists, and documentarians played a key role in social improvement by bringing together their talents to convey a message of social justice, economic progress, and to protect the people's right to work.[21] This program was very influential and a good example of how these sorts of messages were disseminated to the masses. Anthropologist Antonio Lauria-Perricelli has pointed out that DIVEDCO was utopic and full of contradictions, for it encouraged people's self-help attitude while creating a dependency on what was emerging as a welfare state. It fostered *puertorriqueñidad* (or Puerto Ricanness), attributing an integral role to the rural people in its creation of the kin-type of social imagery.[22] As a state institution, DIVEDCO can be seen—as literary critic Catherine Kennerly put it—as a primary example of the marriage between state and intellectual elite in the creation of a new society.[23]

As the UPR played a role in the intellectual rearticulation of national identity, political leadership added a new episode to Puerto Rico's modernization process. A perfect example of how national identity manifested in this decade was seen in the efforts to boost the island's tourist industry and the establishment of Puerto Rican–owned upscale restaurants and entertainment businesses. These types of industries became the perfect setting for locals to enforce new codes of social behavior.

Remarkably, while an American film company and state institutions collaborated to market Puerto Rico as a tropical paradise, hotels in Puerto Rico continued to prohibit Blacks from their premises to appease white American tourists. This is illustrated by an investigation launched by the chairman of the United States section of the Caribbean Commission, Charles W. Taussig. K.M. Ellsworth, the coordinator of Insular Affairs, wrote a letter to Taussig asking him to investigate the challenges facing the tourism industry in the Caribbean. One of the coordinator's concerns was that Puerto Rico was not "in a position to receive any considerable affluence of tourists."[24] Ellsworth pointed out, "another matter which engages our attention is race discrimination." He went on to congratulate the Commission "on its policy declaration (on racial discrimination) concerning this problem." However, he noted, in no place in the report on the proceeding of the Council is it specified how this problem will be solved." It was difficult to implement antiracial discrimination policies because, in Puerto Rico, racial discrimination had become more difficult to address as U.S. colonization increased racial denial. It was problematic for members of the Commission and local hotel owners to admit racial discrimination because the island was showcased as a racially tolerant society.

Drops of Justice

Despite flourishing signs of modernity in Puerto Rico, racial discrimination appears to have persisted, as shown in three incidents covered in the local press. The first one took place on August 14, 1943. First Lieutenant Rafael Muriel with his wife Paula Olavarría, Captain Rafael Pérez-García with his wife Juanita Velázquez (both in uniform), and Jorge Haddock with his wife Ana Delia Cordero were denied access to the trendy middle-class Club Esquire. The excuse of the bouncer was that the club did not allow "people of color."[25] The three friends started arguing with the doorman and demanded to speak with the club owner, Salvador Suazo, who arrived promptly but simply reiterated what his employees said. Muriel warned Suazo that he was violating the law. Suazo responded that as the club's owner he was entitled to do whatever he wanted. Lieutenant Muriel and his friends filed a lawsuit against Suazo on the grounds of racial discrimination and violation of Law 131 (1943), seeking compensation for having suffered mental anguish. The case was eventually taken to the Puerto Rican Supreme Court in 1950, where Suazo's attorney argued that his defendant could not pay compensation for "mental anguish because it was not physical."[26] However, Judge R. Cordovés Arana concluded that the suffering and humiliation experienced by the plaintiffs induced pain, ruling in their favor on March 30, 1951. This ruling was significant as it established for the first time in Puerto Rico that racial discrimination can cause pain and suffering, and that people who violate the law would be punished accordingly. Judge Cordovés Arana ordered Suazo to pay Muriel and his party a total of $3,000 in addition to $300 in legal fees.[27]

The outcome of Lt. Muriel's case also implied that an army uniform would not necessarily give a Black Puerto Rican preferential status. Furthermore, despite the time lapse between the first incident and the court decision, it appears that Lt. Muriel was willing to be patient in order to exercise his rights and finally see justice served. Though he had the resources, his middle-class status and high rank in the army were probably decisive in this matter.

The second and third incidents took place on April 7, 1949, when Club Zero denied "entry and equal treatment" to Dr. Thomas B. Jones, Mario Urdaneta, Evelyn Price, and Irene Hayman because they "did not make reservations."[28] The following day, the same group visited Suazo's Club Esquire and was denied entry on the same grounds. Jones filed a lawsuit against Carlos Vizcarrondo, owner of Club Zero, and Suazo, taking both cases to trial in September 1949, within a week of each another. Despite the similarities in accusations, Vizcarrondo was acquitted due to insufficient evidence while Suazo and his employees were once again found guilty and fined $300. The ruling in Vizcarrondo's favor is of little surprise, considering that at the time people of color were not welcome in locally owned businesses. Nonetheless, given that the owners of the two clubs were Puerto Ricans, racial discrimination in these cases was particularly problematic.

The arbitrary sentencing in one case and the acquittal in the other suggest how difficult it was to establish racial discrimination cases in that period. These cases illustrate how deeply embedded racial discrimination was—and still is—in the Puerto Rican social fabric. Moreover, the attitude of the club owners reflected defiance of the law and the misguided belief that their ownership status allowed them to freely exercise discrimination. Local media coverage of the lawsuits against the owners of the private clubs was a new development. It conveyed an act of self-criticism of Puerto Rican society and a willingness to seriously consider racial issues.

One might compare this example to what Michael Omi and Howard Winant describe as racial formation on a macro level. They argue, "we may notice someone's race, but we cannot act upon that awareness,"[29] as was the case of the two club owners. In other words, experiencing racial discrimination does not necessarily translate to its denouncement and prosecution. However, the state acted with a color-blind filter when Vizcarrondo was acquitted. Again, as Omi and Winant mention in their study, the state "cannot suddenly declare itself 'color-blind' without in fact perpetuating the same type of differential racist treatment. Thus, race continues to signify difference and structure inequality."[30] The ruling highlights that the State assumed its responsibility to solve it and stop the perpetuation of discriminatory practices, instead of ending the pattern of structural racism.

In his book, provocatively titled *Justicia Negra: Casos y cosas* (Black Justice: Cases and Things), Marcos Rivera Ortíz, a prominent Afro-Puerto Rican attorney and activist, compiles stories and newspapers articles from the late 1980s until the 1990s focusing on civil and criminal cases that directly involve Black Puerto Ricans. Rivera Ortíz describes the different ways that the island judicial system handled cases that involved race, racism, or discrimination. Rivera Ortíz may be the first contemporary Black Puerto Rican attorney to take racial discrimination cases and litigate them conscientiously. Because of the nature of racial denial on the island, it is still challenging to prove racial discrimination in Puerto Rico. *Muriel v. Suazo* was a noteworthy exception. The incidents cited in these cases are clear examples of "structural racism," which the Aspen Institute defines as

> a system in which public policies, institutional practices, cultural representations, and other norms work in various, often reinforcing ways to perpetuate racial group inequity. It identifies dimensions of our history and culture that have allowed privileges associated with "whiteness" and disadvantages associated with "color" to endure and adapt over time. Structural racism is not something that a few people or institutions choose to practice.[31]

Applying the concept of structural racism to Puerto Rico, psychologist Marta Cruz-Janzen affirmed that racial discrimination is even denied among many Black Puerto Ricans. Despite the many studies pointing out the close relation between race and poverty, the Puerto Rican government ignores the situation. Cruz-Jenzén sustains that, in Puerto Rico, Blacks living in barrios are more likely to have issues with the legal system. Legal options to deal with this situation are basically ignored because of the belief that racism does not exist. Addressing the issue from a legal point of view seems an uphill battle. Cruz-Janzén asserts, "Clearly Puerto Rico is in its infancy along the lines of recognizing openly addressing the legacy of racism as it has evolved, and more importantly, been maintained on the island."[32] Legal scholar Tanya Hernández examined the disparities of antidiscrimination laws in Puerto Rico, Latin America, and the United States, concluding that in the case of Puerto Rico, despite existing legal framework to address racial discrimination cases, very few were filed from 1940s to 2001.[33] What is apparent from these two assessments is that the denial of racism in Puerto Rico has impacted negativity and discourage possible cases of racial discrimination because the court system has not yet found a common consensus in taking such cases.

Measuring Racial Democracy

Enforcing civil rights was a priority for the Truman administration (1945–1953), which sought its extension in international areas where U.S. companies operated. A few years before *Muriel v. Suazo*, President Harry S. Truman's Committee on Civil Rights initiated an investigation of racial discrimination, both nationwide and within U.S. possessions and territories. Again, officials attempted to measure the island's racial situation against America's racial yardstick. In an official memo, the committee's executive secretary, Robert K. Carr, concluded that, "there is no legal or political discrimination against Negroes in Puerto Rico. Intermarriage is acceptable."[34] Co-author of *To Secure These Rights: The Report of the President's Committee on Civil Rights*, Carr was a political scientist and the driving force behind the accuracy and effectiveness of this document. The outcomes of the civil rights report, which were discussed in detail in the public sphere, illustrate how federal and insular governments were trying to eradicate racial discrimination.

However, Puerto Rican newspapers followed the investigation's results, refuting them on their front pages. A newspaper article written by the American journalist and Pulitzer Prize winner William J. Dorvillier, in *El Mundo*, summarized the study's findings, adding that, despite the considerable number of Blacks on the island, whites occupied most of the important positions. Dorvillier further outlined the Commission's recommendations, which included the establishment of the Civil Rights

Regional Office to monitor issues such as police brutality and working conditions.[35] By publishing the Commission's findings, authors of newspaper articles sought to highlight discriminatory practices, particularly at work and in public places. However, the colonial government did not consider these measures. It took more than two decades to implement civil rights in the United States and its overseas possessions.

Assessing social problems and race relations in Puerto Rico were topics of interest for scholars from different fields. One of them was Dr. Eric Williams, a Caribbean intellectual, head of the Caribbean Commission, and the first prime minister of Trinidad and Tobago. In an article addressing race relations in Puerto Rico and the Virgin Islands, Williams wrote of racial discrimination in these territories, analyzing the Puerto Rican government, the tourist industry, and the University of Puerto Rico.[36]

Williams's sharp assessment reflected the complexities of Puerto Rican race relations. For instance, he attributed the absence of legal racial prejudice to the fact that "racial differences are subordinated to those of class" and that Black Puerto Ricans have attained important roles in the government and the economy.[37] Williams warned the authorities about not allowing American capitalism to break race relations in Puerto Rico.[38] Though he stated that progress had been made to include colored people in the new economy, he also acknowledged that interracial mixing, which the ruling class was promoting, did not "whiten" the island, as many sociologists had predicted.[39] He thus made the following recommendations:

> The Administration must try to formulate policy and practice in accordance with the history and patterns of the area, and not allow itself to be influenced by the national traditions of the interests, which it represents. Given the history and social sentiments of the island, it is not at all impossible for the United States Administration in Puerto Rico to strike blows at race prejudice and to try to develop an official attitude toward race relations in harmony with the aspirations and practice of the colonial areas.[40]

According to Williams, the situation in Puerto Rico reflected a pattern of discrimination in the region that was clearly incompatible with the changes and democratic values promoted by the United States. Nonetheless, many observers and visitors were optimistic and saw a model of racial harmony in Puerto Rican society.

Observing from the Outside

The misinformed views expressed by U.S. and Puerto Rican officials served only to spread the myth of racial democracy on the island, despite the fact that it was clearly absent in reality. Professor Jennie M. Turner, from Madison, Wisconsin, came to teach as an adjunct at the UPR in the spring of 1947. Turner was a member of the Wisconsin State Board of vocational and industrial adult education. She was married to Glenn Turner, an attorney and a socialist. She sent a letter to *The Capital Times* to share her experiences in Puerto Rico with the United States. She saw the U.S. brand of racism as widespread, rampant, and violent. The article reports that Turner saw a "better" and "gentler" form of racism in Puerto Rico. Although no evidence remains of the letter she sent to the newspaper, the Puerto Rican newspaper *El Mundo* reported on her impressions and suggestions for addressing the racial problems in the United States. Turner proposed that Puerto Rico be used as a model of racial harmony.[41] She proposed that the City of Madison recruit Black Puerto Rican teachers to work in the Wisconsin public school system to improve racial tolerance. In so doing, Turner was changing standards for racial discrimination instead of working to solve the problem. According to *El Mundo*, Turner confidently declared that Black Puerto Ricans had equal access to academic jobs on the island and that many of the department chairs in the island's universities were Blacks.[42] The publication of Turner's initiative in *El Mundo* reinforced the myth of successful race relations in Puerto Rican society.

Turner's misinterpretations could be rooted in her notion of race and racial discrimination from an American perspective, which is characterized by segregation and violence. Moreover, Turner clearly failed to recognize that the island had its own racial contract in which Black Puerto Ricans were relegated to a folkloric or subcultural status.[43] It is possible that Turner made racial assessments based solely on phenotypical observation, not realizing that blackness worked differently in Puerto Rico. Perhaps Turner was simply praising the level of educational and economic attainment of Black Puerto Ricans.

It is puzzling that Turner made such a positive assessment of race relations on the island, and particularly in Puerto Rican universities. In contrast to Turner's impressions, the problem of racial discrimination at the University of Puerto Rico (UPR) is well documented and was particularly acute in the 1940s. For example, the study conducted by sociologists José Colombán and Justina Carrión in 1940 revealed that Black Puerto Ricans were excluded from teaching and administrative positions at the University of Puerto Rico. Even in 1974, Isabelo Zenón Cruz pointed out that racism at UPR extended to the faculty and students' fraternities. In fact, Jesús T. Piñero (the first appointed Puerto Rican governor) wrote a letter to Ramón Barreto Pérez, president of the *Unión General de Trabajores* (UGT), supporting a workers' resolution to condemn racial discrimination at UPR.[44] In the same letter, the governor expresses his regret for not being able to attend their historic meeting. Piñero assured Barreto of his intent to implement a resolution banning racial discrimination at UPR. The governor also informed the union leader of his correspondence with UPR's Chancellor, demanding the end of racial discrimination in the public university system. It is clear that the myth of racial harmony was at work.

Chapter 5

Strategizing Modernity

1950–1965

In the mid-1940s, which coincided with the beginning of the Cold War, Puerto Rico transformed from an agriculturally based economy to an industrialized country. Historically, the industrialization process was framed by the creation of the Commonwealth of Puerto Rico, the resurgence of the Nationalist Party, and the implementation of a series of economic reforms on the island called the *Operación Manos a la Obra* but better known as "Operation Bootstraps." These major developments shaped the national culture and politics on the island. On one hand, the industrialization of the island triggered a boom in the economy. On the other, the power exercised by American investors incited the Nationalist Party to challenge the spread of capitalism, which they believed was another form of American imperialism.

The *Partido Popular Demócratico* (PPD) became the main political party, and Luis Muñoz Marín became the governor. The PPD pushed for the passing of Public Law 600 in the United States Congress, which authorized Puerto Ricans to elect their own governor, draft their own Constitution, and create the *Estado Libre Asociado* (ELA), or Commonwealth of Puerto Rico, in 1952. However, the election of Luis Muñoz Marín as the first governor of Puerto Rico did not mean that the United States was distancing itself from the island. On the contrary, in this decade the United States launched a crusade against communism, and Puerto Rico became part of the Truman and Eisenhower Administrations' plan to deter the spread of communism in the Caribbean and around the world.

The PPD focused on bringing social and economic reform to all Puerto Ricans. Luis Muñoz Marín considered industrialization both a vital step for achieving modernity of the island and an indispensable measure to eradicate poverty.[1] To this end, Muñoz Marín played a leading role in a series of economic reforms when, during his terms as a senator and later as governor, he and fellow partisans introduced programs intended to promote U.S. investment on the island through tax incentives. They believed that providing the infrastructure needed for business would support their ultimate goal of decreasing the high unemployment rate.

Puerto Rico followed the trend of many nations in the hemisphere that sought to optimize their social structure. In his influential study about the relationship between modernity and identity, Chilean economist Jorge Larrain identified the period from 1900 to the 1950s as the beginning of industrialization for most Latin American countries. This process paralleled the emergence of populist regimes. The 1950s sat in the second period of economic modernization that began with World War II and ended in the 1970s. During these decades, populist governments consolidated as democratic societies, and political institutions moved to the forefront of modernization through processes such as industrialization, educational projects, and urbanization.[2] This theoretical parenthesis allows us to place Puerto Rico within that historical context. There we can identify patterns that suggest the exclusion of groups that did not necessarily represent the desired mainstream of the modern nation. The PPD Administration of the 1950s prioritized the industrialization of Puerto Rico as a pathway to revitalize the island economy. At the same time, the United States began to solidify its diplomatic relationship with Latin America under the administration of President Dwight D. Eisenhower.

Planning for Industrialization

Rexford G. Tugwell, the last American governor of Puerto Rico (1941–1946), was a liberal, a trained economist, and a former Secretary of Agriculture. He was appointed by President Roosevelt to implement the New Deal in Puerto Rico. Tugwell teamed up with Teodoro Moscoso, a trained pharmacist, to create a plan that would boost the Puerto Rican economy in both the long and short terms. Originally, Tugwell believed that industrialization should be agriculturally based. But Moscoso had another vision. He proposed that the island should go beyond its dependence on agriculture and sugar-based products. To solidify his views on industrialization, Moscoso traveled to the United States to research models of government-run development agencies in France, India, and Canada. A Chilean program titled *Corporación de Fomento de la Producción* (Corporation for the Development and Production) caught his attention. He presented his subsequent plan to Governor Tugwell, who immediately approved it. The result was the creation of Fomento (a development agency) and, later, the Puerto Rican Development Bank.[3]

The first phase of their industrialization plan consisted of items that complemented those things already manufactured on the island. For example, concrete facilitated the construction of buildings. The glass industry eased manufacturing of glass containers to bottle rum, and cardboard provided packing for rum bottles. Moscoso also considered expanding the tourist industry, which was previously proposed by former governor General Winship. He envisioned that tourism could significantly change the island's economic status.[4] The only problem was a lack of hotels. To give some historical background, in the mid-1940s, there were only two hotels in San Juan. During this period, local entrepreneurs attended a conference in New York City sponsored by the Caribbean Commission. A document released from that meeting summarized a plan to develop tourism in the Caribbean. The main tourism issues they discussed were the construction of more hotels and transportation for tourists.[5]

In Puerto Rico, specifically, measures were taken to expand the tourist industry in the 1940s. For example, a partnership between the government and American investors resulted in the contribution of $7 million from the local government to build the Caribe Hilton Hotel, which opened to the public in 1949.[6] The hotel attracted American investors, and many important business transactions took place there. Historian Rafael Bernabe and sociologist César Ayala contend that the tourist industry made urban development difficult because its greatest efforts went into developing the more attractive coastal areas. In addition, the tourist industry "shaped official and commercial representations of Puerto Rico and its people and contributed to the image of Puerto Rico as a model of noncommunist development in the context of the Cold War."[7] The expansion of the tourist industry was one of the most important programs promoted by *Fomento*. This agency promoted the island in American magazines and business newspapers. The government of Puerto Rico opened branch offices in the continental United States for the same purpose.[8]

The final stage that paved the way for industrialization in Puerto Rico was the creation of Bill 184 (signed in May 1948), which granted autonomy to the government of Puerto Rico. The new legislation empowered the

Puerto Rican government to grant income and property tax exemptions to newly established industries for a period of ten years.[9]

A Drop of Ingenuity

As Puerto Rico entered the tourism industry, newly constructed chain hotels and hospitality businesses became social spaces where the elite could display their status as a hegemonic and modern social class. The increase in hotel construction brought with it a flourishing entertainment business. Big musical bands performed in private clubs and hotels, such as the Condado-Vanderbilt. At these venues, the upper social class gathered to dance to music such as *danzas* (Spanish waltz), which were essentially European. Despite the *danzas* European sound, many of their composers were Puerto Ricans of African ancestry, such as Juan Morel Campos. While the upper class enjoyed their *danzas*, the lower class enjoyed *bomba* and *plena*, both genres of Afro-Puerto Rican music. The *plena* music was mostly performed in the public spaces or at working-class events. However, *plena* music was slowly integrated, or rather, appropriated, into the musical repertoire of the upper class.[10] For the upper class, the structure of the hotels became "sanitizing" venues where they could "safely" enjoy themselves under the influences of an Afro-Puerto Rican beat.

In exclusive clubs and high-end hotels, it was the custom that people who did not have a *buena apariencia*[11]—light skin with European features—would rarely hold a key public position or be engaged in customer service. Ruth Fernández was born on May 23, 1919, in the community of Ponce known as Barrio Bélgica. Her father, Santiago Fernández, was of Spanish ancestry and her mother, Rosa María Cortada, shared both Spanish and African heritage. Rosa María died when Ruth was six years old, leaving her and her four sisters to be raised by their maternal grandmother Adela.[12]

Ruth Fernández received her education in Ponce. She wanted to pursue a college degree in social work from the University of Puerto Rico, but like so many Black females in the period, her only option was to become a schoolteacher. Fortunately for Ruth Fernández, she grew up in a household where her father and grandmother were able to provide her with music lessons. Ruth began taking piano lessons at an early age. By fourteen she had her first singing performance, earning fifty cents per show. According to the online *Encyclopedia of Puerto Rican Popular Culture*, at age sixteen, Ruth became the main vocalist of the band Mingo and the Whoopee Kids, which was the most popular band of the period.[13] She remained with the band for eight years, which allowed her to travel to the United States, Latin America, and throughout the island performing in casinos, social clubs, and hotels.

Fernández became the first Black Puerto Rican female leading vocalist in an all-male band in Puerto Rico. Her achievement can be compared to that of the African American jazz vocalist Ella Fitzgerald. What is extraordinary about Ruth Fernández's path is that, at that time, neither art nor music were considered alternative occupations for women, much less for a Black woman. Music careers were mostly limited to men, and women were the exception. Women's place in a patriarchal society is expected to be in private spaces. If that is not the case, they were judged by being in public areas, and for Ruth Fernández, being a musical performer challenged those customs.

Figure 5.1. Puerto Rican singer Ruth Fernández on stage at the Caborrojeño Social Club in New York City, October 17, 1956. Source: Justo A. Martí Photographic Collection, 1948–1985 (JAMA_b51_f04_0001). Center for Puerto Rican Studies Library & Archives, Hunter College, CUNY.

Between 1940 and 1941, Ruth began her recording career with the RCA Victor label. One of her most popular hits was "*Y tu abuela, ¿a'onde está?*" (And Your Grandma, Where's She At?). The song was an adaptation of a satirical poem by Fortunato Vizcarrondo (1895–1977), in which he mocked people who denied their blackness by hiding their African ancestors. Fernández's successful interpretation of the poem became an important achievement for Vizcarrondo, who also was of African descent. Contextualizing Ruth Fernández's artistic trajectory, cultural critic Licia Fiol-Matta unravels the intersections of gender, class, and race in the lives of Fernández and other Puerto Rican female singers in her book *The Great Woman Singer.*

In a chapter devoted to Fernández, Fiol-Matta highlights the relevance of Fernández's performances. Although she also performed Afro-Cuban pieces, Vizcarrondo's poem illustrates the navigations of the artist within the racial narrative of Puerto Rican society. Fernández successfully performed a song in which the lyrics are charged with linguistic sounds from the Black Puerto Rican dialect without perpetuating the negativity associated with the language spoken by uneducated Black Puerto Ricans. Fiol-Matta explains, "It is a performance of blackness following how the elites and popular sectors were codifying racial alterity through literature."[14] The author went on, saying that overall "Fernández bridged the belittling of Afro-Puerto Ricans, on the one hand, and on the other, the discourse investing music performance with a growing stature as a professional, artistic pursuit, aligned with class taste."[15]

In the 1950s, Fernández gained popularity among the newly established Puerto Rican community in New York City. She was known for her strong voice, flamboyant attire, and endurance. In NYC, she also performed songs from another Afro-Puerto Rican composer, Rafael Hernández (1892–1965). According to Fiol-Matta, Fernández's acceptance by the Puerto Rican community was symbolic in the sense that her persona represents two discourses: racial and political. Politically, Fernández was affiliated with the Popular Party, which advocated for the self-determination of Puerto Ricans under the Commonwealth formula in 1952.[16] As a result of her ability to bridge the Puerto Rican diaspora, Fernández gained the epithet *el alma de Puerto Rico hecha canción* (the soul of Puerto Rico made song). What seems paradoxical is that Master of Ceremonies Héctor del Villar gave her the epithet while she was performing in the Teatro Hispano in New York City.[17] This parallels the narrative of Puerto Rican culture, which traditionally has been constructed as Spanish and patriarchal. As Fiol-Matta stated, "The epithet 'El alma de Puerto Rico hecha canción' stresses the spiritual; comes across as *cursi* (tacky) to the present-day ear; and places the icon squarely in the feminine and in the purportedly colorless realm of the soul, reformulating the original icon considerably by placing her at a remove from race and closer to gender."[18]

Fiol-Matta also adds Fernández's role as an artist for modern Puerto Rican society: "At home, she became the unofficial, cultural spokesperson of the PPD and local elites. Abroad she functioned as their cultural ambassador. Her repertoire advertised a vision of Latin America that was calibrated to the Good Neighbor Policy and the Alliance for Progress."[19] In addition to her career as a professional singer, Fernández promoted Puerto Rican culture and sought to establish cultural and political networks with Latin America. However, being a woman of African ancestry made her vulnerable, a situation she was well aware of.

Ruth Fernández shared her stories of racial discrimination in two interviews: one with anthropologist Marvette Pérez and another with journalist Patricia Vargas. Respectively, an abridged version of Perez's interview, which is part of the Latino Music Oral History Project originated by the Smithsonian Institution, was published later in the *Journal of the Center for Puerto Rican Studies*. Vargas published her interview in the newspaper *El Nuevo Día* in 2000. In both recollections, Ruth Fernández mentioned that early in her musical career, the Condado-Vanderbilt Hotel barred Blacks, apart from service workers.[20] She declared in both interviews that regardless of social status, Black performers were required to enter through a designated back door.

Based on Pérez's interview, the singer intercalated her racial experience with issues of gender and class. As a pioneer in the musical business, she confronted prejudice not only because of her skin color—as she identified it—but also because she was one of the few females who gained prominence in a male-dominated circle (the other female performer was Myrta Silva, who was white). Aware of the traditional exclusion of Black Puerto Ricans from society, Fernández's personally complied with this requirement in order to keep her musical profession. Black Puerto Rican women were stigmatized for working in public spaces. Fernández's trajectory sheds light on new trends or exceptional examples in the twentieth-century Puerto Rican society in which Black Puerto Rican women challenged these societal constructions. Fiol-Matta argues that, despite her race, Ruth Fernández managed to construct a persona that was so beloved that, even when she was performing Afro-Puerto Rican musical genres such as *bomba* and *plena,* both the middle class on the island and the Puerto Rican diaspora embraced her. Fernández navigated the political/class arenas and the discourse on blackness by developing behavioral "codes" in her performances and personal life.[21]

On one occasion, however, when she was invited to perform at the Condado-Vanderbilt, Fernández broke the silent rules of racism. On that night, she chose to wear a white dress decorated with sequins and rhinestones. A friend lent her a Packard, driven by a Black chauffeur. When she arrived at the hotel, the doorman, who happened to be Black, was surprised to see a Black person when he opened the car door. According to the artist, the doorman let her in because he thought she was an African queen or a dignitary. She emphasized that the doorman called her "Miss" and did not used the term *negrita* (black girl), which on the island some people use as either a term of endearment or as an insult. After entering the hotel, a waiter graciously directed her to the entrance to the ballroom. Reaching the entrance, she waited until the music stopped and everyone was back at their tables, and then she made a triumphant entrance. She recalled, "I made my entrance with confidence and dignity, not with arrogance."

The terms "confidence" and "dignity" reference the basic rights many Black Puerto Ricans have fought for in society. The upper class commonly associates Black Puerto Ricans' displays of confidence and dignity as signs of disrespect for and defiance of the established social hierarchies. This attitude is commonly known as *manternerse en su sitio* (staying in their place). Racial codes on the island established that Black Puerto Ricans have a place in society, but they should not cross that line. This was even more challenging for Black Puerto Rican women, who had to negotiate their multiple roles as mothers, wives, and providers while ignoring the social taboos related to their constructed position in the society. In addition, Black Puerto Rican women—as stated by historian Dr. Belén Barbosa—have the burden of being Black and poor. This intersectionality places them in a more vulnerable position compared to white Puerto Rican women. Traditionally, Black Puerto Rican females were the most vulnerable subjects of racial discrimination.[22] Black Puerto Rican women have also been sexualized more blatantly than their white peers. For instance, Afro-Puerto Rican women have been subjected to different standards of womanhood that is intertwined with their race. Historian Eileen Suárez-Findlay's study on the politics of race and sexuality in late nineteenth-century and early twentieth-century Ponce, Puerto Rico, offers an excellent analysis of contradiction among working-class people, liberal in terms of women's "rights" and place in society. The study also demonstrated the *machista* ideology that was and still is pervasive in Puerto Rican culture. For women of color, the stigma of slavery and racial prejudice is to blame for creating negative stereotypes of black women and males. It seems that Afro-descendant people are automatically associated as vulgar or as if they lack dignity—a complex situation common to all former slave societies.[23]

While in different social spheres, members of the elite class participated in the exclusion of the African culture and their people. Ironically, in the 1940s and 1950s, the middle class demonstrated its ability to switch from a "European rhythm" to an African beat. Fernández's example demonstrated that in certain physical spaces, Puerto Ricans of African ancestry, particularly women, learned to negotiate the environment of social oppression and racial exclusion. Fernández broke that social norm. Anthropologist and feminist Maritza Quiñones-Rivera used her experience as an Afro-Puerto Rican woman *salsera* (salsa music enthusiast) in Puerto Rico to explore the myths of racial harmony with gender. She noted that on the island, there are markers of differentiations associated with "color, music, language, and class," such as the "cocola"—a feminized and racialized term for salsa music enthusiast. Quiñones-Rivera stated that "cocolas have had to negotiate spaces for ourselves in masculine-dominant domains that are clearly marked by class, race, and gender. Salsa, reggeaton, bomba, and hip-hop provided me with an escape in which the musical rhythms invoke a Spanish-speaking and English-speaking Black culture."[24]

The acceptance of Afro-Puerto Rican music in upper-class clubs should not be considered an indication of an acceptance of Afro-Puerto Rican music or its performers. On the contrary, it represents a social appropriation in which Black Puerto Rican music became acceptable as long it was performed in reputable, privileged spaces, such as private clubs and hotels. According to cultural critic Marilyn Miller, under the American occupation, *plena* music became a weapon of resistance against American hegemony. Her research examined the several instances in which *plena* music composers criticized the colonial establishment. She also noted that people from different social classes negotiated the racial and political implications of this musical genre and its lyrics denounced the colonial establishment.[25] Similarly, cultural theorist Peter Manuel stated that, while mainstream groups such as the elite or upper classes rejected or underestimated Black music, it was a source of cultural affirmation and empowerment for people of the African diaspora.[26]

A Drop of Creation

The boost in the economy triggered by Operation Bootstrap brought many socioeconomic changes. Due to Puerto Rico's strategic position during World War II, the United States built several military bases. This situation, as well as the advocacy of local politicians, prompted the U.S. Congress to include Puerto Rico in its military budget.[27] Federal money poured into the island's economy, directly benefiting both soldiers and personnel working on the military bases. Furthermore, in the 1950s the revolution in Cuba and the political unrest in other Latin American nations made the region vulnerable to the spread of communism.

Puerto Ricans and government institutions accepted their new role in showcasing democratic values and combating communism. The Department of Instruction hurried to implement educational reforms, recruit more teachers with the aim of increasing the student population and decreasing school dropouts to prepare a new generation of leaders, professionals, and educators. In 1949, the insular government under the PPD developed a massive program of community education known as the Division of Community Education (DIVEDCO). It mirrored President Roosevelt's New Deal programs such as the Federal Art Project, which was the humanities division of the Work Projects Administration (WPA). The DIVEDCO program focused on educating mostly rural Puerto Ricans about family, moral values, community empowerment, health, and patriotic values through films, posters, and brochures designed by renowned Puerto Rican artists and writers. Interestingly, all the pedagogical initiatives for rural people involved artistic creation. The DIVEDCO program became extremely popular and elevated the role of visual arts in the Department of Instruction curricula.[28] It is thus not surprising that the public-school curricula considered plastic arts a pedagogical tool to combat school dropouts and criminality, according to the Afro-Puerto Rican artist and educator Cecilia Orta Allende (hereafter Cecilia Orta).

Born in the municipality of Carolina on October 21, 1923, Cecilia Orta Allende was the fifth of eight children (six boys and two girls). Her father, Raymundo Orta, was a skilled construction worker and sculptor. Her mother, Cecilia Allende, was a seamstress-designer and domestic worker. According to Cecilia Orta's biographer, Dr. Aixa Merino Falú, the Orta Allende family resided in Carolina when the municipality was undergoing economic challenges.

By the 1920s and 1930s, in addition to the traditional church and government buildings, there were several schools' buildings, including the Luis Muñoz Rivera and Julio Vizcarrondo Coronado public schools, where Cecilia, affectionately called Cecilín, attended her primary and high school, respectively.[29]

The Orta Allende family traces its origins to Africa via the town of Loíza, a predominantly Black populated town. In fact, Carolina was part of the *partido* or district of Loíza until the end of eighteenth century when they were divided and founded under Trujillo Bajo and in 1857 became the San Fernando de Carolina.[30] Historian Fernando Picó's book on Carolina describes how the town of Trujillo Alto and Carolina became shelters for runaway African slaves, who settled in the region.[31] Merino Falú and Picó record that the town of Carolina was racially mixed due to the constant influx of enslaved and free Africans. Racial hierarchies were prevalent in the structure of the town.

The region's economy depended on sugar production. Sugar mills such as *Progreso* and *Victoria* were key to the urban development of Carolina.[32] Throughout the nineteenth century, the town operated under the leadership of a major who was either Spanish or of Spanish descendant. After the arrival of Americans in 1898, according to Picó, Carolina was referred to as a "Spanish colony." The Spanish families put effort into strengthening their cultural life and influence.[33] Simultaneously Afro-descendant families such as the Ortas made the best of the limited opportunities available to them by securing jobs, educating their children, and developing their own identity as proud residents of Carolina.

The Great Depression and two hurricanes that hit the island—*San Felipe* in 1928 and *San Ciprián* in 1932—negatively impacted the economy and moral of Puerto Ricans. It was a period of socioeconomic adjustment for small towns such as Carolina. According to the U.S. Census of 1930 (also cited in Merino Falú), 13,479 people lived in Carolina, and of that number 43.9 percent were Afro-descendants; 6,524 were Black women.[34] Merino Falú documents that the males from the Orta Allende family used their skills in carpentry and construction to survive the crisis, while her mother contributed her skills as a seamstress.[35]

The life and deeds of Cecilia Orta Allende are an excellent testimony to her family's resilience. While attending high school, Cecilia began showing an interest in art. She was raised in a working-class setting, but the Orta Allende household, according to Merino Falú, experienced a period of significant fortune. For example, they owned two horses, one of which was used for transportation.[36] The Ortas allowed Cecilín to take art classes when she was fifteen. She combined her art courses with her regular school curricula.

With the improved transportation and infrastructure, Carolina began to show its level of modernization. In this regard, historian Fernando Picó wrote that in Carolina "modernity implies the peak of the *centrales* or sugar mills, the displacement of the small *agregado* nucleus and the explosion of new urban enclaves and the creation of new barrios."[37] With the agricultural boom came an increased production of local products. Governor Rexford G. Tugwell introduced a zoning plan based on the concept of a "metropolitan area" in which Carolina would be included with San Juan and Río Piedras.[38] This would greatly benefit the involved municipalities because the public transportation would be absorbed into the metro area. Another characteristic of the modernization of Carolina was the increase in public recreational spaces. The clubs and beaches in Isla Verde were mainly for the rich, while the banks of the Grand River of Loíza were reserved for poor families.[39]

Carolina became even more prominent in the Puerto Rican modernization project with the construction of the international airport of Isla Verde (later renamed Luis Muñoz Marín) and the construction of beachview condos and hotels. According to historian Fernando Picó, the Planning Board drafted a plan for the construction of the airport in the 1940s. However, bureaucracy and the military status of the island delayed the plan. Finally, when construction became inevitable in 1949, poor and Black families living in the areas impacted by the future airport were relocated and given monetary compensation as little as $100 for their land. The construction of the airport and removal of the residents from the land scattered traditional Black Puerto Rican communities throughout Carolina. They were relocated to new neighborhoods such as Sabana Abajo, public housing complexes, and La Cerámica, an industrial park complex.[40] The finalized phase of construction of the airport in 1955 prompted the creation of routes that connected Carolina to Río Piedras, the location of the University of Puerto Rico (UPR). The university created new programs to train Puerto Rican teachers to replace white American teachers. Young women like Cecilia Orta took advantage of this opportunity to pursue a career in education.[41]

In 1941, Cecilia Orta attended the University of Puerto Rico to pursue a degree in the Education Department. According to Merino

Falú, her father Raymundo was against her plans to study art, so she combined her home economics courses with art courses.[42] Cecilia lived in the residence for *señoritas* (young women), although the residence was traditionally reserved for whites.[43] Cecilia graduated on July 1, 1945. In today's terms, it would be fair to say that Cecilia Orta graduated with a major in education, with a focus on home economics, and a minor in art. According to Merino Falú, Cecilia Orta immediately began her career as an educator. Her first positions, teaching home economics and art, were outside of the metropolitan area.

By 1949, she was teaching art courses on a part-time basis. Ten years later, she obtained a five-year teaching certificate from the Department of Instruction.[44] Merino Falú states that Cecilia Orta was one of the rare few Afro-Puerto Rican females who became part of the teaching profession; in the 1930s they made up only 23 percent of the profession.[45] She took advantage of the limited options available to women and people of color.

Cecilia's artistic career continued evolving while she was working as a teacher. She was able to show her work in prominent spaces in San Juan, such as the Ateneo, which was an exclusive institution founded by Spanish and wealthy Creoles in the nineteenth century. Interestingly, Cecilia Orta's exhibitions were covered in mainstream newspaper media and received good reviews. Eventually, differences with the politics of the Department of Instruction led her to resign from teaching in November 1953.[46] The turning point in her career came when she was encouraged by a friend to apply for a grant offered by the U.S.-Mexico Special Cooperation Commission Office to advance her career as a professional artist at the legendary Academia de San Carlos (founded in 1551), which is today part of the Autonomous University of Mexico.[47]

With her move to Mexico City, Cecilia Orta became part of a small group of Puerto Rican artists, including Rafael Tufiño (1922–2008) and Antonio "Tony" Maldonado (1920–2006), both Afro-Puerto Ricans who lived and studied art in Mexico. It seems likely that Cecilia Orta, along with Tufiño, were among the few Afro-Puerto Rican artists of their generation to receive such honor. Their work reflected the influence of the Mexican muralist school, such as Diego Rivera, David Alfaro Siqueiros, and Clemente Orozco.[48] Cecilia Orta graduated from the program in Mexico with high qualifications in the fall of 1954.[49]

When Cecilia Orta returned to Puerto Rico, the island was undergoing significant political and economic progress. For instance, in 1955, the Institute of Puerto Rican Culture (ICP) was created under the directorship of anthropologist Ricardo Alegría. This entity created cultural initiatives and policies to foster Puerto Rican culture and revive Taino-Indian culture. The ICP administration also advanced the politico-cultural agenda of the Popular Party. Remarkably, the ICP emblem is the image of an Indian, Spaniard, and African, the symbols of Puerto Rican's cultural heritage.

Cecilia Orta challenged the pervasive notion of the tri-rooted heritage through her art. For example, the logo she designed for her "Cecilia Orta consultorio de arte" business (figure 5.3) does not take the Hispanic-centric approach of the ICP logo (figure 5.2).

Instead, the artist image places the island of Puerto Rico as the base and over it a *cemí*, a Taino religious figure, and over the *cemí*, a Taino mask (figure 5.3). This appears to show the influence of her studies in Mexico where *indigenismo* was popular in the visual arts. Merino Falú asserted that "the experiences acquired, not only will be reflected in her art but also in her role as an educator and politically as well."[50] One may also observe that African heritage does not appear to be include in the logo. However, many of Cecilia Orta's pieces included Puerto Rico's African heritage, such as in the mural *Añoranzas de mi raza negra* (Longings from

Figure 5.2. "Escudo del ICP." (Emblem of the Institute of Puerto Rican Culture.) Lorenzo Homar. 1955, linoleum. Institute of Puerto Rican Culture Collection.

Figure 5.3. Cecilia Orta's art consultant business logo from a piece of her stationary. Source: Luis Muñoz Marín Foundation and Archives.

My Black Race), a painting that Orta dedicated to her mother Cecilia. Cecilia Orta herself embodied Africanness, demonstrated by the turban she wore both with regular clothing and with the elaborated blouson similar to the traditional West African women clothing in which she painted herself.

The well-being of children from the lower classes was at the heart of Cecilia Orta's social advocacy work. On April 11, 1955, she founded the Puerto Rican Mobile Academy of Plastic Arts and Future Painters, intended to provide a creative space for youths. According to Merino Falú, in an interview with one of Cecilia Orta's brother, Rafael, he revealed, "Cecilia embodied the mobile Academy."[51] The mobile academy consisted of Orta visiting public schools with art equipment, including two cartoon tables, where she invited students to create art. She also trained more advanced students to help with the art workshops. All this was done by coordinating with principals and teachers. Inés Mendoza, the wife of Luis Muñoz Marín, welcomed this initiative. Mendoza was a teacher before becoming Puerto Rico's First Lady. Cecilia Orta's impact on the educational field was covered in local newspapers such as *El Mundo* and *El Imparcial*.[52] Children were learning how to draw and paint, and their artwork was exhibited throughout the island.[53]

In early 1955, Cecilia's marriage to Ángel M. Rondón came to an end. They had married in 1950 and lived in Santurce. Rondón was a white Puerto Rican pursuing a career in engineering at the University of Puerto Rico, Mayagüez campus.[54] In an interview with Cecilia's niece, Marta Cecilia Orta declared that the family of Rondón did not accept Cecilia because she was Black.[55] Cecilia's niece also added that her aunt helped Rondón cover the costs of his studies.[56] This example of white Puerto Rican families opposing biracial marriage indicates that Puerto Rican society was not as racially tolerant as they claimed.

Professionally, Cecilia scored another achievement when she was appointed to be the art teacher at the Luis Muñoz Rivera School of Río Piedras. This position made it possible for Cecilia to expand her mobile academy. She held exhibitions in the San Juan metropolitan area while demanding the Department of Instruction to provide more teaching materials for her art courses. Dissatisfied with their response, she took her fight to a higher level, all the way to the governor's mansion, *La Fortaleza*.

Cecilia Orta sent a series of telegraphs and letters to Governor Luis Muñoz Marín and other public officials requesting personal interviews during which she could ask for additional support for the mobile art academy. In these missives, Orta suggests that her vision of the mobile academy was part of the ELA (Spanish acronym for the Estado Libre Asociado or Commonwealth of Puerto Rico) national project and would complement the role of Puerto Rico in promoting democratic values in the Western Hemisphere. For example, in a telegram addressed to Governor Luis Muñoz Marín dated December 12, 1955, Cecilia Orta introduces herself as a "Puerto Rican teacher in the Department of Instruction and a painter." She requests an interview with the governor before the end of the year to discuss issues pertaining to the education of "our children" and to "inform him about secrets that would help to guide our treasured country through important pathways."[57] What stands out in this communication is that Cecilia Orta highlights that she had two careers: one as a teacher affiliated with the primary government institution dealing with education, and the second as an artist. Education was already an established priority of the Luis Muñoz Marín administration, as was the role of the visual arts in the popular education of poor people.

Also important to note is Cecilia Orta's sense of responsibility when she wrote that she had "important information" that could help the ELA mission. Cecilia Orta used the first-person possessive pronoun "ours" suggesting that education of Puerto Rican children is a collective and mutual concern. Two days after the telegram, Cecilia Orta received a letter from Enrique Rodríguez, the administrative assistant to LMM, stating that the governor asked him to meet with her on January 17 of the following year (1956). It appears she was unable to attend the meeting with Rodríguez. The copy of the letter includes a handwritten note that read "did not show up."[58] Meanwhile, she continued flourishing as an artist.

Six months after the original notification, Cecilia Orta sent another request to Luis Muñoz Marín for a personal interview. She wrote, "I am a Puerto Rican painter from the Black race." She adds that they met back in December 1955 and spoke in the gardens of the governor's mansion. According to the telegram, she insisted on meeting with him privately to discuss matters pertaining to the education of "our children and secrets that would help him to guide our people." In another line she reminds the governor that he promised her the interview. She adds that she worked as a teacher for ten years and resigned because of injustices. The telegram ends with her telling the governor that she has faith in God and in him.[59] In March of 1956, the artist participated in an important art exhibition in the School of Plastic Arts in San Juan that included ninety-two artists, including Rafael Tufiño and Lorenzo Homar.[60]

Cecilia Orta seemed eager to actively participate in the modernization of Puerto Rico. As a Black woman, she placed herself in the position of a confidante and consultant to the governor, who was white. In her telegram she emphasized that she had won a prestigious fellowship with the government of Mexico, with which Muñoz had an excellent relationship. Regarding this period of Cecilia Orta's life, biographer Aixa Merino Falú observes that "Cecilia understood each one of her identities (the Black woman, the educator, the artist and the political activist) as a whole."[61] Her determination drew from what she had already accomplished on her own merit. In this regard, Merino Falú adds, "Her artistic trajectory, pedagogical experience and her academic degree from Mexico were enough credentials to motivate Cecilia Orta to demand government institutions of the period."[62] Therefore, the telegrams, letters, notes, and perhaps calls to La Fortaleza, the Department of Instruction, and other institutions illustrate her right to be heard as an educated Black Puerto Rican.

The boom in the hotel industry, particularly in Isla Verde, Carolina, benefited Cecilia Orta. On January 1, 1958, she inaugurated an art exhibition titled "Arte Borincano" at the newly built San Juan Hotel. As part of the exhibition, she unveiled the mosaic/mural *Añoranzas de mi raza negra* (The Longing of My Black Race), which was supposed to be installed at a restaurant in Isla Verde/Piñones. Her brothers also exhibited wood pieces and crafts.[63] By naming her exhibition "Boricua Art," the artist announced her alignment with the indigenous Borinquén, the original Taino-Arawak name of Puerto Rico. She was not only affirming the precolonial roots of Puerto Rico but also presenting an alternative interpretation to the Hispanic-American discourse embedded in the PPD and the Luis Muñoz Marín administration. Like the labor leader Romero Rosa, her "rhetoric of a Boricua nation imagines a Puerto Rico free of colonialism." These concepts manifested in Cecilia Orta's art throughout her career. The title of her mural *Añoranzas de mi raza negra* suggests she was inspired by her identity as a Black Puerto Rican artist to create her artwork. According to Merino Falú, the artist received good reviews from that art show.[64]

The same year as the exhibition at the San Juan Hotel, Cecilia Orta married Carlos Ojeda Vizcarrondo, a blacksmith and plumber.[65] According to Merino Falú, the marriage did not last long.[66] In 1961, Cecilia Orta returned to teaching with the Department of Instruction. As an activist teacher, she developed a more comprehensive art program for school children free of charge. The same year, in the town of Manatí, she embarked on a mural/mosaic project dedicated to Luis Muñoz Rivera, autonomist leader and father of Luis Muñoz Marín. In 1962, she was hired as an art teacher for an experimental project in Nemesio R. Canales, a public housing project popularly known in Puerto Rico as *caserío*.[67]

On January 14, 1962, the magazine *Bohemia Puertorriqueña* published an article about Cecilia Orta and featured her on the cover (see appendix B).[68] In the article, she explains the art program in detail. She acknowledged that it was sponsored by various government agencies and mentioned the support of the Dean of Humanities of the University of Puerto Rico-Río Piedras. She reiterated the significance of art as a tool for poor children, stating, "Let us give to our youth tools for creating and in that way, we will have a better world."[69] She explained the purpose of the art project, saying, "It is necessary that spare time must turn out into pure and dynamic creativity." In this way, the public school system administrators could prevent children from misbehaving and guide them to positive activities instead of their becoming beggars or engaging in destructive activities. She urged, "Let us extend a hand in favor a crusade of salvation," ending with the quote, "May the children and youth of today become artists and not the criminals of tomorrow."[70] The article ends with the line, "Let us support her."[71]

A caption on one of the photos in the article describes how children from "public urbanizations" (a local euphemism for *caserios*) benefited from the program.[72] Most of the children in the photo appear to be Black. Why did Cecilia Orta imply that these children were in danger of becoming criminals? Regardless of race, level of education, or moral values, negative stereotypes marked the residents of *caserios*. Living at the wrong address could jeopardize your ability to get a good job. The locations the mobile academy visited and the social status of the population she served were part of the reason she had to constantly fight for more resources for her program.

According to Merino Falú, Cecilia Orta was unable to secure a permanent position as an art teacher with the Department of Instruction. In August 1961, the Department assigned her to an experimental project, teaching art at the Nemesio R. Canales public housing project and other *caserios* throughout the metropolitan area, including in her hometown of Carolina. The job was a temporary position. Despite her job changes, Cecilia Orta's mission to make art accessible to low-income children continued.

What could have felt like a career setback became a blessing. While working with children in the *caserios*, Cecilia Orta's artistic career blossomed. She held numerous art exhibitions throughout the island, Mexico, and New York.[73] In 1963, she returned to Mexico to pursue a masters in fine arts from the Academia San Carlos at the Universidad Autónoma de Mexico (UNAM).[74] On her return to Puerto Rico in 1964, Cecilia Orta was promoted to art teacher, and the Nemesio R. Canales public housing project became her laboratory three days a week. The rest of the week she collaborated with the cultural program of the Museum of Central High School in Santurce. In addition to working the equivalent of two part-time jobs, she established an art consultancy business and taught art at the Luis Muñoz Rivera School in Río Piedras.[75] It took Cecilia Orta twenty years to get a full-time job as an art teacher.

In 1961, President John F. Kennedy created the Alliance for Progress. Through this program the United States would invest economically and militarily in key Latin American countries with the aim of eradicating poverty, reducing adult illiteracy, and promoting democratic values.[76] The lack of democratic governments and persistent poverty were perceived as the primary reasons for popular revolts that ended in the infiltration of communist ideals. The United States intended to use Puerto Rico as a model to inspire other Latin American political and intellectual elites. As a bridge between the United States and Latin America, Puerto Rico hosted heads of states, intellectuals, and upper-class military personnel, welcoming them to training programs the Alliance offered at UPR and in other Puerto Rican institutions. Most importantly, Governor Luis Muñõz Marín and Teodoro Moscoso, the President of Fomento, became advisors to President Kennedy in the Alliance for Progress program. Assessing this period in Puerto Rican history, historian Arturo Morales Carrión declared that this was possibly the closest relationship between a Puerto Rican governor and an American president.[77]

In her communication to Governor Muñoz Marín dated June 23, 1964, Cecilia Orta again requested a meeting. She included a design in her handwritten letter.[78] The letter describes a plan to "strengthen and increase the destiny of the Commonwealth of Puerto Rico, within the context of an invigorated America." The design shows a two-way arrow, with the words "Puerto Rico the axis of the U.S." on the top, and below the arrow the words *"Alianza para el Progreso"* (Alliance for Progress). Employing the same language used by politicians of the period, she was clearly subscribing to a discourse of modernization.

Cecilia Orta sent another letter to the governor on August 2, 1964 (figure 5.4). By this time Orta had been writing to the governor for almost a decade. Since her earlier arguments about preventing youth delinquency did not get the result she desired, here she described art as an important tool to prevent youth from being "infested" by communism and the "negative wave of Castro."[79] Cecilia Orta understood that Puerto Rico played an important role in the Western hemisphere and asserted that her art teaching program supplemented the overall mission of the Commonwealth.[80]

The governor's aides misinterpreted her persistence. A handwritten note that reads "crazy" in Spanish appeared on the August 2 letter and was archived "as is" among the governor's correspondence.[81] With the letter she included a newspaper clipping showing a photograph of her wearing a head turban typical of her style. In the photo she looks Black, which gave the people handling the mail another reason to condemn her. What could have been a strategic self-promotional move from Cecilia Orta— sending a newspaper clipping—became a condemnation. Her name also counted against her. In Puerto Rico, the surname "Orta" is traditionally linked with Black people, as are "Clemente" and "Osorio." These family names are commonly associated with Carolina, a racially mixed town. The combination of these racialized signifiers and the tone of her letter

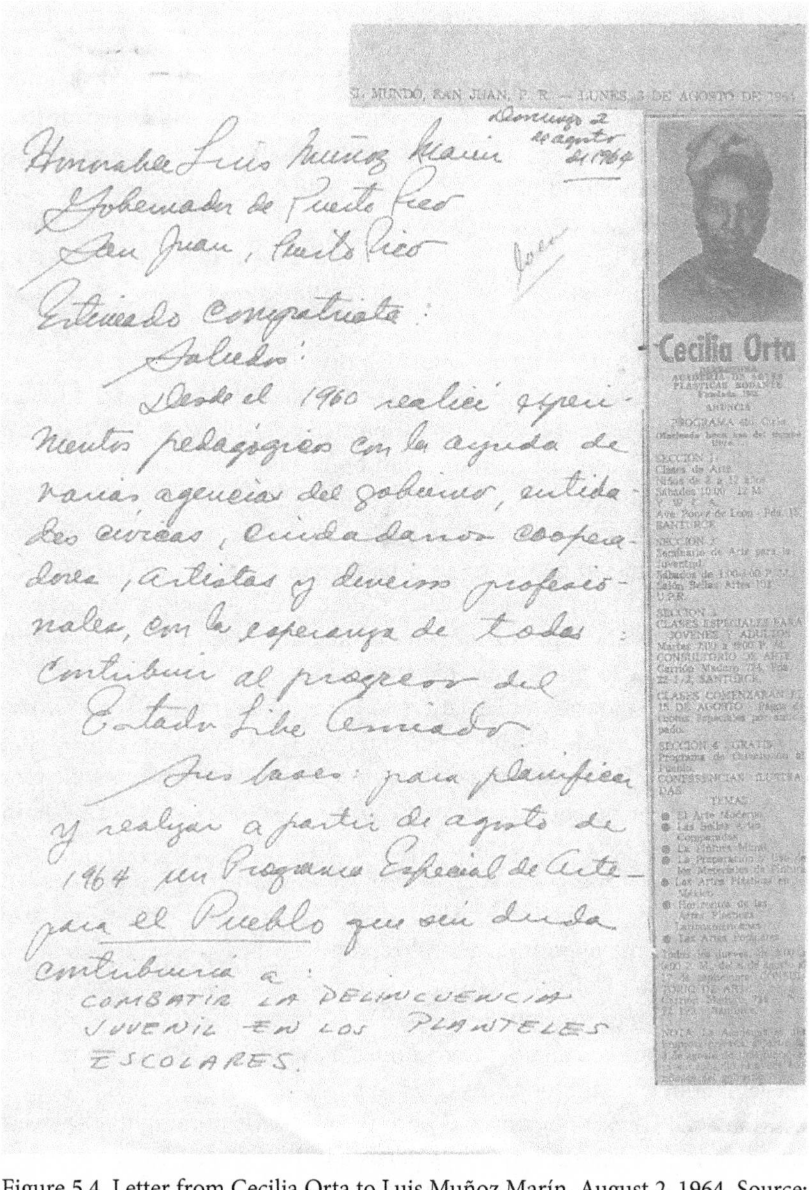

EL MUNDO, SAN JUAN, P. R. — LUNES, 3 DE AGOSTO DE 196

Domingo 2 de agosto de 1964

Honorable Luis Muñoz Marín
Gobernador de Puerto Rico
San Juan, Puerto Rico

Estimado compatriota:

Saludos:

Desde el 1960 realicé experimentos pedagógicos con la ayuda de varias agencias del gobierno, entidades cívicas, ciudadanos cooperadores, artistas y diversos profesionales, con la esperanza de todos: contribuir al progreso del Estado Libre Asociado.

Sus bases: para planificar y realizar a partir de agosto de 1964 un Programa Especial de Arte para el Pueblo que sin duda contribuirá a:

COMBATIR LA DELINCUENCIA JUVENIL EN LOS PLANTELES ESCOLARES.

Cecilia Orta

ANUNCIA

PROGRAMA

SECCION 1
Clases de Arte
Sábados 10:00 - 12 M.
SANTURCE

SECCION 2
Seminario de Arte para la Juventud
U.P.R.

SECCION 3
CLASES ESPECIALES PARA JOVENES Y ADULTOS
CONSULTORIO DE ARTE
SANTURCE

CLASES COMENZARAN EL 15 DE AGOSTO

SECCION 4 - GRATIS
CONFERENCIAS ILUSTRADAS

TEMAS
- El Arte Moderno

Figure 5.4. Letter from Cecilia Orta to Luis Muñoz Marín, August 2, 1964. Source: Luis Muñoz Marín Foundation and Archives.

most likely prompted the reader to label her with the stereotype of the "angry/crazy Black woman."

This negative stereotype mythologizes the behavior of Black women, depicting them as aggressive, ill tempered, and hostile and implying that their "explosive" behavior is without provocation. African American literature and studies on the topic helps to contextualize the case of Cecilia Orta. For instance, psychologist Wendy Ashely, in "The Angry Black Woman," argues that these stereotypes are common in slave societies in the Americas, including Puerto Rico. After the end of slavery, it became common to use the label "angry or mad" whenever free Black women spoke up against discrimination and abuse.[82] The myth undermines the ways in which Black women defended and protected themselves and their families from oppression. This myth infected society's overall perception of Black women, associating them with poor mental health and implying they are a public health menace.[83] The scribbled adjective *loca* (crazy) on Orta's letter is disrespectful and unprofessional. The pejorative comment completely dismissed her desire to helping poor children and advance the social agenda of the Commonwealth of Puerto Rico. Despite the lack of response to her correspondence, she painted a portrait of Muñoz Marín and presented it to him before his term ended in 1965.[84]

Cecilia Orta sent similar letters to other government offices, particularly those that made decisions pertaining to the security and well-being of Puerto Rico. For example, a telegram to request an appointment went to Rafael Rivera Betancourt, assistant to then Secretary of State Roberto Sánchez Vilella. She also sent a letter to the Deputy Secretary of State, Adolfo Porrata Doria.[85] The subject of the note was her new project called "Yellow Crusade." According to her letter, the crusade was an initiative to standardize the appointment and recruitment of teachers and create a sustainable system of teaching art.[86]

Following an incident with the Department of Instruction, Cecilia Orta was admonished and her teaching certification jeopardized. Contesting the situation, she sent letters to officials at the Department of Instruction and the State Department, as well as to the governor, arguing that she was the victim of an injustice. She was persistent. In response to her letters, a memorandum dated August 21, 1964, asked Luis Laboy "to take care of the matter on behalf of Mr. Sánchez Vilella" (the secretary of state). In the same document is a handwritten note that reads, "esta mujer está loca" (this woman is crazy) (see appendix C). Again, the phrase "this woman is crazy" was a condemnation and a warning. It suggests they should not take her seriously. The next person to review the letter would simply dismiss it. Once again, government officials showed gender discrimination and their lack of professionalism.

In 1966, according to Merino Falú, the Department of Instruction suspended Cecilia Orta from her teaching duties because she did not follow recommendations to visit a psychiatrist.[87] The recommendations were made when she supposedly provoked the resignation of the director of the Department of Instruction's Music Program, Dr. María Luisa Muñoz. This time, Cecilia Orta sent a handwritten note implying that Dr. Muñoz, as a music consultant under the payroll of the Department of Instruction, was obligated to organize the musical program with the School of Fine Arts. The program was to honor the legacy of Ernesto Ramos Antonini (1898–1963), the late speaker of the house under the *Partido Popular* and the only Afro-Puerto Rican to have occupied such a prestigious government position in the Puerto Rican government. Ramos Antonini was also an accomplished musician credited with popularizing the study of music with people from low-income backgrounds, similar to Cecilia Orta's efforts with art. Although Orta's letter could be interpreted as a little aggressive, she offered to help Dr. Muñoz with the program.[88] After this incident, she resigned from the Department of Instruction, seemingly to avoid another censor from the government agency.

In the mid-1960s, Cecilia Orta returned to Carolina and spent time with her mother. Her art production and advocacy did not decrease. On the contrary, she turned her family property in Carolina into an art studio/school/gallery. According to oral accounts, her second-floor apartment on the corner of Narciso Font Street and José de Diego Street became a destination for local artists and children. In a telephone conversation, biographer Dr. Aixa Merino Falú suggested to me that Cecilia Orta proclaimed herself, "*la pintora del pueblo*" (the artist of the people), an epithet for which she is still known.[89] In the late 1960s, Cecilia Orta collaborated with the new governor, Luis A. Ferré, whose party advocated for the annexation of Puerto Rico from the United States. She also engaged in projects with the Municipality of Carolina public school system. She continued showing her art throughout the 1970s and 1980s.[90]

In 1986, the Autonomous Municipality of Carolina named Cecilia Orta Allende "Woman of the Year"—just one of such honors she received during her lifetime. Despite suffering from glaucoma, Cecilia Orta continued painting until she passed on October 27, 2000. In the prologue to her biography, Marta Cecilia, Cecilia's niece, shared that Ruth Fernández stopped by the funeral home to pay her respects to the Orta Allende family.[91] Ruth Fernández, "the soul of Puerto Rico made song" and Cecilia Orta, "the artist of the people," were together for perhaps the first and last time.

"Showcasing" Racial Tolerance

In the 1960s, at the height of the civil rights movement, many famous public figures visited the island. In February 1962, Dr. Martin Luther King Jr. made a weeklong visit to Puerto Rico.[92] The Inter-American University in San Germán invited Dr. King to be the keynote speaker for the fiftieth anniversary of the founding of the institution. King's keynote was on February 12, 1962. The Inter, as it is commonly called, is a privately owned ecumenical institution that began as a polytechnic school and was founded by an American reverend in 1912.

Dr. King gave that keynote address and other public speeches for the Puerto Rico chapter of the Fellowship of Reconciliation, an interfaith pacifist organization, located at the Inter-American University. He spent a few days in San Germán, where he met with members of the faculty and graduate students.[93] His other engagements took place in San Juan, one at the theater of the University of Puerto Rico.[94] In the two or three days that Dr. King spent in San Germán, he gave two formal speeches: "The Future of Integration" on February 12 and "The Stride Towards Freedom" on February 15. These events were private, and Inter-American University prepared an itinerary so Dr. King could spend time with the fellows.

According to the transcripts of the lecture titled "The Future of Integration," Dr. King addressed the problem of race relations in the United States, the state of poverty among African Americans, and how racism intertwined with poverty among African Americans. He added that men and women could only solve the issue of racism and segregation if they followed the moral values intrinsic in society. In the second speech, "Strides towards Freedom," Dr. King revisited other problems affecting other parts of the globe, such as colonialism and apartheid in South Africa, as well as how a nonviolent approach could be a solution. In this lecture, King advised leaders, students, and other members of the public to pay attention to how terrible conditions could be eradicated through nonviolence, giving the example of Gandhi in India.

After fulfilling his commitments in San Germán, Dr. King returned to San Juan. There he was invited to address an audience of five hundred people at the theater of the University of Puerto Rico on February 17. Dr. King's visit received wide coverage in the local newspaper, *El Mundo*. According to the newspaper, the title of his speech was "The Challenges of a New Era." The reporter, Roy Godes, described it as "one of the most concise, profound, well thought out, moral, and socially significant speeches given in Puerto Rico."[95] During King's presentation, State Attorney Hiram Cancio declared, "the island shares with Dr. King the same passion for civil rights." He continued, "the people (Puerto Ricans) can count on with his leadership and will take any advice so they can continue living in fraternity."[96] The attorney general's statement reminded the audience of the challenges that some Puerto Ricans faced and that their democratic government had a responsibility to maintain a society where there was no room for discrimination of any kind.

Although no transcript of "The Challenge of a New Era" is available, it is likely that this speech addressed issues that also applied to the political environment in Puerto Rico in the 1960s. After his speech, King was asked his impressions about "racial integration in Puerto Rico," to which he answered: "I am exceedingly pleased to see the high level of fraternity that exists here. However, there still persist subtle ways of racial discrimination, but you Puerto Ricans must be alert to fight against them."

Dr. King's recommendation addressed the concealed issues that could affect any society, even one like Puerto Rico where the banner of racial harmony drew the most attention. Correspondence between Dr. King and Beresford Hayward, a consultant and planning advisor for the Department of Instruction, showed that Dr. King was aware of some of the issues Puerto Rico was facing. Hayward told Dr. King that "there is an indigenous problem of racial prejudice in Puerto Rico." He added, "Class distinctions have traditionally been interpreted in racial terms." In another part of the letter, Hayward acknowledged racial prejudice present in private schools and clubs, marriage arrangements, and other areas. He mentioned that "these social prejudices seem also to limit job and career opportunities" for Black Puerto Ricans. The letter continued acknowledging, "the racial problem and attitude in the States directly affect Puerto Ricans in the states and here. Furthermore, the island itself has revived a striking influx of American capital and personnel, which brings with them American social attitudes."[97] However, Hayward also remarked that, despite all that was going on against Black Puerto Ricans, the apparent intermingling of the different races in public spaces, work groups, churches and so on, "makes Puerto Rico a model of racial ease by any standards in the world, to say nothing of the United States."[98]

With his letter to Dr. King, Hayward included a report titled "Attitude, Knowledge, and Apperception of the Civil Rights in the Puerto Rican Public," written by sociologist Eduardo Seda Bonilla. Originally, the report was part of conference proceedings at the Catholic University in Ponce in 1959. In 1963, the presentation was published under the title *Los derechos civlies en la cultura Puertorriqueña*. The report uncovered racist practices in Puerto Rican society, in government institutions, in the educational system, and in the press, among other places.[99] It is clear that Dr. King was better informed about the reality of race relations in Puerto Rico than the government officials, who wanted to make a good impression, would have preferred. Dr. King's life and crusade for social justice armed him with the ability to identify racial discrimination.[100] His statements were right on target for those in the audience who believed that only blatant acts of discrimination were racist and that Puerto Rico did not operate in that way.

The University of Puerto Rico's participation in Dr. Martin Luther King Jr.'s lecture in San Juan was another example of an influential government institution attempting to validate the state propaganda of racial harmony. In their discussion of the political spectrum of racial formation, sociologists Michael Omi and Howard Winant noted that in societies where race becomes the determinant factor against a racial minority there is the tendency to deny race. They added that the state denial of race could lead to "color-blind" racial politics that every political ideology reinterprets at their convenience." For example, liberal political groups in Latin American societies, including Puerto Rico, recognized racial differences while promoting equality. The neoconservative's politicians took a color-blind stand, establishing a "hands-off" policy.[101] This political strategy did not help to address or seek a solution to racial discrimination. Omni and Winant's theory accurately described what was happening in the political leadership in Puerto Rico during this period. Leaders ignored the issue, refusing to address race or racism. It seems absurd that the "liberal" UPR-PPD administrations denied race or racial discrimination. Like the visits organized by UPR in which Latin American scholars came to the island in the late 1920s and 1940s to validate the island's Hispanic-centered ideology, the intellectual elite used King's public engagements in San Juan to demonstrate that Puerto Rican society was racially tolerant. It appears that the political and intellectual elite believed that Dr. King's visits to Inter-American University and the University of Puerto Rico would endorse their "nothing to hide" attitude.

Godes, the reporter for *El Mundo*, devoted most of his subsequent article to what he called "Diagnosis." The writer used Martin Luther King Jr.'s title "doctor" to imply that Dr. King's warning about racial discrimination in Puerto Rico was a diagnosis of "the diseases affecting our society." Based on the three speeches that Dr. King gave in Puerto Rico, he was indeed diagnosing the illness from which many societies like Puerto Rico were suffering—racial discrimination. Dr. King also prescribed a remedy. He declared that racial discrimination could be fought with nonviolence and that a community that is alert to the implications of racism against its citizens uses its elected officials to enact laws intended to break down artificial barriers that are affecting peoples of African ancestry globally, including in Puerto Rico.

Roberto Clemente (1934–1972), the famous Pittsburgh Pirate baseball player, humanist, and philanthropist from the town of Carolina, also met with Dr. King during his visit in February 1962. Being a Black Hispanic (Puerto Rican) in the major baseball league forced Clemente to test the waters of racial discrimination. In an informal conversation, Clemente's widow, Vera Zabala, told me that Clemente met King before she married Clemente in 1965. According to her story, her husband took Dr. King to his farm in the barrio Martín González in Carolina. In a joyful tone Vera Clemente added, "Roberto idolized Dr. King" because of his stand on racial discrimination and civil rights.[102] Details from the conversations between Clemente and Dr. King have not been made public. However, by reaching out to Dr. King, Clemente was doing his part to address the issues affecting Afro-Puerto Ricans and Afro-diasporic people. For Clemente, Dr. Martin Luther King Jr. was a role model.

In an article published in *El Mundo* only a few days after King's visit, Beresford Hayward questioned whether Puerto Rico needed the type of message that Dr. King delivered.[103] Hayward's main argument was that racial segregation did not exist in Puerto Rico. He echoed the mistakes of social scientists who insisted on measuring racism in Puerto Rico based solely on racial violence and segregation. Instead, Hayward thought that people should have focused on comments about peace. According to Hayward, peace was one of the most important principles of human relations.

Hayward also stated that the presence of U.S. military bases on the island must have seemed like a contradiction to the principles preached by Dr. King and embraced by all Puerto Ricans. However, he rushed to defend the United States' anti-communist agenda when he wrote that a state of alert against the spreading of communism would avoid an "international conflict" and the "possibility of a nuclear war." He concluded that King's visit should have served as a lesson on peace. Hayward considered Puerto Rico an example of the efforts to combat poverty and model democracy. He added that the military presence on the island was securing "peace" in the region.

The excitement created by Dr. King's first visit led to the elevation of Puerto Rico as an economic, democratic, and racial model for the hemisphere. Several political and religious dignitaries visited the island to witness Puerto Rico's "racial harmony" for themselves. One such visitor was Reverend M. Moran Weston, then rector of Saint Phillip's Episcopal Church in Harlem, New York City. Reverend Weston's church was located in the traditional Black community of Harlem, where racial tensions were addressed from different angles, including open demonstrations, art, music, politically, and spiritually. Another visitor was the minister of finance from the Eastern State of Nigeria, E. Mole. In his declaration to the newspaper, Minister Mole came to "observe social and economic programs developed in the island." He also expressed his admiration for Puerto Ricans' racial relations. The Nigerian official saw Puerto Rico as a colony of the United States, in a situation like that of Nigeria and the African continent, where colonial powers ended their rule but left economic challenges in their wake. For both visitors, Puerto Rican society represented an example of how modernity and democracy could operate from a raceless point of view.[104]

Although visitors saw the island as a "racial paradise" when compared to the United States, it was not. The examples discussed by Ruth Fernández and Cecilia Orta Allende demonstrated that Black Puerto Ricans had to navigate racial exclusion and gender discrimination. They are both examples of the many Afro-Puerto Rican people to whom the ideological apparatus of modernity and whiteness hampered their humanity, talents, and efforts. In building a modern society, Puerto Ricans adopted models from many sources, including Latin American countries and the United States. Unfortunately, these models were tainted by systemic racism, so the new "modern" state continued to exclude Afro-descendants from the nation-building process.

Chapter 6

The Liga Opened Pandora's Black Box

1950–1965

Throughout the 1950s and 1960s, articles in the newspaper *El Mundo* continued the debate around racial discrimination in Puerto Rican society. During the summer of 1950, a column by the Peruvian intellectual Ciro Alegría sparked a series of responses on racial discrimination. A visiting scholar at the University of Puerto Rico (UPR), Alegría was a representative of the *indigenista* movement, whose goal was to advocate a return of Amerindian values in opposition to the European cultural heritage. Nonetheless, advocating for Amerindian values did not necessarily translate into their social improvement. According to Alegría's article, Puerto Rico had no racial discrimination only if the U.S. brand of racism—that is, physical violence and physical segregation—was used as the benchmark. Although Alegría believed that racial prejudice in Puerto Rico was "weak" compared to that in the United States, he maintained that Black Puerto Ricans had to prove themselves twice as much as whites to obtain a "good position."[1]

Ten days later, Ciro Alegría published a follow-up articulating his concerns about the increase of racial prejudice on the island. He described several ways that racial prejudice was perceived on the island. Alegría stated that racial discrimination is natural. He also pointed out that the middle and upper classes discriminated against Black people more frequently. Finally, he maintained that while Blacks gained more opportunities for climbing the socioeconomic ladder, a factor that could be fostered by industrialization, white Puerto Ricans would see them as a threat to their control of the island's economy.

125

Enrique Laguerre, a Puerto Rican writer of African ancestry, weighed in with an essay entitled "El problema racial de la isla no es a base de blancos y negros" ("The Race Problem on the Island Is Not Based on Whites and Blacks"), which was part of his recurring column "Hojas Libres" in *El Mundo*. Laguerre responded to Alegría, explaining that the racial situation of the island was different from that of the United States. Laguerre argued that the island did not practice segregation because of its long history of miscegenation. He, like most of his contemporaries, denied such harsh racism because the island did not have the same violent trajectory as other countries. In other words, he was proposing that the island's situation was similar to that of Brazil, where there was a "racial democracy."[2]

The exchange between Laguerre and Alegría represented the mainstream beliefs among the elite class in Puerto Rico and how they marketed the island internationally as not racially conflictive. Using the U.S. brand of racism to assess racism in Puerto Rico did not erase what was already rooted in Puerto Rican society. More importantly, Laguerre's assertion about the nonexistence of segregation on the island and affirming a type of racial democracy was an example of the denial of racial discrimination among many intellectuals. Even when racism is less harsh, it is still racism. During this period, Puerto Rican society exhibited a certain level of socioeconomic progress, but racial discrimination advanced along with economic progress.

Advancing Civil Rights

Puerto Rico's transition from an agrarian-based economy to a modern industrialized state combined the rearticulation of the national identity, which excluded Black Puerto Ricans, and the implementation of the political reforms that would facilitate its new era. There was criticism of the modernization project's trajectory. Juan Falú Zarzuela and the grassroots organization he founded in 1939 continued their advocacy and highlighted in 1951 how Black Puerto Ricans had been "left behind."[3] The *Liga para Promover el Progreso de los Negros en Puerto Rico* (League to Promote the Advancement of Blacks in Puerto Rico, hereafter Liga) criticized policies by Muñoz Marín and his colleagues at Fomento. According to *El Mundo*, Falú Zarzuela accused Teodoro Moscoso, president of Fomento, of being racist because they did not provide equal employment opportunities to

Black Puerto Ricans.[4] Coverage in local newspapers, such as *El Mundo* and *El Diario de Puerto Rico*, reported that Falú Zarzuela also openly accused Moscoso and the commissioner of education, Dr. Mariano Villaronga, of being "too conservative." Moscoso denied Falú Zarzuela's accusations. According to the claim, Moscoso's and Villaronga's stand was "very different from those liberals like Jaime Benítez and Muñoz Marín." The Black activists also claimed that members of the faculty at the University of Puerto Rico blocked Black Puerto Ricans who wanted to pursue graduate degrees at that institution.[5]

The controversy and bitterness that these accusations generated are examples of how the topic of racial discrimination was undermined in Puerto Rico. The reaction of the editor-in-chief of *El Diario de Puerto Rico* corroborated the statements that Puerto Ricans had no race. In his statement, the editor declared:

> All Puerto Ricans, absolutely all, only belong to one race: the human race. The phrase "colored race" revolts the Christian and civilized spirit of this country. For moral reasons, which are out of discussion, and because of the well-proven scientific reasons and by law and because of the position of respect taken by the government towards the people on human values, here does not exist racial discrimination.[6]

It is obvious from this statement that the editor was troubled by the controversy and accusations made by Falú Zarzuela. Moreover, the editor appears uncomfortable with the phrase "*raza* de color," which he openly rejects. The fact that a Black Puerto Rican "dared" to accuse an agency like Fomento of racial discrimination was a stain on the image of the "good" democratic and tolerant state the administrations of the *Partido Popular Democrático* (PPD) wanted to portray. The demands and accusations made by Falú Zarzuela are examples of the actions Black Puerto Ricans undertook to uncover racial discrimination. Unlike the Liga's protests in the 1940s, this time the newspaper headlines gave leading roles to Falú Zarzuela and his group. More importantly, the Liga allegations demonstrated the principles and commitments of a group of strong Black Puerto Ricans fighting to advance their race. Time proved to be Falú Zarzuela's best ally.

The correlation between the industrialization of the Puerto Rican economy and racial exclusion as denounced by Falú Zarzuela and the Liga can be seen in an interview with José L., a former employee of

Fomento and a bodyguard for Governors Luis Muñoz Marín and Roberto Sánchez Vilella. José L. indicated that during the thirty years he worked for Fomento he saw very "few people of color" working in that agency. When asked about his racial identity José L. identified himself as "white."[7] He also commented that it was not customary in those days to hire Blacks in public agencies. As he put it, "cuando yo a voy a las agencias del gobierno hay muy poca gente negra" (when I go to the government agencies, there are very few Black people). He added that, although the government promoted employment to *gente negra* (Black people), when one goes and visits government agencies, there are very few of them. What is important in this interview is that the informant self-identified as a white Puerto Rican and was straightforward in his statements. This offhand glimpse into the situation from an outside observer corroborated Falú Zarzuela's accusations.

At that time, the major political development taking place on the island was the PPD's efforts to draft Puerto Rico's first constitution. The *Asamblea Constituyente* (Constitutional Assembly) was established in July 1951, and the following month ninety-two district representatives debated the main articles to be added to the document. Among the representatives, the only woman, María Libertad Gómez Garriga (1889–1961), was of African ancestry. She was a native of the town of Utuado, traditionally associated with whites and coffee farms. An educator and community leader, she became the vice president of the Asamblea. She was thus the only woman whose signature appeared on the new Constitution.[8] Falú Zarzuela also participated in the sessions of the Asamblea. On October 5, 1951, in front of the Assembly he demanded the creation of a document that would guarantee constitutional rights for Black Puerto Ricans so that they could obtain jobs without being discriminated against. He also argued that racial discrimination should be punished and that the government should not sponsor discriminatory organizations.[9]

Warring Populares

Between 1950 and 1955, while the island was in the process of industrialization, the Nationalist Movement resurrected. The nationalist leader Pedro Albizu Campos had been released from prison in 1947. During his long imprisonment, the new economic boost fostered by Operation Bootstraps had transformed Puerto Rican society. In the urban centers, where the economy had transformed the lives and ideology of the new middle class, Albizu's Hispanophile rhetoric was no longer attractive. However, the economic transformation that benefited the urban centers had not reached the rural areas. For this reason, as historian Fernando Picó explained, Albizu's speeches had a deeper effect on certain groups from the rural areas.[10] These new *Albizuistas* led the way into what has been called the nationalist insurrections of the 1950s.[11]

In November of 1950, a group of nationalists orchestrated simultaneous attacks on law enforcement and government buildings, including La Fortaleza, the official residence of the governor. The shootings left three nationalists dead and six police officers and one nationalist wounded. In an attack on Blair House, the residence of President Truman, a nationalist was killed. Another was later sentenced to life in prison. Following these incidents, the Insular Police occupied the residences of members of the Nationalist Party, including Albizu, who was found guilty of conspiracy to overthrow the government and sentenced to prison. Although Governor Muñoz Marín released him under probation in 1953, Albizu suffered many mysterious illnesses during his three years of imprisonment.[12]

On March 1, 1954, a group of four nationalists (among them a female) led an attack on the U.S. House of Representatives, where six Congressmen were wounded. The incident in the U.S. House of Representatives drew the attention of the American and Latin American public. Due to both political pressure and the damage to his administration's reputation, Governor Luis Muñoz Marín tried to suppress the nationalists by any means. The violence incited by the nationalists also affected the image of the Independence Movement. As a result of the violent acts, the rhetoric about the independence movement was associated with terrorism and communism. In this respect, historian Fernando Picó asserted that the relationship between the *populares* and *independentistas* became more bitter after 1954.[13] The wrath of the PPD against the nationalists was channeled into the persecution of members of the *Partido Independentista*.

The United States did not condemn Muñoz Marín's persecution of the nationalists because they were labeled as communists. In fact, haunted by the threat of the spread of communism in the Western Hemisphere, the Americans pressured Muñoz Marín to the extent that he became a crusader in suppressing nationalist activities on the island, with the assistance of the FBI. Studies document that Albizu Campos's followers were harassed; some of them disappeared mysteriously or simply were killed.[14] Also, media accounts claimed that Albizu was tortured in jail with lasers.

The allegations of physical abuse eventually reached the Latin American media. In a letter from Venezuelan politician Rómulo Betancourt to Muñoz Marín, the former president referenced this issue: "A while ago the *Repertorio* reprinted from *Bohemia* made some statements by Albizu accusing the U.S. army of torturing him with nuclear devices." In the next sentence, Betancourt expresses his support to Muñoz Marín, saying, "You are doing what you consider patriotic, and you are doing it with all the support from the majority of your country's citizens."[15] One may infer from all this negative propaganda that the governor was trying to avoid political turmoil on the island like that taking place in Venezuela at the time. Among the correspondence between Betancourt and Muñoz Marín, newspaper clippings described the wave of terror unleashed by the Pérez Jiménez regime. These newspaper clippings suggest that the governor was aware of what could happen in a country that fell under a "totalitarian regime."[16]

The public and civil rights activists demanded an investigation into the persecution of the nationalists. Between 1950–1955, a thorough investigation into the events took place, and in 1956, the Muñoz Administration created a Civil Rights Commission. The Commission was created with the purpose of "studying all the problematic human rights issues in Puerto Rico, covering the issues that are outlined in the Constitution, in the laws, and in the U.S. federal authority."[17] Members from the academic (professors and students), judicial, and professional communities comprised the Commission, which was charged with conducting investigations into civil rights violations in the field they represented. The Commission also had an advisory group, which included Roger Baldwin, president of the American Civil Liberties Union, and sociologist Eduardo Seda Bonilla. The ACLU took an active role in defending the rights of colonial citizens, such as Puerto Ricans, particularly those like the nacionalistas. Seda Bonilla later published his research in his book *Los derechos Civiles en la cultura puertorriqueña*, (Civil Rights in Puerto Rican Culture), which included a sociological analysis of race in relation to civil rights.[18]

The International League for the Rights of Man and the American Civil Liberties Union (ACLU) uncovered violations of the civil rights of nationalists and of Black Puerto Ricans, throwing the Muñoz Marín administration into the spotlight of public opinion.[19] It appears that the report of the Civil Rights Commission on the island took longer than expected. In a 1958 letter from Roger Baldwin to Dr. Pedro Muñoz Amato (director of the graduate school of public administration), Baldwin expressed his surprise that "after a month of work, I see no indication of an overall plan" from the two commissions. In addition to recommendations about implementing and engaging the public in civil rights surveys, Baldwin offered to share educational material and warned Dr. Muñoz Amato, saying, "You will doubtless face controversy among yourselves on some of these suggested reforms."[20]

It took almost three years for the Commission to gather all the data needed to evaluate the civil rights situation on the island, and in 1959 they published the final report in a document entitled *Informe al Honorable Gobernador* (Report to the Honorable Governor).[21] According to the report, the investigators found a pattern of political and racial discrimination. The Commission based its findings regarding political discrimination on the persecution of nationalists. Suppression measures included imprisonment, torture, and the killing of high-ranking members of the party. In other instances, trials against the suspects were rushed, and some of them remained in jail for lengthy periods of time without being indicted.[22] The profiling of the Nationalist Party by the Insular police began in the 1930s, after Chief of the Insular Police Colonel Francis Riggs was killed in a confrontation between the two parties. In the 1950s, the Insular Police, in conjunction with the FBI, took this tactic further by creating a database—known as *carpetas*—to profile persons believed to be associated with the nationalists' political ideology.[23]

In her study titled *La insureccion nacionalista*, historian Miñi Seijo Bruno suggests that in addition to political persecution, Albizu and other members of the Nationalist Party were also subjected to racial discrimination.[24] Using figures from the 1950s census, she concluded that compared to white Puerto Ricans, Black Puerto Ricans represented a greater percentage of those engaged in the fight for independence.[25] Sociologist Clarence Senior, co-author of *The Puerto Rican Journey*, corroborates the claim that the nationalists were persecuted because of their race, beginning with their leader Pedro Albizu Campos. Senior participated in a conference that took place in New York City in December 1950, where he addressed the issues confronted by minorities in that city, including Puerto Ricans. In a presentation published in *El Mundo*, Senior highlighted that the discrimination against Puerto Ricans in New York was a result of the rooted racial intolerance among many Americans. Although Senior appeared to disagree with Albizu and the nationalists' approach to the colonial situation of Puerto Rico, he acknowledged that the persecution of the nationalist leader was another example of racial discrimination.[26] According to the

El Mundo article, Senior concluded that racism and racial intolerance against the colored race were the reasons behind the recent nationalist rebellion in Puerto Rico. Senior's declaration implied that not only were the nationalists from the "colored race" but that all Puerto Ricans were.

The Commission made eight recommendations regarding political discrimination. In summary, they advocated for the elimination of the police task forces created to undertake surveillance of any person affiliated with the nationalist or communist party on the island, and denounced the role played by the FBI in these persecutions.[27] The Commission condemned all political persecution, citing its incompatibility with the democratic values professed by the ELA. In 1964, five years after the release of the Commission's report, Governor Muñoz Marín created a formal Office of Civil Rights, and in the same year he pardoned Albizu due to his health. The nationalist leader died in 1965.

The Civil Rights Commission also identified five major areas of racial discrimination against Black Puerto Ricans. According to the report, Black Puerto Ricans were discriminated against in schools, fraternities, housing, private businesses, private clubs, and the armed forces.[28] The pattern of racial discrimination was confirmed as widespread. For example, college fraternities did not allow Black Puerto Ricans to become members.[29] The Commission recommended that the directors of college fraternities improve their efforts to avoid racial discrimination at Commonwealth University.[30]

The government had more motivation and power to intervene in this particular case because sororities, fraternities, and private clubs were under tax-exemption laws. It seems that tax-exempted organizations were to be held to a higher standard. In contrast, racial discrimination had been going on for decades in private clubs with no intervention from authorities, a situation that the ACLU and the International League for the Rights of Man were prompted to investigate as well.

Muñoz Marín was aware of the negative impact that the allegations of racial discrimination could have on his political career. The governor held several meetings during the summer of 1956 to discuss his administration's image.[31] According to minutes from one of those meetings, the governor stated it was important that the ELA's campaign create a "favorable impression of Puerto Rico in the United States." A favorable image was a significant issue for Muñoz Marín because the United States was restructuring its diplomatic relations with Latin America. One of the goals of the restructuring, known as the Point Four Program, was to provide so-called underdeveloped countries with technical assistance and show Latin America the benefits of United States' "Good Neighbor" policy. With Puerto Rico's role as a "cultural bridge" between Latin America and the United States, it was critical that Muñoz Marín maintain a "favorable impression before the Americans." Without its image of a good democratic administration, the Commonwealth might be unable to continue to subsidize the socioeconomic programs embedded in Operation Bootstraps.

A four-page letter from Roger Baldwin, Chairman of the International League, to the Secretary General of the United Nations, also demonstrated Muñoz Marín's concern about his public image. This letter stated that it was Muñoz Marín who invited Baldwin to conduct a "survey" on human rights within the Commonwealth.[32] The letter also mentions that Muñoz Marín was highly cooperative since his "expressed purpose was to examine the actual operation of the provisions for the human rights to determine how effectively they worked and to recommend reforms in law or practice to bring human rights to the highest possible level."[33] It is apparent from Muñoz Marín and his assistants' efforts to keep track of the issues raised by civil rights investigations that they were concerned because the Commonwealth was being heavily scrutinized.

This report served two important purposes. First, Muñoz Marín was looking for United Nations' approval to demonstrate to the United States that Puerto Ricans were qualified to govern themselves. The presumed "inability" of Puerto Ricans to govern themselves was the reason the United States had given to keep the island under its "tutelage" since 1898. Second, the issue of civil rights in Puerto Rico could also affect the United States' image internationally. Although the island achieved a certain level of autonomy with the creation of the Commonwealth in 1952, island affairs were still strongly subjugated by the United States. This situation with apparent civil rights violations is a good example of the mistrust between the United States and Puerto Rico. Since the United States was in the middle of an anti-communist crusade, it would have been a public relations disaster for Puerto Rico—the United States' frequently extolled example of democracy—to experience civil rights violations.

Consolidating the Raceless Nation

In 1958, after involvement of the International League and ACLU led to the results of the Report of the Commission, members of Muñoz Marín's cabinet, specifically the Planning Board asked the director of the Census

Bureau to grant the Puerto Rico Planning Board "maximum responsibility for the planning and conduct of the various censuses of Puerto Rico."[34]

The proposed agreement included the charge to conduct the 1960 census of the population, housing, and agriculture. In the agreement's second appendix, the third provision specified that "it is assumed that a substantial number of census items will be covered on a sample basis. For population, only basic items, such as name, relationship, sex, age, place of birth, and marital status will be included in the 100% schedule."[35] Based on provision number three, the race question was eliminated. The elimination of racial classifications from the censuses conducted in Puerto Rico beginning with the 1960 became systematic. One may suggest that, for the local administration, Puerto Rico's racial situation was too complex and that removing racial classifications could avoid exposing further discriminatory practices. One could suggest that if the Puerto Rican government controlled the questionnaire, particularly the race question, it could perpetuate the myth of a raceless society that the political elite had so meticulously constructed. Economic inequalities could be based on class criteria, disregarding the racial aspects. The Bureau of the Census agreed with the Planning Board recommendation in recognition of the "special needs of Puerto Rico."[36] So from 1960 until 2000, the censuses in Puerto Rico did not report racial or color data.

The elimination of the racial classification in Puerto Rico's censuses has been the subject of more contemporary analysis. Dr. Palmira Rios, president of the Puerto Rican Civil Rights Commission from 2003 to 2008, pointed out in 2000 that the PPD always saw race as "divisive." When the U.S. Census Bureau agreed to eliminate the race question from the census, it gave Muñoz Marín and his party a "degree of autonomy" that would allow them to pursue their national project.[37] Anthropologist Jorge Duany added that the U.S. Census Bureau agreed to such requests because Puerto Rico's racial classifications "were incompatible with the dominant U.S. scheme of racial classification" (limited to only Black or white).[38] He added, "Furthermore, Commonwealth officials were not interested in dividing the Puerto Rican population by race but in uniting it under a common nationality."[39] Further, Eliseo Combas Guerra, in his column at the newspaper *El Mundo* noted such changes. At the same time, Luis Sánchez Cappa affirmed that a "new Federal Agency would process information and census data in the 1960 census."[40] It appears that eliminating the racial classification from the Puerto Rican census was critical for the national project because it dismissed the entire infrastructure of racial hierarchies and promoted a "color-blind" society despite historical evidence that clearly demonstrated that Puerto Rican society was racially driven. Finally, leaving the racial classification would lead to further investigations or give root to more civil rights activism on the island.

Erasing Blackness

The selective elimination of the Black race from government records such as the census had a precedent in the island's history. According to historian Luis Díaz Soler, in January of 1867, the Spanish colonial government on the island was evaluating the arguments for the abolition of slavery. A delegation from Puerto Rico and Cuba presented their arguments at the Cortes (Spanish Parliament). For the Puerto Rican delegation, the argument established the justification to abolish slavery, which already represented a nonprofitable business and a moral issue for some. The delegation included reformists José Julián Acosta, Segundo Ruiz Belvis, and Francisco Mariano Quiñones, as well as the conservative Manuel Zeno y Correa. The conservative faction, which included Peninsulares, aimed to maintain positions of power. The main points discussed were (1) should slavery be abolished, Black people would outnumber whites, and (2) how to solve the problem with *jornaleros* (free white laborers) who were regulated by the *libreta* system or notebook system. The jornaleros on many occasions were abused physically by their employers, and many had issues with discipline and were accused of "vagrancy."[41] In response to the concerns about Blacks outnumbering whites, the Puerto Rican delegates agreed to bring more white Spaniards to the island. They also proposed to prohibit interracial marriages, but that was rejected. Another proposal included deporting Blacks, which Zeno y Correa opposed, arguing that it seemed like a punishment. Further, they proposed the elimination of racial distinctions from birth certificates, to which all the delegates agreed.[42] Eliminating the "racial difference" in birth certificates—although there is no evidence of its implementation—connects with the discussion about eliminating racial classification in the census of Puerto Rico after 1960. Analyzing that historical fact, Díaz Soler concluded, "at the end, the reformist commissioners of Puerto Rico were against any discriminatory measure, *preventing the raising of a racial problem that did not exist* on the island."[43]

This historical capsule and its interpretation by a leading scholar on the topic of slavery in Puerto Rico is another example of the denial of racial discrimination and the perpetuation of a color-blind society by politicians and academics. At a glance, the Puerto Rican delegates at the Cortes did not want to create traumatic experiences for Blacks by expatriating them to a land where most of them did not have a connection. While it seems benign that the delegates opposed banning interracial intermarriages, they agreed to increase the white population by promoting Spanish migration. The discussions to abolish slavery in Puerto Rico uncovered that even for the most moderate politicians, eliminating racial difference in an official document was acceptable. Although in this example the political setting was under the Spanish colonial regime, the efforts to eliminate racial differences and erase Blackness—a concerted effort to create a raceless society but at the same time make it whiter—were equally a travesty. As Omni and Winant stated, the formation of a color-blind society couldn't be achieved overnight since "state actions in the past and present have treated people in very different ways according to their race."[44]

The measures proposed by the ruling class on the eve of the abolition of slavery resemble the strategies employed by the PPD with the racial classification of the census. In both instances, the island was under colonial administrations, first by the Spanish and then by the Americans. Equally, race became an obstacle for those who wanted to implement their national project. Finally, the elimination of racial classifications meant the perpetuation of the idea of a "grand Puerto Rican family" and the creation of the Caribbean version of a racial democracy.

Creating and fostering a color-blind society is indeed what Puerto Ricans have been practicing throughout the island's two colonial periods. These examples illustrate a specific but not unique type of *blanquiamiento* (whitening) to maintain hegemonic control and a reinforcement of racial hierarchies by manipulating "official documents." This strategy not only attempts to override peoples' lives by erasing their racial identity or their entire existence from official documents, it also intentionally creates the illusion of an open, race-free society. In the process, this type of so-called color-blind state forces the proliferation of a false identity in which—as Omi and Winant asserted—"race continues to signify difference and structure inequality."[45] In this context, Puerto Ricans' efforts to become a color-blind state led to the marginalization of those not included under the umbrella of whiteness.

Investigating Racial Discrimination

Falú Zarzuela's challenges in the early 1950s to the government, along with the coverage in the local press, and the civil rights report triggered an investigation by the Puerto Rican House of Representatives. This investigation led to allegations of racial discrimination against Black people in the private and public sector.[46] The Commission of the Senate initiated an investigation in March 1962 and appointed an independent counsel named Miguel Velázquez Álvarez to lead the investigation. The hearings took place on July 22–23, 1963. Due to the seriousness of this topic, numerous articles about racial discrimination occupied the headlines of *El Mundo*.

In the opening statement of the hearing, the chairman of the Commission, Jorge Font Saldaña, pointed out the "delicate nature" of the hearings and that the investigation would be limited to banks with business operations in Puerto Rico.[47] The introduction continues with a comparison of the racial situations in the United States and Puerto Rico. As had been the case before, the common sentiment was that the island had evolved socially and economically so that regarding intellectual and political achievement, race was not a factor. Those achievements were not racialized and the successful person was Puerto Rican without racial labels.[48] In the hearings, eight people (seven men and one woman) testified.

Drops of Experience

The first witness was José Miranda-Pratts, a cashier from the Banco Popular. During the first round of questioning, Miranda-Pratts explained his duties in the bank as well as his race and color, which he described as "*de color negro*." The interrogation asked about Miranda's service at the bank and how he applied for his job. The independent counsel asked Miranda-Pratts specifically if he feared he would not get the job because of his race. He answered, "Well, I was afraid."[49] Miranda-Pratts pointed out that his fears were based on his experiences and knowledge of the way things were on the island. He also mentioned that, prior to applying for the job, he visited branches of the Banco Popular and never saw a Black person employed there. Miranda-Pratts explained that he went to the Human Resources office and applied for the job. A month later he was notified that he was to take an exam, which he passed. The witness explained that he also applied to other financial institutions, such as the Chase Manhattan Bank and the Banco de Ponce, but never received a call back from them. The witness also stated that for all the institutions to which he applied the employer asked him to submit a photograph.[50]

They also asked Miranda-Pratts if he saw another *persona de color* (person of color) while he was in training. The witness answered that he saw only two mulattos and one Black. He added to his answer that he was the first *negro* working as a cashier in the Banco Popular.[51] With regard to his experiences at the bank, the independent counsel asked Miranda-Pratts if he noted anything unusual on the job, such as harassment or discrimination. He answered, "No." Interestingly, he did comment that the bank's customers were surprised that he was working as a teller. He added that some customers asked him how he was treated and how long he had been working at the bank. He further added in his declaration that he received words of encouragement from Black customers.[52]

The second witness to testify, Manuel Rivera-Osorio, a thirty-four-year-old Black man, began working as a cashier at the Banco Popular San José branch on February 1, 1963. When asked about his race, Rivera-Osorio responded that he was a "colored person." After he provided his educational background, the independent counsel asked Rivera-Osorio if he had classmates who were *de color*, to which he gave a positive answer. Then the interrogation continued with the question, "Podría usted explicar si con anterioridad a comenzar a trabajar para el Banco había recibido alguna impresión o temor, o actitud en relación con la posibilidad de que su solicitud fuera rechazada? ¿Cuál era su situación? (Could you explain if before you began working in the bank you had the impression, fear or attitude that your application would be rejected? What was your situation?) Rivera-Osorio answered, "Bueno, yo tenía la duda, ¿verdad? Como yo no había visto a una persona de color trabajando en un Banco, pues yo creía que si yo solicitaba mi solicitud iba a ir al canasto. O sea, esa era la impresión que yo tenía" (Well, truthfully, I had doubts. Since I had never seen a Black person working in a bank, I thought that if I applied my application was going into the trashcan. At least, that's the impression I had).[53] He also had to present a photograph of himself to Human Resources and was asked to return and take an exam.[54]

Both Rivera-Osorio and Miranda-Pratts began working with the Banco Popular in 1963, the same year that the House of Representatives began an investigation into racial discrimination in Puerto Rico's financial institutions. From the time the investigation was announced (March 1962) until the hearings (July 1963), the hiring of Black Puerto Ricans took place around nine months later. It seems that the banks under scrutiny were alerted and applied damage control measures. Like Miranda-Pratt, Rivera-Osorio was the only "persona negra" working in that branch, even though he worked in San José, a predominately mulatto community. Also, like Miranda-Pratts, Rivera-Osorio received words of encouragement from customers. In one instance, a woman asked him when the policy of not hiring *personas de color* had changed.[55] The customers' reactions to Black men working as bank tellers indicated that Blacks were considered outsiders in the corporate environment.

These testimonies are quintessential examples of Puerto Rican society's unique racial discourse. It is evident from the declarations that Black Puerto Ricans knew they were subjected to racial discrimination. But instead of concretely articulating their experiences, such actions are internalized and normalized as part of customs, language, and traditions. The experiences of Rivera-Osorio and Miranda-Pratts affirm that racial discrimination was a common practice and that excluding Blacks from jobs that required contact with the public was the acknowledged norm. Of course, the term "persona de color" is a clear euphemism for Black. Based on those declarations, it was a common term used to refer to non-whites. Anthropologist Isar Goudreau identified this as language that, "allows for a multidimensional interpretation of power relationship in everyday encounters."[56]

Defining *Persona de Color*

During the proceedings, the chairman of the Commission asked the Counsel to define what he meant by *persona de color*. Before the answer was given, the chairman, Jorge Font Saldaña, provided his own definition of a person without color. He declared, "se considera blanco a todo el que no tenga características negroides" (an individual who does not possess "Negroid" features is considered white).[57] The chairman's explanation reflects the essential racial understanding of Puerto Rican society at that time. Then the Counsel provided its own definition of a "persona de color":

> In the sense that they are Blacks, absence of dark hue of color or people that we in Puerto Rico classify as "Indian." In other words, a colored person, with dark complexion, but he or she

has straight hair, or a person that we consider a mulatto. There
is a variable on those physical characteristics, the person that
has "Negroid" features,' but she or he could have a "white"
complexion. This includes the hair, lips, and other "Negroid"
features. When I refer to an "Indian," I mean by that a person with straight hair. A "mulatto" is any person who is not
classified as "white" in the sense of the physical appearance
shows "Negroid" features.[58]

The responses of both the chairman of the Special Commission and the
independent counsel reflect racial classification based on concepts used
by the United States.

During his testimony, Samuel Hernández the vice president and
comptroller of Banco de San Juan, was also asked to clarify his racial
terminology. He very specifically differentiated between *blanco* and *negro*.
Hernández did so by establishing physical and skin color characteristics
that may differentiate the two races. He also said that, while he was in
the army, the Americans labeled his race as "Puerto Rican white." Another
member of the Commission, Congressman Roig-Vélez, stated that in
Puerto Rico although people might look white this does not necessarily
mean they are white. He, like Hernández, was trying to sort out that being
"Spanish or Puerto Rican white" was not the same as being "American
white." This brought up *raja*, which means background. These statements
confirmed that while race and color in Puerto Rico were based on physical
appearances, they were not the only criteria. For those who were proud of
their whiteness, Roig-Vélez's comments served as a reminder that "Puerto
Rican white" was not equal to Caucasian but was instead a subcategory
of U.S. racial schemes. The irony of this exchange is that they did not
appear to realize that they were racializing themselves.

Requiring *Buena Apariencia*

Samuel Hernández's testimony sheds more light on racial discrimination
in the workplace from a managerial point of view. Hernández was asked
that for anyone who wanted to apply for a position at that bank if it was
a requirement "tener buena apariencia" (to have a good appearance). The
witness answered that it was, and added, "No podemos negar que nos

fijamos en la apariencia de la persona" (We cannot deny that we look at the physical appearance of the person).[59] Further in his testimony, Hernández explained that a photograph was required with the application for two reasons. First, if the employee stole from the bank the administration would be able to provide the FBI and the Insular Police with a description of the suspect. Second, the photograph could expedite the issuance of an identification card in case he or she was hired.[60]

These elaborate discriminatory practices were rampant in Puerto Rico. For example, job advertisements in *El Mundo* specified that applicants must have a "buena apariencia" or "preferiblemente española" (preferably Spanish/ European) in advertisements seeking a babysitter or a maid."[61] In another advertisement, a single man looking for a cook required the applicant to tell her age and race.[62] In other instances, the advertisement was specific, requesting a "niñera blanca, de buena salud" (a white babysitter, in good health). The so-called requirement of a "good appearance" is another euphemism for "white." The word "race" may not be used, but it is implied. The good appearance epitomizes Omi and Winant's debate about aesthetics and the social fabric based on racially charged codes.[63] The need to look white is imbedded in Puerto Rico's racial discourse and cultural norms. As the vice president of a bank, Hernández clearly affirmed this in his testimony.

Coding Residence

During his testimony, Hernández stumbled when asked if the bank took applicants' place of residence into consideration during employee selection. Rather than answer directly, Hernández explained that while the bank required a background check in Puerto Rico (which according to him was not a requirement in the United States), the requirements were much stricter in countries like Mexico.[64] In a second round of questions, another member of the Commission addressed the class issue. Hernández concurred that they took an applicant's social class into consideration during the selection process. He explained that the place of residence was an important way to evaluate "the customs and manners of the person . . . his family background and whether or not they have had drug problems."[65] These are stereotypes assigned to residents of low-income housing such as a *caserío* (public housing) or a *barriada* (shantytown) who undoubtedly would not be hired to work in a financial institution. Clearly, the social class biases that criminalized an often racialized social class also prevented the bank from hiring people from those neighborhoods.

In her groundbreaking study on public housing, sociologist Zaire Dinzey-Flores showed that the Puerto Rican government's push in the 1960s for low-income public housing was intended to foster ownership among working- and middle-class families. The study examined the different strategies the government employed.[66] This was a complex decision for the Muñoz Marín administration because the construction of low-income public housing, whether single-family homes or multifamily complexes, was confronted by myths related to living in *caseríos*. The Muñoz Marín administration made several educational efforts to assure Puerto Rican families that the *caseríos* were a temporary residence and it was expected that they would eventually move into private homes. One of the PPD's public relation tactics was the "spatial integration" of the structures instead of "isolating" them or "creating ghettos," as was the case of many low-income public housing buildings in major U.S. cities. Instead, Muñoz Marín suggested that these structures could co-exist spatially within the same visual landscape with more affluent development. Thus, today Puerto Rican *caseríos* are surrounded by or are next to upper-class private developments.[67] Muñoz Marín received several complaints from members of the upper class opposing his spatial integration plan. He solved that problem by reminding the upper class that they had a responsibility to "teach and educate" the less fortunate class and to show them how to become dignified homeowners.

Another important tactic was to change the semantics of the stereotyped structures. For example, "caserío público" (public housing) was changed to "residenciales" (residences) or "urbanización pública" (public urbanization).[68] This approach to soften the name of public housing is similar to what occurs in parts of the United States where inner-city, low-income projects are called "houses" with the name of a public figure or geographic feature, such as the "Jefferson Houses" or the "Marble Hills Houses." For instance, there was the "Residencial Nemesio R. Canales" and the "Residencial Luis Llorens Torres," to name just two. These semantic approaches to calming fears and lowering opposition resembled the "softening" approach used in the island's racial lexicon. It appears that again Puerto Ricans resorted to linguistic strategies to smooth over controversial issues that, in this case, pointed to the intersectionality of race and class.

Once Muñoz Marín's urban planning was put into effect, it was common to see the lower class in *caseríos* while private housing was reserved for the middle class. Roy Simón Bryce-Laporte's study "Urban Relocation and Family Adaptation in Puerto Rico" explained that the *caserío* "was operated under certain legislation and policies, which were modified by the insular corporation and its administrator to 'suit' the local situation."[69] The local situation consisted of residents who were predominately racially mixed, had little income, and in some cases were forced to live in the same place for two or three generations without the possibility of moving to the suburbs, which was an ideal in Puerto Rico at this time.[70]

Over the years, public housing became true homes for many Puerto Rican families. There were many reasons for staying in the *caseríos* instead of becoming homeowners, so in many cases the residents stayed "by choice." Among the reasons were the lack of economic means to move out and the sense of a community that, ironically, the temporary housing created.[71] This issue also illustrates that the residents of the *caseríos* in some way were marginalized *in situ* because, although this housing was "temporary," as Dinzey-Flores argues, the majority of residents remained living there due to a lack of resources.[72] Working-class people had little choice but to occupy undesirable living conditions induced by spatial discrimination. Thus, merely the "physical address of a residence" located in a *caserio* stigmatized people, often making it difficult for them to find good jobs or simply negatively associating them with criminals.[73] This pattern of social exclusion was taking shape parallel to the modernization of the island.

Offering Unreasonable Solutions

When the independent counsel asked Samuel Hernández why he thought only a few Blacks applied for jobs in financial institutions, he answered, "White Puerto Ricans apply in higher proportions than Blacks." Hernández added that Black Puerto Ricans were missing from this particular private sector because "it seems to me that is a result of that [inferiority] complex, and second it is because the banks did not hire Blacks in previous years, or it may be because they [Blacks] did not apply."[74] He added that in his bank, the legal advisor was *una persona de color, un negro*. And the other Black employee was a woman who resigned for a job in another institution.

When asked to provide a suggestion for increasing the number of Blacks applying for jobs in the financial sector, Hernández responded, "Well, my suggestion is that there should be a major campaign, which does not exist, well, a campaign to eliminate that [inferiority] complex that they [Blacks] have." Hernández was in denial about racial discrimination. Rather than acknowledge the racial and class discrimination in his workplace, he blamed Black Puerto Ricans for the island's racist systems.

To increase their job opportunities, Hernández also suggested that *la persona de color* needed a better education. A high school diploma was not enough, since financial institutions were evolving with new technology.[75] He pointed out that his bank was providing training workshops or, alternatively, they could take courses at the Inter-American University, which was a private institution. Hernández's suggestion that candidates take courses in a private institution to build their resumes was not realistic. Average working-class Puerto Rican families did not have the means to pay for enrollment at the Inter-American University. Sadly, the Inter-American University and other private institutions of higher education were servicing students from working-class families. The enrollment at UPR, a state institution, became more oriented to middle-class students.

The testimonies provided in these hearings were excellent examples of the elusiveness of the Puerto Rican conceptualization of race and color. By adhering to cultural norms that (1) refuse to use concrete terms to describe a person's race and that (2) presume their interactions with *gente de color* is not discriminatory simply because the patterns differ from the United States or other Latin American societies, they deny the lived reality of Black Puerto Ricans. Sociologists Omi and Winant explain the social dynamics at play: "Conversely, our ongoing interpretation of our experience in racial terms shapes our relations to the institutions and organizations through which we are embedded in social structure." Because racial codes encourage people to make assumptions about physical differences, which include skin color, these codes can influence an individual's "confidence and trust in others."[76] These coded euphemisms became "racially coded simply because we live in a society where racial awareness is so pervasive."[77] In other words, the financial institutions created and sponsored by the government reflected the racialization process because they were codifying applicants based on race, appearance, and neighborhood origins (social class). Those in positions of power, such as Samuel Hernández, had a racialized mindset about Black people. These racial codes could activate at any moment to prevent those in power from hiring or recruiting people of color.

Assessing Results

In 1975, Judge Jeannette Ramos analyzed the findings and results of the 1963 hearings. Her report also provided quantitative data on the employment practices of the island's financial sector. The Commission's investigation showed that, in 1962, only one of 942 employees at the Banco Popular was a Black Puerto Rican. According to Ramos, after the investigation, this bank hired only four Black Puerto Ricans. There were no Black Puerto Ricans working at the Banco de Crédito de Ahorro Ponceño. Interestingly, both banks were locally owned and operated. The American banks showed a more expected outcome. Before the investigation, the then First National City Bank had no Black Puerto Ricans among its 653 employees. After the investigation, the number of employees increased to 1,000, and only thirty-four were Black Puerto Ricans. From that figure, only one Afro-Puerto Rican reached a highly ranked position, compared to the 269 white Puerto Ricans in similar positions. The other thirty-three Afro-Puerto Ricans performed clerical and office positions that kept them out of public view. The Bank of Nova Scotia had no Black Puerto Ricans on staff. However, the elevator operator and the chauffer were Black Puerto Ricans. In another bank with 106 employees, only two were of African ancestry. Finally, no Black Puerto Ricans were working in the Chase Manhattan Bank, the Banco de San Juan, Roig Bank, or the United Federal Savings.[78]

Jeannette Ramos's study went on to evaluate hiring practices and representation of Puerto Ricans of African ancestry in the private sector in the 1970s, particularly in the banking sector. She investigated forty-two corporations.[79] It appears that nothing had changed for Black Puerto Ricans since 1963. The study revealed that in the banking and private sectors only 8.6 percent of Black or "colored" Puerto Ricans were represented in the industry or white-collar jobs, while they made up 29.6 percent of blue-collar jobs. Black Puerto Ricans were also proportionally overrepresented in retail and entertainment businesses, showing 25.2 and 20.3 percent, respectively. Ramos noted that jobs that required face-to-face interaction were given mostly to "mulattoes" or light-skinned applicants rather than dark-skinned Puerto Ricans. The preference for light-skinned people in these types of jobs suggest that colorism continued to be part of the social fabric. Another important figure is that only 6.5 percent of Black Puerto Ricans held highly ranked positions in technical and administrative jobs.

From Jeannette Ramos's study, one may infer that between 1963 and 1975 some changes were made to include Black Puerto Ricans in the new economy. However, those changes were altogether insufficient, continuing the patterns that codified socioeconomic disparities between Black and white Puerto Ricans. The report concluded: "Blacks in Puerto Rico are excessively underrepresented in financial institutions" and "categorically we can declare that occupational segregation and exclusion against blacks is not accidental but, rather, consistent and systematic."[80] Respecting the involvement of the government, the study added, "the official stand is obvious in the fact that there are not specific recommendations to alleviate this problem."[81] In other words, the discrimination against Puerto Ricans of African ancestry was openly recognized, but when it came to a plan of action, nothing was done until the situation caught the attention of the federal authorities and human rights activists in the 1960s.

Epilogue

Drop by Drop

At first glance, Puerto Ricans celebrate their racial diversity, but this study has shown that their approach is far more complex. Puerto Rico is not a racial paradise. Puerto Rican society has dealt with race and racism by combining the Spanish and American racial hierarchies to create a system uniquely their own. This formula is grounded in a narrative of denial passed on from one generation to another.

I began this research to delve into the complexities of racism in Puerto Rico and to uncover the Black stories that I knew had to exist. The existence of racial denial matters to me because, as an Afro-Puerto Rican historian, not uncovering racism contributes to the perpetuation of a system of exclusion and oppression. By developing this book, I join other scholars' efforts in dismantling the myths of the *gran familia puertorriqueña* and *armonía racial* (the great Puerto Rican family and racial harmony).

Through this book, I wanted to give readers a more critical view of race relations on the island. The Afro-Puerto Rican men and women whose stories I share in each chapter represent the people who have been subjected to racial hierarchies in periods from 1898 to 1965. These Afro-descendants denounced, navigated, and negotiated racism and secured a place in society. Each in their own way defeated the oppressive exclusion of racism. This study pays homage to them.

It is my hope that knowing the stories of what many Afro-Puerto Rican men and women have endured will encourage the current generation of Afro-Boricuas. Representation matters. Through this book and the stories told, I aim to promote a community of people whose Black lives matter. They must be recognized as part of Puerto Rican history, national identity, and development. For Afro-Boricuas, these stories validate our families' history and pride in our hometowns. The historic accounts of these Afro-Puerto Rican trailblazers show how much of an impact one person can have whether their career is in advocacy, banking, civil rights activism, education, law enforcement, literature, military, music, performance, plastic arts, politics, or another pursuit. Each one of the Afro-Puerto Rican men and women mentioned in this book stood up for their rights and dignity, insisting on their own inclusion. They refused to become victims and found ways to break out of racial, class, and gender stereotypes. In their way, they defeated the system of racial hierarchies embedded through 500-plus years of colonization.

Drops of Inclusivity is not the first book to address the myths of racial relations in Puerto Rico. Other studies have focused on education, the labor movement, semantics, literature, and other subject areas. This book frames race and racism by combining a chronological historical narrative with the stories of specific individuals. While the book's voice is historical, it also incorporates oral history, genealogy, and social history to broaden the framework. History itself is vibrant and contradictory. For me, it was essential to develop a dynamic narrative to reflect those diverse undercurrents.

As a historian, my goal was not only to document racially loaded aspects of the process of modernization in Puerto Rico but also to insert the history of Afro-Puerto Ricans who took part in that process. While applying a historical lens, I also gathered, analyzed, and recorded in writing the narratives from an Afro-Puerto Rican–centered perspective. I have aimed to underline the moral, demographic, cultural, intellectual, economic, developmental, and political contributions of Black Puerto Ricans. At its heart, this book historicizes the lives of Afro-Puerto Rican men and women whom conventional history has silenced.

I hope those who read this book will gain tools to help them think more critically about Puerto Rican history and race relations. A common saying claims that "history repeats itself," and I agree. Throughout the decades at the scope of this study, examples of racial prejudice against Afro-Puerto Ricans run rampant. Whether its manifestations are implicit or explicit, racial prejudice erodes peoples' lives and humanity. Racism remains a problem in Puerto Rican society. We must ensure that mistakes and injustices from the past do not continue to corrupt our society. In that context, this book seeks to educate and establish a constructive narrative that can be applied today. Whether in the Puerto Rican diaspora or on the island, each one of us can contribute to making a better society.

At the beginning of the book, I cited the metaphor *Gota a gota, se llena el vaso* (Drop by drop, you fill the glass). In the past, the glass of Afro-Puerto Rican history was kept empty through erasure and exclusion. The drops we need to fill this glass are the untold stories of the thousands of Afro-Puerto Ricans, some of whose lives are represented here. More need to be documented. Their resilience, determination, authority, leadership, ingenuity, perseverance, and sense of justice fills the glass. In the battle against erasure, silence, and denial, each drop, each person, each story matters. Perhaps when we have filled the glass to overflowing, we can all drink freely from the cup of equality and justice.

Appendix A

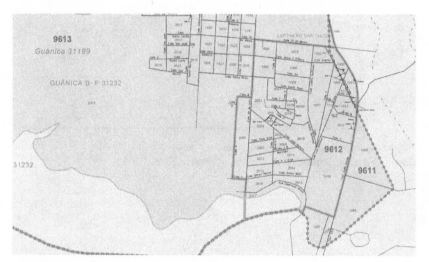

Appendix A. Map of the town of Guánica's, including Simón Mejil Street (blocks 2013 and 2014). Source: U.S. Census of Puerto Rico, 2000.

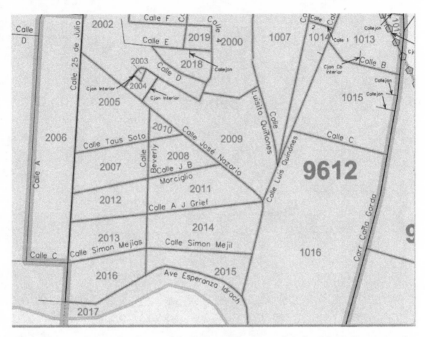

Appendix A.1. Detail of map of Guánica showing Simón Mejil Street in the downtown area. Source: U.S. Census of Puerto Rico, 2000.

Appendix B

Appendix B. Cover of *Bohemia Puertorriqueña* (1962) featuring Cecilia Orta Allende and students from her art program. Source: Luis Muñoz Marín Foundation and Archives.

Appendix C

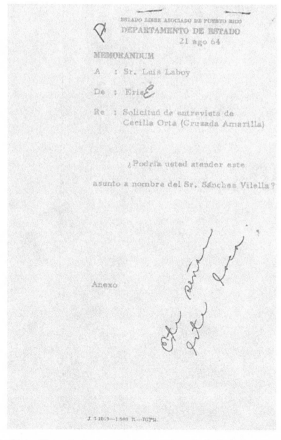

Appendix C. State Department note instructing Luis Laboy to answer Cecilia Orta's request for an interview with Roberto Sánchez Vilella. Note the words "this woman is crazy" handwritten in Spanish. Source: Luis Muñoz Marín Foundation and Archives.

Notes

Introduction

1. See Jorge Larrain, *Identity and Modernity in Latin America* (Cambridge, UK: Polity Press, 2001).

2. See Kelvin Santiago-Valles, " 'Still Longing for the Plantation': The Visual Parodies and Racial National Imaginary of United States Overseas Expansionism, 1898–1903," *American Studies International* 37, no. 3 (October 1999): 18–43; Ileana Rodríguez-Silva. *Silencing Race: Disentangling Blackness, Colonialism, and National Identities in Puerto Rico* (New York: Palgrave Macmillan, 2012).

3. Jay Kinsbruner, *Not of Pure Blood. The Free People of Color and Racial Prejudice in Nineteenth Century Puerto Rico* (Durham, NC: Duke University Press, 1996).

4. Isar P. Godreau. *Scripts of Blackness: Race, Cultural Nationalism, and U.S. Colonialism in Puerto Rico* (Urbana: University of Illinois Press, 2015).

5. Isar P. Godrau et al. "The Lessons of Slavery: Discourse of Slavery, *Mestizaje* and *Blanqueamiento* in an Elementary School in Puerto Rico," *American Ethnologist* 35, no. 1 (February 2008): 115–135.

6. See Arcadio Díaz Quiñones, "Tomás Blanco: Racismo, historia y esclavitud," in Tomás Blanco, *El prejuicio racial en Puerto Rico* (Río Piedras: Ediciones Huracán, 1985), 13–91; Michael Omi and Howard Winant, *Racial Formation in the United States. From the 1960s to the 1990s*, 2nd ed. (New York: Routledge, 1994), 53.

7. See James H. Sweet. "The Iberian Roots of American Racist Thought." *The Mary and William Quarterly* (3rd series) 54, no. 1 (January 1997): 143–166.

8. The original quote reads: "Los mulatos, de que se compone la mayor parte de la población de la isla, son los hijos de blanco y negra. Su color es oscuro desagradable, sus ojos turbios, son altos y bien formados, más fuertes y acostumbrados al trabajo mas que los blancos criollos, quienes los tratan con desprecio." Fray Iñigo Abbad y Lasierra, *Historia geográfica, civil y natural de la isla de San*

Juan Bautista de Puerto Rico. Estudio preliminar por Isabel Gutierrez del Arroyo (San Juan,1970), 100. The book was first published in 1788.

9. Díaz Quiñones, "Tomás Blanco: Racismo, historia y esclavitud," in Tomás Blanco, *El prejuicio racial en Puerto Rico,* 66.

10. For works related to the impact of the Haitian Revolution in Puerto Rico, see Guillermo Baralt, *Esclavos rebeldes, conspiraciones y sublevaciones de esclavos en Puerto Rico (1795–1873)*; Arturo Morales Carrión, "El reflujo en Puerto Rico de la crisis Dominico-Haitana," *Revista Eme y Eme* (República Dominicana, 1976); and Milagros Denis, "Interpretations and Consequences of the Haitian Revolution in Puerto Rico: Resistance and Racism" (MA thesis, Cornell University, 1999).

11. The Spanish version reads: "Son ciudadanos aquellos españoles que por ambas líneas traen su origen de los dominios españoles de ambos hemisferios, y están, avecinados en cualquier pueblo de los mismos dominios." *Constitución política de la monarquía española promulgada en Cádiz a 19 de marzo de 1812.* www.congreso.es/docu/constituciones/1812/ce1812_cd.pdf

12. ". . . a los españoles que por cualquier línea son habidos y reputados originarios del Africa, se les daría carta de ciudadanía siempre y cuando hiciesen servicios calificativos a la Patria o que se distiguiesen por su talento, aplicación y conducta siempre que fuesen hijos de legítimo matrimonio." *Constitución política.*

13. See that discussion in David M. Stark. "Discovering the Invisible Puerto Rican Slave Family: Demographic Evidence from the Eighteenth Century," *Journal of Family History* 21, no. 4 (1996).

14. See the works of Rosa E. Carrasquillo, *Our Landless Patria: Marginal Citizenship and Race in Caguas, Puerto Rico, 1880–1910* (University of Nebraska Press, 2005); Mariano Negrón Portillo and Raúl Mayo Santana, *La esclavitud menor: la esclavitud en los municipios del interior de Puerto Rico siglo XIX. Estudio del Registro de Esclavos de 1872: segunda parte* (Río Piedras: Centro de Investigaciones Sociales/Universidad de Puerto Rico, 2007); Luis A. Figueroa. *Sugar, Slavery, and Freedom in Nineteenth-Century Puerto Rico* (Chapel Hill: University of North Carolina Press, 2005).

15. Michael Omi and Howard Winant, *Racial Formation,* 55; Mervyn C. Alleyne, *The Construction and Representation of Race and Ethnicity in the Caribbean and the World* (University of West Indies Press, 2000), 2.

16. Isar P. Godreau, "Slippery Semantics: Race Talks and Everyday Use of Racial Terminology in Puerto Rico," *Centro. Journal of the Center of Puerto Rican Studies* 20, no. 2 (Fall 2008): 6.

17. See the influential works by Luis M. Díaz Soler, *Historia de la esclavitud negra en Puerto Rico* (San Juan: Editorial de la Universidad de Puerto Rico, 1959); and Emilio S. Belaval, *Problemas de la cultura puertorriqueña* (Rio Piedras: Editorial Cultural Edil, 1977). The book was first published in 1935.

18. See the poetry by Luis Palés Matos, *Tuntún de pasa y grifería* (Río Piedras: Editorial de la Universidad de Puerto Rico, 1993). The book was first

published in 1937. I see in Palés Matos a parallel of this approach to the effort made by Gilberto Freyre in Brazil and Fernando Ortíz in Cuba. Adjudicating a "folklore status" did not endanger the process of modernity within the Iberian roots of the Puerto Rican society or solve the debate of *negritud* or blackness on the island. Literary school represented by the work of Zenón Cruz, *Narciso descubre su trasero*. 2 vols. (Humacao: Editorial Furidi, 1974) and José Luis González, *El país de cuatro pisos y otros ensayos* (Río Piedras: Ediciones Huracán, 1989) lead a challenge to this approach.

19. See Kelvin Santiago-Valles. " 'Still Longing for the Plantation': The Visual Parodies and Racial National Imaginary of United States Overseas Expansionism, 1898–1903," *American Studies International* 37, no. 3 (October 1999): 18–43; Ileana Rodríguez-Silva. *Silencing Race: Disentangling Blackness, Colonialism, and National Identities in Puerto Rico* (New York: Palgrave Macmillan, 2012).

20. I use the historical analysis by Nancy P. Appelbaum et al. *Race and Nation in Modern Latin America* (2003); Mervyn C. Alleyne, *The Construction and Representation of Race and Ethnicity in the Caribbean and the World* (Chapel Hill: University of North Carolina Press, 2002); Richard Graham, *The Idea of Race in Latin America,* (Austin: University of Texas Press, 1990); Winthrop R. Wright, *Café con leche: Race, Class, and National Image in Venezuela* (Austin: University of Texas Press, 1990); Emilia Viotti da Costa, *The Brazilian Empire: Myths and Histories*. Rev. ed. (Chapel Hill: University of North Carolina Press, 2000).

21. Abbad y Lasierra, *Historia geográfica*; González, *El país*; Zenón Cruz, *Narciso Descubre*; and Aixa Merino Falú, *Raza, género y clase social. El discrimen contra las mujeres afropuertorriqueñas* (San Juan: Oficina de la Procuradora de las Mujeres, 2004).

22. See Blanco, *El prejuicio racial*; Díaz Soler, *Historia de la esclavitud*.

23. "The Prejudice of Not Having Prejudice in Puerto Rico," *The Rican. A Journal of Contemporary Puerto Rican Thought*, nos. 2–3 (Winter 1972–Spring 1973): 41–54, 23–37, 42.

24. Contemporary documentation of the period: United States War Department. *Report of the Island of Porto Rico; Its Population, Civil Government, commerce, Industries, Productions, Roads, Tariff, and Currency*, with Recommendations by Henry K. Carroll (Washington, DC: Government Printing Office, 1899). Groundbreaking scholarship of this period including critical analysis of this data from U.S. reports are found in Kelvin Santiago-Valles, *Subject People and Colonial Discourses: Economic Transformation and Social Disorder in Puerto Rico* (Albany, NY: SUNY Press, 1994); Lanny Thompson, *Nuestra isla y su gente. La construcción del "otro" puertorriqueño en "Our Islands and Their People* (San Juan: Centro de Investigaciones Sociales, 1995); Pedro A. Cabán, *Constructing Colonial People: Puerto Rico and the United States, 1898–1932* (Boulder, CO: Westview Press, 1999); José Anazagasty Rodríguez and Mario R. Cancel, eds., *"We the People." La represenatación Americana de los puertorriqueños, 1898–1926*

(Fundación Puertorriqueña de las Humanidades, 2008); and Jorge Duany, *The Puerto Rican Nation on the Move. Identities on the Island and in the United States* (Chapel Hill: University of North Carolina, 2002), among others.

Chapter 1

1. Arturo Morales Carrión, "The Hope and the Trauma," in *Puerto Rico. A Political and Cultural History*, ed. Arturo Morales Carrión (New York: W.W. Norton, 1983), 141.

2. The United States was very reluctant to intervene in the conflict between Spain and Cuba. It was not until December 7, 1897, that President Cleveland, a Republican, announced his interest in the conflict. In addition, the United States had big investments in Cuba. This fact and the imperialist agenda of the United States accelerated U.S. intervention in the conflict. On this subject, see Evan Thomas, *The War Lovers: Roosevelt, Lodge, Hearst, and the Rush to Empire, 1898* (New York: Back Bay Books, 2010); David Trask, *The War with Spain in 1898* (New York: McMillan Publishing, Co., 1981); and Philip S. Foner, *The Spanish-Cuban-American War and the Birth of American Imperialism* (New York: Monthly Review Press, 1972).

3. This aspect of the War of 1898 is amply discussed in Carmelo Rosario Natal, *Los pobres del '98 puertorriqueño. Lo que le pasó a la gente* (San Juan: Producciones Históricas, 1998).

4. The U.S. Naval Institute, *Log of the U.S. Gunboat Gloucester. Commanded by Lt. Richard Wainwright and the Official Reports of the Principal Events of Her Cruise during the Late War with Spain* (Annapolis: The Navy Department, 1898), 91. www.google.com/books/edition/Log_of_the_U_S_Gunboat_Gloucester/obx CAAAAYAAJ?hl=en&gbpv=1&dq=Lieutenant+H.+P.+House+of+the+Gloucester &pg=PA90-IA3&printsec=frontcover

5. Trask, *The War with Spain*, 365–366; Olga Jiménez, *Puerto Rico: An Interpretative History from Pre-Columbian Times to 1900* (Princeton, NJ: Markus Wiener Publishers, 1998), 204.

6. Ángel Rivero, *Crónica de la Guerra Hispanoamericana en Puerto Rico* (New York: Plus Ultra, 1973), 210. This first edition of the book was in 1922. Rivero, a journalist and writer, wrote the book after his retirement in 1899.

7. Rivero, *Crónica*, 210.

8. Rivero, *Crónica*, 211.

9. Rivero, *Crónica*, 211.

10. According to Díaz Soler, in 1870 this requirement was abolished. In many cases the priest was the person who certified the purity of blood of the individual in question. *Historia de la esclavitud negra en Puerto Rico* (Río Piedras, 2000), 169, 300.

11. Rivero, *Crónica*, 210.

12. The census of 1910 shows Mejil's native language was English and that his father was born in Venezuela and his mother in "Holland" (probably the Caribbean Dutch colonies).

13. Puerto Rico Civil Registrations, 1885–2001.

14. U.S. Bureau of the Census, *Guánica, Puerto Rico. Block Map. 2000.* www2.census.gov/geo/maps/blk2000/st72_PuertoRico_sp/Place/7231189_Guanica/CBP7231189_002_sp.pdf

15. Trask, *The War with Spain*, 365–366; Olga Jiménez, *Puerto Rico*, 204.

16. Cited in Raúl Martín Berrio, "1898: Intervencionismo militar de los EE.UU. sobre Puerto Rico y Cuba." *Quinto Centenario*, no. 16 (1990): 261.

17. José de Oliveras, *Our Islands and Their People as Seen with Camera and Pencil: Embracing Perfect Photographic and Descriptive Representations of the People and the Islands Hawaii & the Philippines*. With an Introduction by Major-General Joseph Wheeler. Vol. 1 (St. Louis/Chicago/New York/Atlanta: N.D. Thompson Publishers, 1899), 265.

18. This tendency is not new but perhaps the best example is the expansion of the Spanish Empire and then followed by the British, French, and other growing nations. In the Americas, interestingly, this role is going to be replicated by the United States in different stages of its nation-building process.

19. For scholarship on this theme, see Lanny Thompson, *Nuestra isla y su gente. La construcción del "otro" puertorriqueño en "Our Islands and Their People* (San Juan: Centro de Investigaciones Sociales, 1995); a classic on this genre, Marie Louis Pratt, *Imperial Eyes: Travel Writing and Transculturation* (New York: Routledge, 1991); and Richard Hofstadter, *Social Darwinism in American Thought.* With an Introduction by Eric Foner (Boston: Beacon Press, 1992).

20. Charles M. Taylor. *Modern Social Imaginaries* (Durham, NC: Duke University Press, 2004), chapters 1 and 2.

21. For analysis of this literature from a historical point of view, see Félix Matos Rodríguez, "The Invasion of Puerto Rico: Writings By Journalists and Other Observers from the United States, 1898," *Centro: Journal of the Center of Puerto Rican Studies* 10, no. 1–2 (Fall 1998): 96–122.

22. Trask, *The War with Spain*, 366.

23. The study from Juan Hernández Cruz, *La invasión de Puerto Rico: consideraciones histórico-sociológicas* (San Germán: Editorial Xaguey, 1992) provides a better perspective on this issue.

24. Hernández Cruz, *La invasión*, 23.

25. Jorge Duany, *Puerto Rican Nation on the Move* (Chapel Hill: University of North Carolina Press, 2002) and Lanny Thompson, *Nuestra isla y su gente*, which was mentioned earlier, provide the best analysis of the paternalistic point of view of the Americans. For other important points of view on this period, see Kelvin Santiago-Valle, *"Subject People" and Colonial Discourses: Economic Transformation*

and Social Disorder in Puerto Rico (Albany, NY: SUNY Press, 1994); and José Anazagasty Rodríguez and Mario R. Cancel, eds. *"We the People." La representación americana de los puertorriqueños, 1898-1926* (UPR-Mayagüez: 2008).

26. Rivero, *Crónica*, 26–28. See also, Carrión, "The Hope and the Trauma," 142. Part of the supporting group was the Puerto Rican chapter of the Partido de la Revolución Cubana with its headquarters in New York City.

27. Jiménez, *Puerto Rico*, 204. For a relatively fresh interpretation of this "warfare" zeal from the American point of view, see Evan Thomas, *The War Lovers: Roosevelt, Lodge, Hearst, and the Rush to Empire, 1898* (New York: Little, Brown and Company, 2010).

28. Jiménez, *Puerto Rico*, 206–208; Mariano Negrón Portillo, *Las turbas republicanas*, 32–33.

29. Carrión, "The Hope and the Trauma," 142. See also, Lillian Guerra, "The Promise and Disillusion of Americanization: Surveying the Socioeconomic Terrain of Early Twentieth-Century Puerto Rico," *Centro: Journal of the Center for Puerto Rican Studies* 11, no. 1 (Fall 1999): 10.

30. Gervasio García. "El otro es uno: Puerto Rico en la Mirada norteamericana de 1898," *Revista de Indias* 57, no. 211 (1997): 739–759.

31. For a better perspective on the labor movement under the Spanish system, see Gervasio L. Garcia and A.G. Quintero, *Desafío y solidadridad: breve historia del movimiento obrero puertorriqueño* (Rio Piedras: Ediciones Huracán, 1982).

32. On the discussion of expectation of the Puerto Rican population during the invasion, see César J. Ayala and Rafael Bernabe, *Puerto Rico in the American Century: A History since 1898* (Chapel Hill: University of North Carolina Press, 2007), 20–25; Lillian Guerra, "The Promise and Disillusion of Americanization," *Centro: Journal of the Center for Puerto Rican Studies* 11, no. 1 (Fall 1999): 8–31; Carrión, "The Hope and the Trauma," 129–151.

33. Jiménez, *Puerto Rico*, 204.

34. I found some discrepancies with the number of generals that governed Puerto Rico. Olga Jiménez in *Puerto Rico* has listed three generals beginning with the takeover of San Juan, on October 18, 1898. María E. Estades in *La presencia militar de Estados Unidos* (Río Piedras: Ediciones Huracán, 1999) describes the military ruling from July 25, 1898, the date of the invasion of Guánica. I understand that during any invasion, until the main city is taken over, the invader party cannot proclaim total domination of the place invaded. For instance, General Miles did not reach San Juan until October of that year. The War Department in its publication *Military Government of Puerto Rico* stipulates the beginning of the military rule as October 18, 1898.

35. Luis Muñoz Rivera (1859–1916) played an important role during the autonomist movement. He was the political opponent of Dr. José Celso Barbosa, a Black Puerto Rican who founded the pro-annexation Party later known as Republican Party. Muñoz Rivera was committed to obtaining full citizenship for

all Puerto Ricans. He traveled to Washington, DC, as a delegate for the citizenship hearings. Muñoz Rivera returned very disappointed when he discovered the racist bias of Americans in granting citizenship to Puerto Ricans. The newspaper "La Democracia" became a political forum for Muñoz Rivera and, later, his son Luis Muñoz-Marín to expose the ambivalence of the United States' administration of the island.

36. The information on these American civilians can be found in the *Official Register of the United States* (Washington, DC: U.S. Government Printing Office, 1909), National Archives and Records Administration (NARA), Washington, DC.

37. Jiménez, *Puerto Rico*, 214–215. The criminalization of the local traditions is discussed in Fernando Picó's *Los gallos peleados*, 3rd ed. (Rio Piedras: Ediciones Huracán, 2003), chapter 3.

38. Jiménez, *Puerto Rico*, 217.

39. On the subject of the immediate impact of American arrival, see Mariano Negrón Portillo, *Las turbas republicanas, 1900–1904* (Rio Piedras, PR: Ediciones Huracán, 1990); Fernando Picó, *La guerra después de la guerra* (Rio Piedras: Ediciones Huracán, 1987); and Carmelo Rosario Natal, *Los pobres del '98 puertorriqueño. Lo que le pasó a la gente* (San Juan: Producciones Históricas, 1998).

40. Natal, *Los pobres del '98*, 42. Rosario argues that the blockade was ineffective because Spain found ways to deceive the Americans.

41. Carrión, "The Hope," 146.

42. Carrión, "The Hope," 147; Jiménez, *Puerto Rico*, 217.

43. This measure recalls the Cortes of Cadiz. While in the constitution of Cadiz, the right to vote was conditioned by citizenship; under the Americans, the right to vote was conditioned by literacy and ownership. Figures on the level of literacy are not complete. In the census of 1860, in a population of 583,181, only 51,250 persons were literate, while 531,931 were illiterate. In other words, 90 percent of the population of the island was illiterate. The census of 1899 shows that only between 18 to 20 percent of the population was literate.

44. Estades, *La presencia militar*, 91; Mariano Negrón-Portillo, *Las turbas republicanas 1900–1904* (Río Piedras: Ediciones Huracán, 1990), 40. Before the Insular Police, there was the Guardia Civil.

45. Jiménez, *Puerto Rico*, 210. The letter of proclamation written by General Miles suggested that the American mission was to "bear the banner of freedom" and "to crush the enemies of our country and yours." The enemy was Spain.

46. Negrón-Portillo, *Las turbas*, 40.

47. Negrón-Portillo, *Las turbas*, 40.

48. Henry K. Carroll, *Report of the Island of Porto Rico: Its Population, Civil Government, Commerce, Industries, Productions, Roads, Tariff, and Currency* (Washington, DC: Government Printing Office, 1899). Hereafter cited as "Report of Porto Rico." This document is commonly known as "The Census of 1899." Carroll wrote a similar report on Cuba.

49. Aida Negrón de Montilla, *La Americanización de Puerto Rico y el Sistema de Instrucción Pública*, 2nd ed. (Rio Piedras: Editorial de la Universidad de Puerto Rico, 1990).

50. Original quote: "el proceso por el cual los pueblos de cultura extranjera adquieren los sistemas y costumbres de vida americanos y la lealtad nacional; o la asimilación de la cultura americana por los pueblos de nacimiento o herencia extranjeros," in Montilla, *La Americanización*, 7.

51. See John M. Faragher et al., *Out of Many: A History of American People* (New Jersey: Prentice Hall, 2004), chapter 20; Hazel M. McFerson, *The Racial Dimensions of American Overseas Colonial Policy* (Westport, CT: Greenwood Press, 1997), chapter 4; Philip W. Kennedy, "Race and American Expansion in Cuba and Puerto Rico, 1898–1905," *Journal of Black Studies* 1, no. 3 (1971): 306–316.

52. Faragher et al., 400; Gary B. Nash et al., *The American People*, vol. 2 (New York: Longman, 2000), 523.

53. In this context I used the American spelling of "Porto Rico" instead of "Puerto" because of its colonial connotation.

54. Samuel Silva-Gotay, *Protestantismo y política en Puerto Rico 1898–1930*, 2nd ed. (Río Piedras: Editorial de la Universidad de Puerto Rico, 1998), 59.

55. Silva-Gotay, *Protestantismo y politica*, 198–199, 201. A few years later, American teachers and then Puerto Ricans trained in the United States will substitute the role of the missionaries.

56. Carroll, *Report*, 32. Osuna made similar observations in *A History of Education in Puerto Rico*, 2nd ed. (Río Piedras: Editorial de la Universidad de Puerto Rico, 1949), 25.

57. Carroll, *Report*, 32.

58. Sociedad Histórica de Puerto Rico, *Puerto Rico: 1897–1917 y un apéndice* (San Juan: Sociedad Histórica de Puerto Rico, 1998); "Foraker Act," 98.

59. César J. Ayala and Rafael Bernabe. *Puerto Rico in the American Century: A History since 1898* (Chapel Hill: The University of North Carolina Press, 2007), 25.

60. Ayala and Bernabe, *Puerto Rico in the American Century*, 29.

61. These are the main categories. In the work *Cadenas de esclavitud*, Mayo-Santana and Negrón-Portillo list at least thirty-two classifications based on skin color. These classifications were used to describe the slave population. After the abolition of slavery in 1873, the descriptions diminished because there was no longer a need to be specific in describing what was considered "property."

62. Among them are Christina Burnett and Burke Marshall, eds., *Foreign in a Domestic Sense: Puerto Rico, American Expansion and the Constitution* (Durham, NC: Duke University Press, 2001); Kelvin Santiago-Valle. " 'Still Longing for the Plantation': The Visual Parodies and Racial National Imaginary of United States Overseas Expansionism, 1898–1903," *American Studies International* 37, no. 3 (October 1999): 18–43; Rubin F. Weston, *Racism in United States Imperialism: The Influence of Racial Assumptions on American Foreign Policy, 1893–1946* (Columbia:

University of South Carolina Press, 1972).

63. Juan F. Perea, "Fulfilling Manifest Destiny: Conquest, Race, and the Insular Cases," in Burnett and Marshall, *Foreign in a Domestic Sense*, 141.

64. Perea, "Fulfilling," 149. After a series of appeals, the court managed to grant full citizenship; Mexicans were not allowed to vote but did hold representation in Congress.

65. Quoted in Perea, "Fulfilling," 153.

66. Perea, "Fulfilling," 155.

67. Weston, *Racism in U.S. Imperialism*, 193.

68. Cited in Weston, *Racism*, 194.

69. Cited in Weston, *Racism*, 195.

70. Cited in Weston, *Racism*, 195.

71. Cited in Elihu Root, *The Military and Colonial Policy of the United States*, eds. Robert Bacon and James Brown Scott (New York: AMS Press, 1970), 163–165. Also see Weston, *Racism*, 185.

72. Weston, *Racism*, 185.

73. Carroll, *Report*, 63.

74. Amílcar Tirado Avilés, Jr., "Ramón Romero Rosa. Su participación en las luchas obreras," *Revista Caribe* Año 2, no. 2–3 (1980–1): 3–15.

75. Cited in Tirado, "Ramón Romero Rosa," 9.

76. The letter "A los negros puertorriqueños" was released in the union newspaper *La Miseria* on March 29, 1901, and reprinted in History Task Force, *Sources for the Study of Puerto Rican Migration, 1879–1930* (New York: Centro de Estudios Puertorriqueños, 1982), 30–33. For this discussion, the reprinted version is used.

77. Ileana M. Rodríguez-Silva, *Silencing Race: Disentangling Blackness, Colonialism, and National Identities in Puerto Rico* (New York: Palgrave-Macmillan, 2012), 150.

78. The implementation of a sugar-oriented economy on the island required a massive restructuring of legislation dealing with tax revenue codes (in the Foraker Act of 1900) that would pave the way for American companies to begin processing and exporting sugar, tobacco, and other small crops to the United States.

79. Ramón Romero Rosa, "A los negros puertorriqueños," 30–33.

80. Romero Rosa, "A los negros puertorriqueños," 31.

81. On the subject, see Rodríguez-Silva, *Silencing Race*; Avilés, "Ramón Romero Rosa"; Reinaldo L. Román, "Scandalous Race: Garveyism, the Bomba, and the Discourses of Blackness in 1920s Puerto Rico," *Caribbean Studies* 31, no. 1 (January–June 2003): 225–230.

82. The excerpt read as follows: "And now we go straight to revisit history. It was the slave trade the hopeless African people, whose eradication some people are still seeking in Puerto Rico, the one that populates that region with those unfortunate ones (the Taínos) in their piece of earth, was snatched by the

cursed merchants, which although they showed the whiteness in the face, carried a blackened insides and heart."

83. David P. Geggus, *Haitian Revolution Studies* (Bloomington: Indiana University Press, 2002).

84. Romero Rosa, "A los puertorriqueños negros," 31. My translation. See Gabriel Haslip-Viera, ed., *Taino Revival: Critical Perspectives on Puerto Rican Identity and Cultural Politics* (New York: Centro de Estudios Puertorriqueños, 1999).

85. Isabelo Zenón Cruz, *Narciso descubre su trasero: el negro en la cultura puertorriqueña*. 2 vols. (Humacao: Editorial Furidi, 1974), 98–105.

86. Roberto Ramos-Perea, *Literatura puertorriqueña negra del siglo XIX escrita por negros. Obras encontradas de Eleuterio Derkes, Manuel Alonso Pizarro y José Ramos y Brans* (San Juan: Publicaciones Gaviota, 2011).

87. José Elías Levis, "La raza de color y Mariano Abril," in Roberto Ramos-Perea, *Literatura puertorriquena negra del siglo XIX escrita por negros*, 461–462. This piece was originally published on June 27, 1898.

88. Ramos-Perea, *Literatura puertorriqueña*, 6.

Chapter 2

1. Samuel Silva-Gotay, *Protestantismo y política en Puerto Rico, 1898–1930. Hacia una historia revisada del protestantismo evangélico en Puerto Rico.* 2nd ed. (Río Piedras: Editorial de la Universidad de Puerto Rico, 1997), 203.

2. Aida Negrón de Montilla, *La americanización de Puerto Rico y el sistema de instrucción pública, 1900–1930* (Río Piedras: Editorial de la Universidad de Puerto Rico, 1977), 9.

3. Historian Lillian Guerra pointed out that the dissolution of child labor was another American promise that never came to fruition. She observed that the American capitalist model collided with their Project of Americanization. The American promise that the next generation of Puerto Rican children born under colonial rule would be better off than their parents turned out to be another contradiction in colonial policy. Most schools built after 1898 competed with the greater number of sugar plantations demanding laborers, making it challenging to reinforce the mandate to send children to school. Although various segments from the Puerto Rican population (rich and poor) welcomed the Americans, Guerra judged that within only a few years the hopes and expectations among Puerto Ricans vanished. Lillian Guerra, "The Promise and Disillusion of Americanization: Surveying the Socio-Economic Terrain of Early Twentieth Century Puerto Rico," *Centro: Journal of the Center of Puerto Rican Studies* 11, no. 1 (Fall 1999): 19.

4. Juan José Osuna, *A History of Education in Puerto Rico* (Río Piedras: Editorial de la Universidad de Puerto Rico, 1949), 158. Osuna did not specify

what went wrong, but by that time the United States was sending Puerto Ricans to schools established only for Native Americans and African Americans.

5. *Report of Commissioner of Education of Porto Rico to the Secretary of Interior* (Washington DC: Government Printing Office, 1907), 45, 62.

6. Negrón de Montilla, *La Americanización*, 112–114.

7. Del Moral, *Negotiating Empire*, chapter 2.

8. Osuna, *A History*, 225–228; Navarro, 198–199.

9. In the 1910 census, Tirado was living with his parents, Juan and Lorenza, and siblings. The census listed all the members of the family as "mulattos."

10. In 1910 the census figures for Coamo were the following: White 8,954, Negro 8,205, Black 220, and Mulatto 7,985. U.S. Department of Commerce, Bureau of the Census. Report of the Thirteenth Decennial Census of the United States. National Archives and Records Administration (NARA) (Washington, DC, 1933), table 38, page 65.

11. Author's interview with Amílcar Tirado Jr., July 2014.

12. Mara Loveman and Jerónimo O. Muñiz, "How Puerto Rico Became White: Boundary Dynamics and Intercensus Racial Classifications" *American Sociological Review* 72 (December 2007): 5–7.

13. 1920 U.S. Federal Census.

14. Information about Rizalina is unclear. In the census of the 1940s, Andrés appears living in Ponce; perhaps he was living in a pension. In the census the name of people living in the property had different surnames. Andrés's mother Lorenza died in 1945. Amílcar Tirado-Santiago became a renowned artist, educator, and filmmaker; for his biography, see Miguel López Ortíz, "Amílcar Tirado," *Fundación Nacional para la Cultura Popular* (San Juan). https://prpop.org/biografias/amilcar-tirado

15. Booker T. Washington Papers, Tuskegee Records (Library of Congress. Manuscript Division), Catalog 1906–1907.

16. Booker T. Washington Papers, Tuskegee Records, Students Files, 1906. The names of the students were cross-listed with the catalog and all of them were Puerto Ricans. They are Salvador Barea (San Germán), Isidro Colón Polanco (Guayama), Onofre Torres (Aibonito), Eduardo Dávila (Yabucoa), Andrés Tirado (Coamo), Pedro Concepción (Fajardo), and Tomás Montes Rivera (Arecibo).

17. Two provisions promoted scholarships for Puerto Ricans to study in the United States. The first, "House Bill 35, which supported study abroad for twenty-five young men at the University of Maryland, University of Leigh, and the Massachusetts Institute of Technology. This program began in 1901. The other government-sponsored scholarship was under Council Bill 15, in which ten young men and ten young women were given scholarships to study in vocational institutions such as the Indian Carlisle, the Hampton Institute, and the Tuskegee Normal and Industrial Institute. *Report of Commissioner of Education of Porto*

Rico to the Secretary of Interior (Washington, DC: Government Printing Office, 1906), 14–15.

18. Author's interview with Amílcar Tirado Jr., July 2014.

19. *The Porto Rico School Review/Revista Escolar de Puerto Rico* 7, no. 2 (April 1922): 30. www.google.com/books/edition/The_Porto_Rico_school_review/PI8QAA AAYAAJ?hl=en&gbpv=1&bsq=Andres%20Tirado%20Sanchez%2

20. Solsiree del Moral, *Negotiating Empire: The Cultural Politics of Schools in Puerto Rico, 1898–1952* (Madison: University of Wisconsin Press, 2013), 70.

21. Aixa Merino Falú, *Raza, género y clase social. El discrimen contra las mujeres afropuertorriqueñas* (San Juan: Oficina de la Procuradora de las Mujeres, 1992), 156.

22. James Dietz, *Economic History of Puerto Rico: Institutional Change and Capitalist Development* (Princeton, NJ: Princeton University Press, 1986), 154–158.

23. Osuna, *A History*, 131.

24. José Manuel Navarro, *Creating Tropical Yankees: Social Science Textbooks and the U.S. Ideological Control in Puerto Rico, 1898–1908* (New York: Routledge, 2002), chapter 3. According to Navarro, from 1898 through 1908 the majority of the Puerto Rican school system received an elementary education that extended to sixth grade. This was the same model used in Hampton, Tuskegee, and Carlisle. Nonetheless there were exceptions in which Puerto Rican students were sent abroad to high schools and universities.

25. Navarro, *Creating Tropical Yankees*, 198. An important reference of this experiment for the Cuban case is seen in the work of Frank A. Guridy, *Forging Diaspora: Afro-Cubans and African Americans in a World of Empire and Jim Crow (Envisioning Cuba)* (Chapel Hill: University of North Carolina Press, 2010).

26. Department of Commerce. United States Census Bureau, *Thirteenth Census of the United States. Taken in 1910. Statistics for Porto Rico* (Washington, DC: Government Printing Office, 1913), 30.

27. Booker T. Washington Papers, reel 685, "Students Files" applications A–K, 1910–1912.

28. The Booker T. Washington Papers, Reel 685, Tuskegee Records, "Letter from Lino Padrón-Rivera to Dr. Washington," December 10, 1910. Originally this letter was written in Spanish; however, there is a translation of it. In the next chapter, I refer again to Padrón-Rivera and his letter. He eventually became a prominent labor union leader in the 1920s.

29. Booker T. Washington Papers, "Students Files" applications A–K, 1910.

30. Padrón-Rivera ultimately stayed in Puerto Rico and attended public schools in Bayamón and Fajardo, and then studied at the University of Puerto Rico-Mayagüez in 1910. He became co-founder of the Socialist Party and moved up through the party ranks and became a senator.

31. "Letter from Joseph Forney Johnston to Booker T. Washington," June 28, 1899, in Louis Harlan et al., eds., *The Booker T. Washington Papers (1898–1898)*

14 vols. (Chicago: University of Illinois Press, 1975), vol. 5, 140.

32. Harlan et al., *Booker T. Washington* Papers, 140.

33. See the discussion by Eric Williams, "Race Relations in Puerto Rico and the Virgin Islands," *Foreign Affairs. An American Quarterly Review* 23 (January 1945) and Mervyn C. Alleyne, *The Construction and Representation of Race and Identity in the Caribbean and the World* (Kingston: University of West Indies Press, 2002).

34. Frank A. Guridy, *Forging Diaspora*, 19. A parallel study is also found in the "Pensionado Program," which was created to encourage Filipinos to come to the United States to study and receive college and vocational education in selected U.S. institutions.

35. The biographical data disclosed in this segment is based on Antonio S. Pedreira, *Un hombre del pueblo: La obra de José Celso Barbosa*, 4th ed. (San Juan: Model Offset Printing, Inc., 1990) and information provided throughout the anthology on Barbosa's writings published by his daughter Pilar Barbosa, ed. *Problema de Razas. La obra de José Celso Barbosa* (San Juan: Model Offset Printing, Inc., 1984). In addition, I am using Miriam Jiménez-Román's essay "Un hombre (negro) del pueblo: José Celso Barbosa and the Puerto Rican 'Race' towards Whiteness," *Centro: Journal of the Center of Puerto Rican Studies*13, no. 1–2 (1996): 8–29.

36. Pedreira, *Un hombre del pueblo*, 24.

37. John M. Faragher, Mary Jo Buhle, Daniel Czitrom and Susan H. Armitage. *Out of Many. A History of American People*, 4th ed. (New Jersey: Prentice Hall, 2004), 391–392.

38. Jiménez-Román, "Un hombre (negro) del pueblo," 18; Pedreira, *Un hombre del pueblo*, 25. Barbosa wrote a synopsis of the American Republican Party in *Problema de Razas*, 92–97.

39. Pedreira, *Un hombre del pueblo*, 31.

40. Pedreira, *Un hombre del pueblo*, 31.

41. Pedreira, *Un hombre del pueblo*, 32.

42. Guillermo A. Baralt, *Tradición de futuro: El primer siglo del Banco Popular* (San Juan: Centro de Investigaciones Carimar, 1993), 25.

43. Jiménez-Román, "Un hombre (negro) del pueblo," 17.

44. María Teresa Cortés-Zavala, "Barbosa, José Celso," in *Dictionary of Caribbean Afro-Latin American Biography*, Vol. 1, eds. Franklin W. Knight and Henry Louis Gates, Jr. (New York: Oxford University Press, 2016), 217.

45. Pedreira, *Un hombre del pueblo*, 144.

46. Pedreira, *Un hombre del pueblo*, 144.

47. These writings are compiled under the title *Problemas de Razas*, ed. Pilar Barbosa, *Problema de Razas. La obra de José Celso Barbosa*, Vol. 1, III (San Juan: Model Offset Printing, Inc., 1984).

48. Barbosa, *Problema de razas*, 31.

49. Samuel Betances, "The Prejudice of Having No Prejudice in Puerto

Rico," *The Rican: A Journal of Contemporary Puerto Rican Thought* 1, no. 2 (Winter 1972): 51.

50. Barbosa, *Problema de razas*, 31–32. Original citation reads, "si el elemento de color procura evitar por todos lo medios posible el entablar lucha alguna de raza; ni afianzar sus derechos en cuestión de raza; ni exigir benevolencias por cuestión de raza, ni considerar como un favor los actos de justicia que con los hombres de color se realicen."

51. J.C. Barbosa, 85. Parts of the English translation of these passages were taken from Jiménez-Román's essay. Original citation: La raza negra ha tenido solamente la oportunidad de demostrar sus condiciones, para adaptarse ala civilización actual en los Estados Unidos, pues en los países de Sud América, en las Antillas y aún en Europa, personas de sangre negra han ganado altas distinciones, tantos políticas como civiles, y han brillado en las artes y en las letras, pero se han movido en un ambiente de tolerancia que les ha aceptado en iguales términos, y en cuanto han sobresalido han dejado de ser exponentes de la raza africana para pasar a ocupar un puesto de alta distinción en la exponencia de la gran cultura latina, confundiéndose dentro de la heterogeneidad que se llama *civilización latina*, y, transformando su descendencia, por amalgamación, por cruces, han pasado a ser calificados como de la raza blanca, y, de ese modo, no pueden ser presentados como exponentes de los adelantos y progresos de la raza africana

52. Pilar Barbosa, *Problema de razas*, "Introducción," 8.

53. Barbosa, *Problemas de razas*, 19.

54. Pilar Barbosa, *Problema de razas*, "Introducción," 9.

55. Gervasio L. García and Ángel G. Quintero, *Desafío y solidaridad: breve historia del movimiento obrero puertorriqueño* (Río Piedras: Ediciones Huracán, 1982), 33, 36–37.

56. Personal communication with author, July 31, 2002.

57. Henry K. Carroll, *Report of the Island of Porto Rico; its Population, Civil Government, Commerce, Industries, Productions, Roads, Tariff, and Currency* (Washington, DC: Government Printing Office, 1899), 63.

58. Sam Erman, *Almost Citizens: Puerto Rico, the U.S. Constitution, and the Empire* (Cambridge: Cambridge University Press, 2019), 16.

59. César J. Ayala and Rafael Bernabé, *Puerto Rico in the American Century: A History since 1898* (Chapel Hill: University of North Carolina Press, 2007), 25.

60. Rubin F. Weston. *Racism in United States Imperialism. The Influence of Racial Assumptions on American Foreign Policy, 1893–1946* (Columbia: University of South Carolina Press, 1972), 197.

61. Weston, *Racism*, 197.

62. Quoted in Weston, *Racism*, 199.

63. Quoted in Weston, *Racism*, 200–202.

64. On the creation of the "one-drop of blood standard" in the United States,

see Scott L. Malcomson, *One Drop of Blood. The American Misadventure of Race* (New York: Farrar, Straus and Giroux, 2000) and Jack D. Forbes, *Africans and Native Americans. The Language of Race and the Evolution of Red-Black Peoples*, 2nd ed. (Chicago: University of Illinois Press, 1993).

65. Efrén Rivera-Ramos, *The Legal Construction of Identity. The Judicial and Social Legacy of American Colonialism in Puerto Rico* (Washington, DC: American Psychological Association, 2001), 151–154; see also, Sam Erman, *Almost Citizens. Puerto Ricans, the U. S. Constitution and the Empire* (Cambridge: Cambridge University Press, 2019).

66. For the United States dilemma of European presence in the Caribbean, see Fitzroy Baptiste, *War, Cooperation, and Conflict: The European Possessions in the Caribbean, 1939–1945* (New York: Greenwood Press, 1988).

67. For a discussion of the significance of drafting Puerto Ricans during World War I, see Estades-Font, *La presencia militar*, 214–215. For a comparative approach to the case between Puerto Rico and the Philippines, see Julian Go, "The Chains of the Empire: State Building and 'Political Education' in Puerto Rico and the Philippines," in *The American Colonial State and the Philippines*, eds. Julian Go and Anne L. Foster (Durham, NC: Duke University Press, 2003), 182–216.

Chapter 3

1. Antonio S. Pedreira. *Insularismo* (Río Piedras: Editorial Edil, 1972). For this section I am summarizing the main argument of Pedreira's essay. On Pedreira's biography, see Grupo Editorial EPRL, "Antonio Salvador Pedreira." *Enciclopedia de Puerto Rico online.* https://enciclopediapr.org/content/antonio-pedreira

2. Juan Flores, *Insularismo e ideología en Antonio Pedreira* (Río Piedras: Ediciones Huracán, 1979), 63. Original quote: "cuenta entre sus premisas sub-yacentes no sólo el poder determinate de la raza, sino la inferioridad inherente de las razas indígenas y africanas respecto de los europeos y de los españoles en particular. . . . Pedreira habla de los negros como "raza inferior," capaz de trabajar forzosamente, pero carente de la "inteligencia del blanco." In reference to this intellectual current in Latin América, see José Vasconcelos's *La Raza Cósmica* (Baltimore: Johns Hopkins University Press, 1997) and *Indología. Una interpretación de la cultura Ibero-Americana* (Barcelona: Agencia Mundial de Librería, 1927).

3. Flores, *Insularismo e ideología*, 63.

4. Benedict Anderson, *Imagined Communities* (New York: Verso, 1983), 101.

5. Jorge Larrain, *Identity and Modernity in Latin America* (Cambridge: Polity, 2001), 35.

6. See a detailed analysis of Palés Matos's work in the introduction to *Tuntún de Pasa y grifería*. Edición de Mercedes López Baralt (Río Piedras: Instituto

de Cultura Puertorriqueña/Editorial de la UPR, 1993), 21–53.

7. Dr. Isabelo Zenón Cruz (1939–2002) was a passionate philosopher and literary critic who taught for many decades at the University of Puerto Rico (UPR). The UPR-Río Piedras campus became the forum for Zenon Cruz's criticism and ideological dissemination. His groundbreaking work *Narciso descubre su tresero. El negro en la cultura puertorriqueña* shook up the field of literary criticism and cultural theory because he harshly denounced the discrimination to which Black Puerto Ricans were subjected. The book features "List(s)" that named Puerto Ricans who did not want to reveal their African ancestry. Zenón Cruz, *Narciso descubre su trasero: el negro en la cultura puertorriqueña*, 2 vols. (Humacao: Editorial Furidi, 1974).

8. Zenón Cruz, *Narciso*, vol. 1, 47–48. My translation.

9. Tomás Blanco, *El prejuicio racial en Puerto Rico*. Con estudio preliminar de Arcadio Díaz Quiñones (Río Piedras: Ediciones Huracán, 1985), 105.

10. Francisco A. Scarano. "The Jíbaro Masquerade and Subaltern Politics of Creole Identity Formation in Puerto Rico, 1745–1823," *American Historical Review* 101, no. 105 (December 1996): 1398–1431.

11. Scarano, "The Jibaro Masquerade," 1407.

12. *El Mundo*, December 1, 1938, 10. Judge Gaetán Barbosa's family was a cadre of professionals. For instance, in 1938, his wife Sara Roberts-Gaetán was the principal of a school named after Dr. José Celso Barbosa. They had three children: Pura Gaetán Izquierdo, Godofredo Gaetán, an attorney, and Libertad Gaetán, a medical doctor. There is a school in San Juan district named after him located on Roberto H. Todd Stop 18, Santurce.

13. Solsiree Del Moral, "Race, Science and Nation: The Cultural Politics of Schools in Colonial Puerto Rico, 1917–1938" (PhD dissertation, University of Wisconsin-Madison, 2006), 130. Del Moral published a revised versión of her dissertation titled *Negotiating Empire: The Cultural Politics of Schools in Puerto Rico, 1898–1952* (Madison: University of Wisconsin Press, 2013). For this specific argument I use a chapter in her dissertation not included in the book version. Also see Ramos-Perea, *Literatura puertorriqueña negra*, 483. Enrique Lefebre was born in the town of Guayama in 1880. In addition to having a law degree, Lefebre was a journalist and wrote in important journals of the period. He founded a modernist journal, *Claro de Luna*, and in 1918 published *Paisajes mentales*. According to Ramos-Perea, with this piece Lefebre solidified his status as one of the "most important literary critics of 1920s Puerto Rico," 483. Ramos-Perea's research shows that Lefebre has an unpublished anthology titled *Las clases y las razas de nuestro ambiente* (Races and Classes of Our Environment).

14. Georgina Falú, "Falú Zarzuela, Juan 'Juanín,'" in *Dictionary of Caribbean and Afro-Latin American Biography*, vol 2., eds. Franklin W. Knight and Henry Louis Gates Jr. (New York: Oxford University Press, 2016), 492.

15. Falú, "Falú Zarzuela, Juan 'Juanín.'" Falú was a very close political ally of Dr. Barbosa. It could be assumed that Falú Zarzuela also was reading the same

materials on African Americans organizations that Barbosa did.

16. AGPR, Fondo Departamento de Estado, caja 58A, file 1015.

17. Falú, "Falú Zarzuela, 'Juan Juanín,'" 492.

18. I use the term in the context in which sociologists have applied it: to identify ideology justifying the racialization and exclusion of non-white groups. Important publications on this topic include Michael Omi and Howard Winant, *Racial Formation in the United States: From the 1960s to the 1990s*, 2nd ed. (New York: Routledge, 1994) and Eduardo Bonilla Silva, *White Supremacy and Racism in the Post-Civil Rights Era* (Boulder: Lynne Rienner Publishers, 2001).

19. The Liga Annual Report, AGPR, Fondo Departamento de Estado, caja 58A, file 1015.

20. The Liga Annual Report, AGPR, Fondo Departamento de Estado, caja 58A, file 1015.

21. Ada Ferrer, *Insurgent Cuba: Race, Nation, and Revolution, 1868–1898* (Chapel Hill: University of North Carolina Press, 1999), 9.

22. Lillian Guerra, *Popular Expression and National Identity in Puerto Rico* (Gainesville: University Press of Florida, 1998), chapter 3.

23. Falú, 493. In 2005, this family embarked on the task of tracing their African roots and discovered a connection to Senegal. They have since started a foundation to promote awareness of and research into African heritage in Puerto Rico.

24. See the discussion of Manuel Maldonado-Denis, *Hacia una historia marxista de la historia de Puerto Rico y otros ensayos* (Río Piedras: Editorial Antillana, 1977), 139.

25. Tendencies toward either position (independence or statehood) were often triggered by the policies of the regime. As a result of disagreements on the issue of independence, members of the *Partido de Unión* broke away and, in 1922, created the *Partido Nacionalista,* presided over by José Alegría.

26. Marisa Rosado, *Las llamas de la aurora, acercamiento a una biografía de Pedro Albizu Campos* (San Juan/Santo Domingo: Editora Corripio, 1992), 12.

27. Rosado, *Las llamas de la aurora,* 28–30.

28. Laura Meneses held a doctoral degree in natural sciences. She was the daughter of Colonel Juan Rosas Meneses, a high-ranking Peruvian military officer who participated in the Guerra del Pacífico of 1879.

29. Rosado, *Las llamas,* 36–40, 58–64.

30. See Taller de Formación Política, *La cuestion nacional: El partido nacionalista y el movimiento obrero puertorriqueño* (Río Piedras: Ediciones Huracán, 1982), chapter 11. Albizu's speeches given in this meeting are published in four volumes edited by Benjamín Torres, *Pedro Albizu Campos: obras escogidas* (Río Piedras: Editorial Jelofe, 1982), vol. 2. See also, Juan Antonio Corretjer, *Albizu Campos y las huelgas en los años '30* (Guaynabo: Private publisher, 1969).

31. Center for Puerto Rican Studies, Franklin Delano Roosevelt Papers, Reel 1, documents pertaining to Puerto Rico, letter July 19, 1933.

32. Laura Meneses de Albizu Campos, *Dr. Albizu Campos y la independencia de Puerto Rico* (San Juan: Partido Nacionalista de Puerto Rico, 1961), 19.

33. In this particular conjuncture, see Juan Manuel Carrión, Juan Manuel, Teresa C. García Ruiz, and Carlos Rodríguez Fraticelli, eds., *La nación puertorriqueña: ensayos en torno a Pedro Albizu Campos* (Río Piedras: Editorial de la Universidad de Puerto Rico, 1993); Maldonado-Denis, *Hacia una historia* marxista, 144; Anthony Stevens-Arroyo, *Catholicism as Civilization: Contemporary Reflections on the Political Philosophy of Pedro Albizu Campos* (San Germán: Inter-American University, 1992), 5.

34. Ferrao and Stevens-Arroyo lead a debate regarding the intellectual origins of Albizu's Catholicism. On the one hand, Stevens-Arroyo argues that Albizu learned and converted to Catholicism during his years as a student in Boston. In that city he was influenced by the Irish nationalist movement, which integrated Catholicism in its political platform. On the other hand, Ferrao contends that Albizu's ideology derived from the Perea brothers, two active members of the party. Luis Angel Ferrao, *Pedro Albizu Campos y el nacionalismo puertorriqueño* (San Juan: Editorial Cultural, 1990), 257–260; Stevens-Arroyo, *Catholicism as Civilization*, 1992).

35. Albizu's Hispanophile bent could be compared with the Francophile position adopted by the Haitian elite when the Americans proposed to the Haitian government the construction of a military base in Molê Saint-Nicolas. In a study on Haitian patriotism, historian Watson Denis revealed that Haitians looked unfavorably upon American influences and value systems. Therefore, to distinguish themselves, Haitians sought refuge in their French ancestry. Puerto Rican nationalists adopted a similar approach when the Americans established colonial government on the island. See, Denis Watson, "Miradas de mutua desconfianza entre dos Repúblicas americanas: el expansionismo marítimo de Estados Unidos frente a la francofilia haitiana, 1888–1898" (PhD dissertation, Universidad de Puerto Rico, Río Piedras, 2004).

36. Excerpt from Torres, *Pedro Albizu Campos*, vol. 2, 118–119.

37. Michael Omi and Howard Winant, *Racial Formation in the United States* (New York & London: Routledge, 1996), 37, 41. According to these sociologists, "national culturalism" is a concept that can be applied to African Americans, who invoked their African past to develop a Black national discourse in response to U.S. racism and exclusion. Its application was expanded to the Chicano movement. It found its manifestation in the 1970s under the "back to Aztlán" rhetoric or glorification of the Mexican indigenous past, which "evoked traditional Mexican cultural values untainted by U.S. domination."

38. One may compare Albizu's cultural definition of race to the U.S. Census Bureau's definition of "Hispanic/Latino" used in 2000. The Census Bureau uses the term to refer to "any person of Cuban, Mexican, Puerto Rican, South or Central American or other Spanish culture or origin regardless of race." The application

of the term "Hispanic" is raceless, with culture as the common denominator. This differs from the common U.S. perception of race as a biological condition. U.S. Census Bureau, "The Hispanic Population: 2010," *Census Briefs*, 2. Online report: www.census.gov/prod/cen2010/briefs/c2010br-03.pdf

39. Kelvin Santiago-Valles, "Our Race Today (Is) the Only Hope for the World": An African Spaniard as Chieftain of the Struggle against 'Sugar Slavery' in Puerto Rico (1926–1934)," *Caribbean Studies* 35, no. 1 (2007): 107–140.

40. Solsiree del Moral, "Race, Science, and Nation: The Cultural Politics of Schools in Colonial Puerto Rico, 1917–1938" (PhD dissertation, University of Wisconsin-Madison, 2006), 129.

41. Omi and Winant, *Racial Formation*, 55.

42. Luis Muñoz Marín, *Historia del Partido Popular Democrático* (San Juan: Editorial El Batey 1984), 73. Muñoz Marín was born into a political family. The local Republican Party between 1900 and 1905 forced his father, Luis Muñoz Rivera, a member of the political opposition and former Commissioner Resident, out of Puerto Rico. As a result, Muñoz Rivera moved his family to New York, where the young Luis attended public schools and mastered the English language. Muñoz Marín went on to study at Georgetown and Columbia Universities, where he took courses in law and journalism. He frequented intellectual circles and made acquaintances, forming networks and contacts that became important later in his life. In the United States, Muñoz met the feminist writer Muna Lee and later married her. The couple socialized in intellectual circles in New York and Washington, DC, until their return to Puerto Rico in 1931. Besides being a prolific writer, Muna Lee was a feminist and political activist. Her opinions on Puerto Rico's political and economic situation are gathered in her correspondence with the American journalist Ruby Black, a personal friend of the Roosevelts. When Mrs. Roosevelt visited Puerto Rico in 1934, Black was assigned as United Press correspondent to cover Mrs. Roosevelt's trip. The Ruby Black Collection is housed in the Centro de Investigaciones Históricas of the University of Puerto Rico. On Muñoz Marín as journalist and writer, see Amalia Lluch Vélez, *Luis Muñoz Marín: poesía, periodismo y revolución, 1915–1930* (Caguas: Universidad del Sagrado Corazón/Fundación LMM, 1999). In the mid-1920s, his advocacy on behalf of the labor movement took him to Venezuela, where he protested against the dictatorship of General Gómez and co-founded the *Unión Obrera Venezolana* "with the objective of giving participation to the masses." His involvement in Venezuela played a formative role in his evolution as a populist leader and his work toward the establishment of an inter-Latin American connection between Puerto Rico and other nations. See Luis Muñoz Marín, *Historia del Partido Popular Democrático* (San Juan: Editorial El Batey, 1984), 78. Muñoz Marín was an admirer of Venezuela's modernization process. He developed a personal relationship with Romulo Betancourt, and the two maintained communication for many decades.

43. LMM Papers Series: LMM: El Político. See also Ruby Black Collection, file 7, document 161, "Luis Muñoz Marín to Ruby Black," September 13, 1933. In this collection, several letters describe the planning of a meeting between Muñoz Marín and President Roosevelt (box 1, file B, document 242) and a proposal for a tropical version of the New Deal in Puerto Rico, better known as "Plan Chardón" (box 2, folder 9, document 31).

44. Muñoz Marín, *Historia*, chapter 9.

45. Muñoz Marín, *Historia*, 30.

46. Muñoz Marín, *Historia*, 84.

47. José Luis González, *Puerto Rico: The Four-Storeyed Country: The Question of an Afro-Mestizo Culture*. Translated by Gerald Guinness (Princeton, NJ: Markus Wiener, 1993), 12–20.

48. González, *Puerto Rico*, 10. González was responding to a question raised by a group of students in a symposium about Caribbean identities at the Mexican National University.

49. González, *Puerto Rico*, 10.

50. An array of new studies deals with the challenges faced by freed slaves' post-abolition. Sources cited in introduction and chapter 2.

51. González's statement is based on the fact that many of the Corsican, Canarian, and other poor immigrants arrived in the late eighteenth century and—in massive numbers—in the nineteenth century. In "Etnia, raza y la nacionalidad puertorriqueña," Juan Manuel Carrión suggested that González contradicted himself and the ideology of the Independentist Party, of which González was a member. Carrión pointed out that the PIP (Partido Independentista Puertorriqueño) is intrinsically Hispanophile. See more on this discussion in *La nación puertorriqueña: ensayos entorno a Pedro Albizu Campos* (Río Piedras: Editorial de la UPR, 1993) and Juan Flores, "The Puerto Rico that José Luis González Built," *Latin American Perspectives* 11, no. 3 (Summer 1984): 173–184. Another critique to González came from the field of archeology: Reniel Rodríguez Ramos's book, *Rethinking Puerto Rican Precolonial History* (Tuscaloosa: University of Alabama Press, 2010), in which he suggests a counterpoint to González's interpretation of Puerto Rican national identity as essentially Afro-Antillean (this is the first floor of the house). Rodríguez Ramos proposed a more preeminent role for the indigenous population in the make-up of the island's national identity.

52. Nathaniel I. Córdova, "In His Image and Likeness: The Puerto Rican *Jíbaro* as Political Icon," *Centro: Journal of the Center of Puerto Rican Studies* 25, no. 2 (2005): 170–195. The debate surrounding the symbolic use of the *jíbaro*, it is important to trace the etymology of the word. On a basic level, the *jíbaro* is defined as a naïve, white peasant. Indeed, in Puerto Rican literature, the *jíbaro* is descended from the Catalans, Corsicans, Asturians, Basque, or Navarrese who settled in the nineteenth century under favorable immigration laws set by the Spanish colonial government. Manuel Alonso also began the tradition of overem-

phasizing the white peasant in his novel *El Gíbaro* (1849), developing a literary movement known as *criollismo* celebrating the Creole identity. The Creole class emphasized the dignity and good character of the *jíbaros* as they were victimized by the Spanish colonial rule. It could be said that in the mid–nineteenth century, the discussion of what is considered "the Creole" versus "the Spanish" permeated the intellectual and political debate. María Vaquero, *Tesoro Lexicográfico del español de Puerto Rico* (San Juan: Editorial Plaza Mayor, 2005), 434.

53. Córdova, "In His Image," 177–180.

54. Córdova, "In His Image," 176.

55. Córdova, "In His Image," 177.

56. Muñoz Marín, *Historia*, 92–93.

57. Silvia Álvarez-Curbelo, "La conflictividad en el discurso político de Luis Muñoz Marín: 1926–1936." Silvia Álvarez-Curbelo and María Elena Rodríguez Castro, eds., *Del nacionalismo al populismo: cultura y política en Puerto Rico* (Río Piedras: Ediciones Huracán, 1993), 13–35.

58. Muñoz Marín, *Historia*, 21.

59. Muñoz Marín, *Historia*, 24.

60. Córdova, "In His Image," 181.

61. Murray Edelman, *From Arts to Politics* (Chicago: University of Chicago Press, 1995), 104.

62. Edelman, *From Arts to Politics*, 2.

63. The demographic profile of the municipality of Culebra is totally different from that of Barranquita, the birthplace of the PPD, which was characterized by the presence of white rural communities' descendants of Spanish migrants. In contrast, Culebra's racial composition is comparable to that of other municipalities in which people of African ancestry constitute a high proportion of the population. But Culebra was always different—in its geographical separation from the main island, its fishing-based economy, and its mulatto racial identity. In this context, the inclusion of Culebra in the PPD's campaign is a testament to the inclusive populist nature of the party.

64. AGPR. Fondo Oficina del Gobernador, box 635, file, "Partidos políticos."

65. AGPR. Fondo Oficina del Gobernador, box 635, file, "Partidos políticos."

66. AGPR, box 176. In this regard he quoted Manuel Álvarez Nazario and his study about the language of rural Puerto Ricans.

67. I make particular reference to the documents generated in 1870, known as the "Slave Register," which consisted of a physical inventory of the plantations in Puerto Rico. In the document planters detailed information of the enslaved population. For a thorough analysis of the Slave Register, see Mariano Negrón Portillo and Raúl Mayo Santana, *La esclavitud menor: la esclavitud en los municipios del interior de Puerto Rico siglo XIX: Estudio del Registro de Esclavos de 1872: segunda parte* (Río Piedras: Centro de Investigaciones Sociales/Universidad de Puerto Rico, 2007).

68. Omi and Winant, *Racial Formation*, 53.

69. Córdova, "In His Image," 179.

70. Edelman, *From Art to Politics*, 50.

71. Edelman, *From Art to Politics*, 101.

72. The sociologists declared, "racial formation is a process of historically situated *projects* [their emphasis] in which human bodies and social structures are represented and organized." Omi and Winant, *Racial Formation*, 55.

73. United States Department of Commerce, Puerto Rican Relief Emergency Administration, *1935 Census* (Washington, DC: Government Printing Office, 1937), 1.

74. Noel Allende-Goitia, *De Margarita al Cumbanchero: Vida musical, imaginación racial y discurso histórico en la sociedad puertorriqueña (1898–1940)* (San Juan: Ediciones Puerto, 2010), 354.

75. On the dichotomies of race and national identity in Puerto Rican music of the twentieth century, see Ruth Glasser's classic, *My Music Is My Flag: Puerto Rican Musicians and Their New York Communities, 1917–1940* (Berkeley: University of California Press: 1997).

76. Allende-Goitía, *De Margarita a El Cumbanchero*, 355.

77. Mercedes López-Baralt, "La tercera salida de 'Tuntún de Pasa y grifería,'" in Luis Palés Matos, *Tuntún de Pasa y grifería*. Edición de Mercedes López-Baralt (San Juan: Instituto de Cultura Puertorriqueña/Universidad de Puerto Rico, 1993), 42.

78. Larrain, *Modernity and Identity*, 34.

Chapter 4

1. Earl S. Garver and Ernest B. Fincher, *Puerto Rico: Unsolved Problem* (Elgin: The Elgin Press, 1945), 23. In addition to presenting American views on Puerto Rico's problem, the book depicts illustrations of Puerto Ricans.

2. Garver and Fincher, *Puerto Rico*, 25.

3. Garver and Fincher, *Puerto Rico*, 100–103.

4. Alejandro de la Fuente, "Myths of Racial Democracy in Cuba, 1900–1912," *Latin American Research Review* 34, no. 3 (1999): 43.

5. See Eduardo Seda-Bonilla, *Requiem por una Cultura. Ensayos sobre la socialización del puertorriqueño en su cultura y en el ámbito del poder neocolonial* (Río Piedras: Editorial Edil, 1970). For this section I used the essays from eds. Nancy P. Appelbaum, Anne S. Macpherson, and Karin Alejandra Rosemblatt, *Race and Nation in Modern Latin America* (Chapel Hill: University of North Carolina Press, 2003).

6. In Puerto Rico, white migration was also used as a way to "balance" the numbers of Blacks on the island during the nineteenth century.

7. De la Fuente, "Myths of Racial Democracy in Cuba," 41.

8. Writer and physician Tomás Blanco led this school of thought. He discussed issues of politics and cultures through some of his publications. His views were widely accepted among his contemporaries. In his essay *El prejucio racial en Puerto Rico*, he stated, "In Puerto Rico, we do not know yet what is racial prejudice." Tomás Blanco, *El prejuicio racial en Puerto Rico*, Con estudio prelimnar de Arcadio Díaz Quiñones (Rio Piedras: Ediciones Huracán, 1985), 105.

9. María E. Rodríguez Castro, "Foro de 1940: las pasiones e intereses se dan de la mano," in *Del nacionalismo al populismo: Cultura y política en Puerto Rico*, eds. Silvia Álvarez-Curbelo and María Elena Rodríguez Castro, 61–105.

10. The idea of the great family encompasses several views. It also involves the construction of people as "others," as Americans did upon their arrival to the island. In her study analyzing visual images, anthropologist Hilda Lloréns explores the impact of negative stereotypes of Puerto Ricans and how the new social imaginary will be contested by Black Puerto Ricans. Hilda Lloréns, *Imagining the Great Puerto Rican Family. Framing Nation, Race, and Gender during the American Century* (Lanham, MD: Lexington Books, 2014).

11. Angel G. Quintero Rivera, "La ideología populista y la institucionalización univesitaria de las ciencias sociales," in Álvarez-Curbelo and Rodríguez Castro, *Del nacionalismo al populismo*, 107–145.

12. Jorge Larrain, *Modernity and Identity*, 34.

13. María E. Rodríguez Castro, "Foro de 1940," 73.

14. Mariano Picón-Salas, *Apología de la pequeña nación. Discurso pronunciado en la cuadragésima segunda colación de grados de la Universidad de Puerto Rico.* (San Juan: Imprenta Venezuela, 1946), 20.

15. Picón-Salas, 9.

16. Picón-Salas, 4.

17. Picón-Salas, 3.

18. AGPR, Fondo Oficina del Gobernador, box 454, "Asociación de dueños de hoteles," letter April 29, 1947. Follow-up to the discussion is in two letters from July 31, 1947. The negotiation of the project included a meeting with the President of Twentieth Century Fox.

19. Although marketing Puerto Rican culture as essentially Spanish/European was introduced in the 1930s; see Richard Rosa, "Business as Pleasure: Culture, Tourism, and Nation in Puerto Rico in the 1930s," *Nepantla: Views from South* 2, no. 3 (2001). Rosa explores the industry's parallel development with politics and national identity. Government campaigns helped by magazines such as *Puerto Rico Illustrado* created an image of Puerto Rico as an essential Spanish/European destination.

20. AGPR, Fondo Oficina del Gobernador, box 454, letter April 25, 1947.

21. The University of Puerto Rico's strategies resembled the combination of

state agencies that President Roosevelt organized through the WPA under the New Deal program. It also had some similarities with the program *Partido de Acción Democrática* in Venezuela, in which the state prioritized its reformist agenda by implementing cultural reforms.

22. Antonio Lauria-Perricelli, "Images and Contradictions. DIVEDCO's Portrayal of Puerto Rican Life," *Centro: Journal of the Center for Puerto Rican Studies* 3, no. 1 (Winter 1990–91), 93.

23. For an expanded analysis of the role of literature in this social project, see Catherine Marsh Kennerly, *Negociaciones culutrales. Los intelectuales y el proyecto pedagógico del estado muñocista.* (San Juan: Ediciones Callejón, 2009), 251.

24. AGPR, Fondo Oficina del Gobernador, box 454, file "Asociación de dueños de hoteles," letter October 28, 1946.

25. The Puerto Rican Supreme Court, *Muriel v. Suazo* 72 DPR 370 (1951).

26. *Muriel v. Suazo*, 5.

27. *Muriel v. Suazo*, 5.

28. M. Nieves-Rivera, "El Juez Bennazar Decidió Caso de Zero Club Distinto al Esquife," *El Mundo*, September 24, 1949, 5.

29. Omi and Winant, *Racial Formation,* 57.

30. Omi and Winant, *Racial Formation,* 57.

31. K. Lawrence and T. Keleher, "Structural Racism." Proceedings from the Race and Public Policy Conference, Aspen Institute, Aspen, Colorado, 2004. www.intergroupresources.com/rc/Definitions of Racism.pdf

32. Marta I. Cruz-Janzen, "Out of the Closet: Racial Amnesia, Avoidance, and Denial—Racism among Puerto Ricans," *Race, Gender and* Class 10, no. 3. (2003): 80.

33. Tanya K. Hernández, "Multiracial Matrix: The Role of Race Ideology in the Enforcement of Antidiscrimination Laws, a United States-Latin America Comparison," *Cornell Law Review* 87, no. 5 (July 2002): 1145.

34. Harry S. Truman Papers, Committee on Civil Rights (PPCR), group 220, box 17. This commission was established December 1946. The President of the Commission was Charles E. Wilson, who was also the president of the General Electric Company. The Commission's report was later published under the title *To Secure These Rights* (Washington, DC: Government Printing Office, 1947).

35. William J. Dorvillier, "Afirman que hay discrimen racial en la isla," *El Mundo*, October 30, 1947, 1.

36. The facts related to the criminal law suit were published in the local newspaper *El Mundo*, September 19, 1949. Also, Eric Williams, who visited Puerto Rico at this time, wrote about these events in the article "Race Relations in Puerto Rico and the Virgin Islands," *Foreign Affairs: An American Quarterly Review* 23 (January 1945): 314, 315.

37. Williams, 312.

38. Williams, 314.

39. Williams, 316.

40. Williams, 317.

41. Editorial. "Sugiere llevar maestros boricuas al continente," *El Mundo*, January 19, 1947, 3.

42. Editorial. "Sugiere llevar maestros boricuas al continente," 3.

43. See the discussions about the folklorization of Black Puerto Rican culture in Petra R. Rivera-Rideau, "From Carolina to Loíza: Race, Place and Puerto Rican Racial Democracy," *Identities* 20, no. 5 (Fall 2013): 616–632; Hilda Lloréns, *Imagining the Great Puerto Rican Family: Framing Nation, Race, and Gender during the American Century* (Lanham, MD: Lexington Books, 2014), chapter 5; and Isar P. Godreau, *Scripts of Blackness Race, Cultural Nationalism, and US Colonialism in Puerto Rico* (Chicago: University of Illinois Press, 2015), chapter 6.

44. AGPR, Fondo Oficina del Gobernador, box 455, letter April 16, 1947.

Chapter 5

1. Aspects related to the PPD and its main founder toward the industrialization of Puerto Rico are found in the LMM papers section pertaining to his role as the president of the Puerto Rican Senate (1940–1948) and as the governor of Puerto Rico (1948–1964).

2. Jorge Larrain, *Modernity and Identity* (Cambridge: Polity Press, 2001), 22–23.

3. A complete history and references of the facts related to the involvement of Moscoso in the modernization of the island is described in A.W. Maldonado's, *Teodoro Moscoso and Puerto Rico's Operation Bootstraps* (Gainesville: University of Florida Press, 1997), chapter 3; see also the LMM paper, section V. On the role played by Tugwell, see Michael Vincent Namorato, *The Diary of Rexford G. Tugwell* (New York: Greenwood Press, 1992). From Tugwell authorship, see *Puerto Rican Public Papers* (Puerto Rico: Service Office of the Government of Puerto Rico, 1945) and *The Stricken Land: The Story of Puerto Rico* (Garden City: Doubleday, 1947).

4. A.W. Maldonado, *Teodoro Moscoso*, 28.

5. AGPR, Fondo Oficina del Gobernador, box 454, file "Asociación de dueños de hoteles."

6. Blanca G. Silvestrini and María Dolores Luque, *Historia de Puerto Rico: Trayectoria de un pueblo* (San Juan: Ediciones Cultural Panamericana, 1991), 509.

7. César J. Ayala and Rafael Bernabe, *Puerto Rico in the American Century: A History since 1898* (Chapel Hill: University of North Carolina Press, 2007), 193.

8. Fernando Picó, *Historia general de Puerto Rico*, chapter 14; Ayala and Bernabe, *Puerto Rico in the American Century*, 195–197.

9. For more details on the implementation of the industrialization, see A.W. Maldonado, *Teodoro Moscoso*, chapters 3 and 6. Also see, Eliezer Curet

Cuevas, *El desarrollo económico de Puerto Rico: 1940 a 1972* (Hato Rey: Management Aid Center, 1976); and Henry Wells, *The Modernization of Puerto Rico: A Political Study of Changing Values and Institutions* (Cambridge, MA: Harvard University Press, 1969).

10. On the role of Afro-Puerto Ricans during this period, see the phenomenal study by Noel Allende-Goitía, *De Margarita a El Cumbanchero. Vida musical, imaginación racial y discurso histórico en la sociedad puertorriqueña (1898–1940)* (San Juan: Ediciones Puerto, 2010).

11. See discussion of another applicability to "buena apariencia" phenomena in chapter 3.

12. María Soledad Romero, "Fernández Cortada, Ruth Noemí," in *Dictionary of Caribbean and Afro-Latin American Biography*, vol. 2, eds. Franklin W. Knight and Henry Luis Gates, Jr. (New York: Oxford University Press, 2016), 5–7.

13. Josean Ramos. "Ruth Fernández." *Fundación Nacional para la Cultura Popular*. http://prpop.org/biografias/ruth-fernández

14. Licia Fiol-Matta. *The Great Woman Singer: Gender and Voice in Puerto Rican Music* (Durham, NC: Duke University Press, 2017), 73.

15. Fiol-Matta, *The Great Woman Singer*, 74.

16. Fiol-Matta, *The Great Woman Singer*, 77.

17. María Soledad Romero, "Fernández Cortada, Ruth Noemí," 2.

18. Fiol-Matta, *The Great Woman Singer*, 79.

19. Fiol-Matta, *The Great Woman Singer*, 91.

20. Marvette Pérez, "La negra de Ponce: una entrevista con Ruth Fernández (el alma de Puerto Rico hecha canción). *Centro: Journal of the Center for Puerto Rican Studies* 16, no. 1 (Spring 2004): 61–67; Patricia Vargas, "Negra ¿y qué? *El Nuevo Día*, October 12, 2000.

21. Fiol-Matta, *The Great Woman Singer*, 70–75.

22. Dr. Belén Barbosa, "La mujer negra," *Revista de Estudios Generales* 8, no. 8 (June 1993–June 1994), 353–367.

23. Eileen Suárez-Findlay, *Imposing Decency. The Politics of Sexuality and Race in Puerto Rico, 1870–1920.* (Durham, NC: Duke University Press, 1999), 3, 6–10.

24. Maritza Quiñones-Rivera, "From Trigueñita to Afro-Puerto Rican: Intersections of the Racialized, Gendered and Sexualized Body in Puerto Rico and in the U. S. Mainland," *Meridians: Feminism, Race, Transnationalism* 7, no. 1 (2006), 169.

25. Marilyn Miller, "Plena and the Negotiation of 'National' Identity in Puerto Rico," *Centro: Journal of the Center for Puerto Rican Studies* 16, no. 1 (Spring 2004): 45–48. This article made a very good analysis of the lyrics as they denounced American colonial establishment.

26. Peter Manuel et al., *Caribbean Currents: Caribbean Music from Rumba to Reggae.* Revised and expanded edition (Philadelphia: Temple University Press,

2006), 77–79. In addition, the empowering virtue of Black music is analyzed from the African American angle by Stuart Hall, "What Is the 'Black' in Black Popular Culture?" in *Black Popular Culture*, eds. Michele Wallace and Gina Dent (New York: New York Press, 1992), 27–28.

27. Further research documents on this matter are found in AGPR, Fondo Oficina del Gobernador, box 1855, file "Planificación de la defensa pública."

28. On the role of DIVEDCO as part of the PPD platform, see *Art at the Service of the People: Posters and Books from Puerto Rico's Division of Community Education (DIVEDCO)*. Catalog of Exhibition at Site Museum of Art (Notre Dame, Indiana, January 22–March 11, 2012); Catherine Marsh Kennerly, *Negociaciones culturales. Los intelectuales y el proyecto pedagógico del estado muñocista* (San Juan: Ediciones Callejón, 2009), chapter 4; Mariam Colón Pizarro, "Poetic Pragmatism: The Puerto Rican Division of Community Education (DIVEDCO) and the Politics of Cultural Production, 1949–1968," University of Michigan, PhD Dissertation, 2011.

29. Introduction, Aixa Merino Falú, *Cecilia Orta Allende: La pintora del pueblo* (Puerto Rico: Imprenta, Imprenta, 2006), 1–6.

30. Merino Falú, *Cecilia Orta Allende*, 1. Also cited in Fernando Picó, *San Fernando de la Carolina: identidades y representaciones* (Municipio Autónomo de Carolina, 2003), 32.

31. Merino Falú, *Cecilia Orta Allende*, 1; Picó, *San Fernando*, 22–25.

32. Picó, *San Fernando*, 87.

33. Picó, *San Fernando*, 88.

34. United States Census 1930; Merino Falú, *Cecilia Orta Allende*, 14.

35. Merino Falú, *Cecilia Orta Allende*, 13.

36. Merino Falú, *Cecilia Orta Allende*, 3.

37. Picó, *San Fernando*, 134.

38. Pico, *San Fernando*, 134.

39. Picó, *San Fernando*, 137.

40. Picó, *San Fernando de la Carolina*, 146–147. See also Merino Falú, *Cecilia Orta Allende*, 48.

41. Picó, *San Fernando*, 89.

42. Merino Falú, *Cecilia Orta Allende*, 16.

43. Declaration of Orta's niece, Marta Cecilia Orta. Cited in Jorge Rodríguez "En busca de la pintora del pueblo," *Escenario*, June 3, 2006, 6–7. Supplement of local newspaper *El Nuevo Día*.

44. Merino Falú, *Cecilia Orta Allende*, 18, 21.

45. Merino Falú, *Cecilia Orta Allende*, 20.

46. Merino Falú, *Cecilia Orta Allende*, 24.

47. Merino Falú, *Cecilia Orta Allende*, 24.

48. Merino Falú, *Cecilia Orta Allende*, 25–30.

49. Merino Falú, *Cecilia Orta Allende*, 38.

50. Merino Falú, *Cecilia Orta Allende*, 38.

51. Merino Falú, *Cecilia Orta Allende*, 40.

52. Merino Falú, *Cecilia Orta Allende*, 40–44.

53. Merino Falú, *Cecilia Orta Allende*, 45.

54. Marriage certificate. Merino Falú states that they were married in 1952, *Cecilia Orta Allende*, 44; however, the certificate shows that Orta and Rondón married on June 20, 1950.

55. Merino Falú, *Cecilia Orta Allende*, 23.

56. Merino Falú, *Cecilia Orta Allende*, 23.

57. Luis Muñoz Marín correspondence (hereafter LMM), "Telegram to LMM" Carolina, 12 Dec. 1955."

58. LMM, "Letter" December 14, 1955. Handwritten annotation has a January 17, 1956, date. Interpretations differ on whether Orta attended this meeting. The handwritten note is the evidence.

59. "Cecilia Orta Telegram to LMM," Telegram, June 16, 1955.

60. Merino Falú, *Cecilia Orta Allende*, 47.

61. Merino Falú, *Cecilia Orta Allende*, 44.

62. Merino Falú, *Cecilia Orta Allende*, 45.

63. Merino Falú, *Cecilia Orta Allende*, 48.

64. Although outside of the timeframe of this study, it is noteworthy to highlight that in 1972 Orta held a very important exhibition, "Panorama pictórico de la cultura puertorriqueña" (Pictorial Overview of the Puerto Rican Culture). It consisted of twenty-one paintings depicting themes focusing on the Tainos, African, and the island's landscapes. They were part of the Mobile Art Gallery. She presented seminars and workshops throughout the island.

65. Merino Falú, *Cecilia Orta Allende*, 49.

66. Merino Falú, *Cecilia Orta Allende*, vi.

67. Merino Falú, *Cecilia Orta Allende*, 74.

68. Miguel Salas Herrero, "Un interesante experimento en Puerto Rico," *Bohemia Libre Puertorriqueña*, January 14, 1962, 3–5.

69. Herrero, "Un interesante experimento," 4.

70. Herrero, "Un interesante experimento," 4–5.

71. Herrero, "Un interesante experimento," 5.

72. Herrero, "Un interesante experimento," 5.

73. Merino Falú, *Cecilia Orta Allende*, 77, 78. In the spring of 1962 Orta exhibited at the UPR, Río Piedras and Mayagüez Campuses, the Santurce Central High, and the Miramar Hotel.

74. Relevant here is the fact that Vasconcelos developed the logo of UNAM "por mi raza hablará mi espíritu" (For my race will speak my spirit), an emblem that clearly would be reflected in Cecilia Orta's work.

75. Merino Falú, *Cecilia Orta Allende*, 79.

76. In 1949, President Harry S. Truman in his inaugural speech proposed

a similar project for developing countries, known as the Point Four Program. It consisted of providing technical assistance to nations in Europe in need of improving industrial and technical infrastructure. The main goal was to establish an international coalition against the then Soviet Union. The Harry S. Truman Presidential Library. www.trumanlibrary.org/hstpaper/psf.htm

77. Arturo Morales Carrión, "The PPD Democratic Hegemony (1944–1969). In *Puerto Rico: A Political and Cultural History*, ed. Arturo Morales Carrión (New York: W.W. Norton & Company, Inc., 1983), 256–307.

78. Letter Governor Muñoz Marín," LMM Correspondence, June 23, 1964.

79. Letter Governor Muñoz Marín," LMM Correspondence, June 23, 1964.

80. Merino Falú, *Cecilia Orta Allende*, 80.

81. Letter to Governor Luis Muñoz Marín," LMM Correspondence, August 2, 1964.

82. For a contemporary perspective on the subject, see Michael Hanchard, ed., *Racial Politics in Contemporary Brazil* (Durham, NC: Duke University Press, 1999).

83. Wendy Ashley, "The Angry Black Woman: The Impact of Pejorative Stereotypes on Psychotherapy with Black Women," *Social Work in Public Health* 29, no. 1 (2014): 27–34. On the stereotypes associated with Black men and women, also see Aida Harvey Wingfield, "The Modern Mamy and the Angry Black Man: African American Professionals' Experiences with Gendered Racism in the Workplace," *Race, Gender and Class* 14, no. 1–2 (2007): 196–212.

84. Merino Falú, *Cecilia Orta Allende*, 100.

85. "Letter to Roberto Sánchez Vilella"; "Letter to Adolfo Porrata Doria," LMM Correspondence, August 21, 1964.

86. Merino Falú, *Cecilia Orta Allende*, 81.

87. Merino Falú, *Cecilia Orta Allende*, 82. Merino Falú's book has a transcript of this letter.

88. "Letter to Dr. María Luisa Muñoz," LMM Correspondence, October 16, 1965. María Luisa Muñoz was also an educator and a writer. She published several books on Puerto Rican music in the 1950s and 1960s.

89. Author's phone conversation with Dr. Aixa Merino Falú, December 8, 2018.

90. Between 1965 and 1975, Cecilia Orta held approximately fifteen art exhibitions in different galleries, museums UPR campuses, and city halls. All of them were a part of her mobile art gallery project and were covered in newspapers.

91. Marta Cecilia Orta, "Prologue," in Merino Falú, *Cecilia Orta Allende*, vi.

92. Tensish Armstrong, ed., *The Papers of Martin Luther King, Jr.* Vol. 7 (Oakland: University of California Press, 2014), 399.

93. This information of his visit is a little sketchy. I was able to connect newspaper coverage of the visit with some of the correspondence found at his online archives. MLK Archives, Correspondence, "Letter from Beresford Hayward to MLK," February 7, 1962, 1–4. The King Center Digital Archives.

Latinorebels.com made the transcripts of his speeches in San Germán available. They are titled "Strides towards Freedom" and "The Future of Integration." www. latinorebels.com/2014/01/20/when-martin-luther-king-jr-visited-puerto-rico. Part of the itinerary included engagements at the Inter-American University in San Germán. Dr. King spent two days there and met Kenyan graduate student James M. Kansongi. King wrote a letter to Kansongi on April 16, 1962, thanking him for the conversation they had at the Inter-American University.

94. This information was published in *El Mundo* on February 5 and 24, 1962.

95. Roy Godes, "Martin Luther King elogia la fraternidad racial de Puerto Rico," *El Mundo*, February 19, 1962, 5.

96. Godes, "Martin Luther King elogia," 5.

97. MLK Archives, Correspondence, "Letter from Beresford Hayward to MLK," February 7, 1962, 1–4. The King Center Digital Archives.

98. MLK Archives, Correspondence, "Letter from Beresford Hayward to MLK," February 7, 1962, 2.

99. The report, "Attitude, Knowledge, and Apperception of the Civil Rights in the Puerto Rican Public," was originally delivered in a conference at the Catholic University in Ponce Puerto Rico. A complete version was then published in one of the most influential of Seda's works, *Los derechos civlies en la cultura Puertorriqueña*, 5th ed. (Río Píedras: Ediciones Bayoán, 1991[1963]). A follow-up study can be found in *Requien para una cultura: ensayos sobre la socialización del puertorriqueño en su cultura y en ámbito del poder neocolonial* (Río Piedras: Ediciones Bayán, 1980).

100. Godes, "Martin Luther King elogia," *El Mundo*, 5.

101. Michael Omi and Howard Winant, *Racial Formation*, 58–59.

102. Conversation with author at the Clemente Zabala residence, Río Piedras, Puerto Rico, August 27, 2018. In his 2006 charming biography on Clemente, David Maraniss mentions that King was one of Clemente's "heroes"; Clemente also referred to King as "one of the people he admired." *Clemente: The Passion and Grace of Baseball's Last Hero* (New York: Simon and Schuster, 2006), 148. On the same subject, Puerto Rican baseball commentator Josie Alvarado wrote, "Martin Luther King's fight inspired [Clemente] to take a stronger . . . position against racism." "Clemente Walker, Roberto," in *Dictionary of Caribbean and Afro-Latin American Biography*, vol 2, eds. Franklin W. Knight and Henry Louis Gates, Jr. (New York: 2016), 172.

103. Beresford Hayward, "Martin Luther King ¿Qué significa su visita a Puerto Rico? *El Mundo*, February 24, 1962, 6.

104. See Ralph Ober, "Párroco destaca ausencias barreras raciales en isla," *El Mundo*, January 29, 1963. Also, Jerónimo Berenguer, "Sin prejuicios raciales. Aconsejan maestros que visitaran la isla," *El Mundo*, July 5,1963, 4; Darío Carlo, "Líder Político Africano se siente feliz porque aquí no existe discrimen racial," *El Mundo*, July 15, 1963, 7.

Chapter 6

1. Ciro Alegría, "Algunas anotaciones más acerca del prejuicio racial en la isla," *El Mundo*, June 18, 1950.

2. Enrique Laguerre, "El problema racial de la isla no es a base de blancos y negros," *El Mundo*, August 13, 1950, 11.

3. AGPR, Fondo Departamento de Estado, box 58A, file 1015.

4. *El Mundo*, July 14, 23, 25, 1951; *El Diario de Puerto Rico*, July 9, 1951.

5. "Falú Zarzuela pide Villaronga y Moscoso le muestren 'hechos,'" *El Mundo*, July 25, 1951, 7.

6. "La Raza de color," *El Diario de Puerto Rico*, Monday, July 9, 1951. Editorial note, 4. Original quote: "Los Puertorriquenos, todos, absolutamente todos, pertenecemos a una sola raza: la raza humana. La frase 'raza de color' repugna el espíritu Cristiano y civilizado de este pueblo. Por razones morales que no admiten discusión, y también por razones científicas bien probadas, y además por la ley y por la actitud de respeto del gobierno del pueblo ante los valores humanos, aquí no existe el cáncer del discrimen racial."

7. The name of the informant was changed in order to protect his identity. Telephonic conversation, February 2003.

8. On Gómez Garriga's life and role in the Assembly, see Aixa Merino Falú, *María Libertad Gómez Garriga. Una mujer con volutad de acero* (San Juan: Oficina Procuradora de las mujeres, 2004), 25–30.

9. Estado Libre Asociado de Puerto Rico. *Diario de la Convención Constituyente* (Oxford: Equity Publishing Corporation, 1961), 264, www.oslpr.org/v2/PDFS/DiarioConvencionConstituyente.pdf; "Declaran plantearán problemas de color sin eufemismos," *El Mundo*, July 14, 1951; Georgina Falú, "Falú Zarzuela, Juan "Juanín," in *Dictionary of Caribbean and Afro-Latin American Biography*, vol. 2, eds. Franklin W. Knight and Henry Louis Gates Jr. (New York: Oxford University Press, 2016), 493.

10. Fernando Picó, *Historia General*, 267; Ayala and Bernabe, *Puerto Rico in the American Century*, 167–171.

11. For a summary of the nationalist insurrections, I alternately use Pico's *Historia general de Puerto Rico*, 267–268, and Miñi Seijo Bruno, *La insurrección nacionalista en Puerto Rico, 1950* (Río Piedras: Editorial Edil, 1989).

12. The physical health of Albizu deteriorated during his imprisonment. The local media suggested that he was losing his mind. See the publications in *El Diario de Puerto Rico* and *El Mundo* (1950–1952). Recent publications suggest that his torture was premeditated with the purpose of altering the state of mind of the nationalist leader. On this issue, see "The Ruth Reynolds Papers" at the Center for Puerto Rican Studies, New York. The "Roger Nash Baldwin Oral History Project," Columbia University; Pedro Aponte Vázquez, ¡*Yo Acuso!: tortura y asesinato de don Pedro Albizu Campos* (Río Piedras: Publicaciones René, 1991);

Carmelo Rosario Natal, ed., *Albizu Campos: preso en Atlanta, historia del reo #51298-A: correspondencia* (San Juan: Producciones Históricas, 2001).

13. Picó, *Historia General*, 268.

14. Seijo Bruno, *La insurrección nacionalista*, "Introduction."

15. LMM Papers, section 5, series 2, Correspondencia Particular, letter Romulo Betancourt to Luis Muñoz Marín, San José, April 20, 1954. Original quote: "Hace poco tiempo publicó *Repertorio Americano* unas declaraciones suyas (Albizu), mejor un artículo, calcado en lo que (Albizu) dijo *Bohemia* 'el ejército de USA lo estaba asesinando, con rayos atómicos.' Tu estas haciendo lo que consideres patriótico, y lo estas haciendo con el libre apoyo de la mayoría ciudadana de tu país." On the involvement of the FBI in the persecution and torture of the nationalist leader, see Pedro Aponte Vázquez, *Pedro Albizu Campos: su persecusión por el F.B.I* (San Juan: Publicaciones René, 1975).

16. LMM Papers, Section, Series (Correspondence with Rómulo Betancourt), "Informaciones Venezolanas," September 1953. This newsletter included a cover letter from Betancourt dated September 20, 1953.

17. A draft from a report of this long investigation originally was submitted to the governor as "Informe al Honorable Gobernador del Estado Libre Asociado" (San Juan, 1959). Later it was published by Comisión de Derechos Civiles de Puerto Rico under the title *Informes de la Comisión de Derechos Civiles del Estado Libre Asociado de Puerto Rico*. There are several editions of this report. For this segment I am using the 1973 edition, vol. 1 (1959–1968), xi.

18. Eduardo Seda Bonilla, *Los derechos civiles en la cultura puertorriqueña* (Rio Piedras, Puerto Rico: Editorial Universitaria, 1963).

19. Issues pertaining to the Civil Rights Commission created in 1956 are found in LMM Papers, section 5, series, "Comisión de Derechos Civiles," file 36. (Hereafter cited LMM Papers, "Comisión").

20. "Letter of Roger Baldwin to Muñoz Amato," April 23, 1958, 2. LMM Papers, Section 5, series "Comisión de Derechos Civiles," file 36.

21. *Informes*, Preface.

22. *Informes*, 85–94.

23. *United States, Federal Bureau of Investigation* (Washington, DC). Copies of these documents were released to the Government of Puerto Rico under the Freedom of Information Act.

24. Seijo Bruno, *La insurrección nacionalista*, chapter 16. This study was conducted in the late 1980s.

25. Seijo Bruno, *La insurrección*, 227.

26. "Senior señaló en Nueva York caso de Albizu," *El Mundo*, December 5, 1950, 3.

27. *Informes*, 97–98.

28. These findings are included in Seda Bonilla's study and at the Centro de Investigaciones Sociales at the University of Puerto Rico.

29. This fact was corroborated not only by evidence collected by the

Centro de Investigaciones Sociales but also by testimonies given in special hearings conducted by the Puerto Rican House of Representatives in 1965. See the Commission, *Informes*, 104–105. The hearing transcripts are under the title *Declaraciones prestadas en la vista celebrada por la comisión especial de la Camara de Representantes para escuchar testimonios en relación con la R. de la C., sobre discrimen racial en las fraternidades y sororidades* (San Juan, 1965).

30. *Informes*, 105.

31. LMM Papers, section 5, series 4, "Reunion de Gabinete," July 11, 1956, 3.

32. LMM Papers, section 5, series 4, Correspondencia Particular, Comisión de Derechos Civiles, letter "Roger Baldwin to UN Secretary General," January 20, 1960, 1.

33. "Roger Baldwin to UN General-Secretary," 1. One must question to what degree Roger N. Baldwin entered into a conflict of interest while supervising the investigation. He became a good friend of Muñoz and even wrote some remarks in one of Muñoz's biographies, along with Romulo Betancourt. For deeper insight into this matter, see Carmelo Rosario Natal, "Luis Muñoz Marín, Arthur Garfield Hays y la Masacre de Ponce: una revelación documental inedita." Also see Rosario Natal in "Boletín Mumorista" LMM (www.flmm.org/boletin.htm).

34. This agreement between the United States Department of Commerce Bureau of the Census and the Commonwealth of Puerto Rico was signed on November 10, 1958. Thanks to then director of the Puerto Rico Office of the Census, Mrs. Lillian Torres, for providing me with a copy of this document.

35. "Memorandum of Agreement on the Conduct of the 1960 Censuses of the Population, Housing and Agriculture in Puerto Rico," United States Department of Commerce, and the Government of the Commonwealth of Puerto Rico; U.S. Department of Commerce, October 29, 1958, appendix 2, item 3. Document was signed by Candido Oliveras, Chairman of the Puerto Rico Planning Board and Robert W. Burgess, Director of the Bureau of the Census.

36. "Agreement between the Bureau of the Census, United States Department of Commerce, and the Government of the Commonwealth of Puerto Rico Concerning the Conduct of Censuses in Puerto Rico," U.S. Department of Commerce, November 10, 1958, 1, item 1.

37. Palmira Ríos, "Are We Racists? Building a National Agenda against Racism in Puerto Rico." Paper delivered at the 2000 LASA Meeting, March 16–18, 2000, 3.

38. Jorge Duany, *The Puerto Rican Nation on the Move: Identities on the Island and in the United States* (Chapel Hill: University of North Carolina Press, 2002), 257–258. Duany stated that the gathering of racial data stated in 1950, but I could not confirm his statement.

39. Duany, *The Puerto Rican Nation*.

40. Eliseo Combas Guerra, column "En torno a la Fortaleza," *El Mundo*, April 7, 1960, 6; Luis Sánchez Cappa, "Nueva agencia Federal procesará información y datos censo 1960," *El Mundo*, August, 11, 1960, 24.

41. Luis M. Díaz Soler, *Historia de la esclavitud negra en Puerto Rico* (Río

Piedras: Editorial UPR, 2000), 260–261.

42. Díaz Soler, *Historia*, 260.

43. Díaz Soler, *Historia*, 260–261, my emphasis. The Spanish citation reads, "leen fin, os comisionados reformistas de Puerto Rico se mostraron contrarios a toda medida discriminatoria, evitando que se planteara un problema racial que no existía en la isla."

44. Omi and Winant, *Racial Formation*, 57.

45. Omi and Winant, *Racial Formation*, 57.

46. "*Vista Pública*" (hereafter *Vista*).

47. *Vista*, 3.

48. *Vista*, 4.

49. *Vista*, 10.

50. *Vista*, 13.

51. *Vista*, 16.

52. *Vista*, 32.

53. *Vista*, 35.

54. *Vista*, 37.

55. *Vista*, 40.

56. Isar P. Godreau, "Slippery Semantics: Race Talk and Everyday Uses of Racial Terminology in Puerto Rico," *Centro Journal* 20, no. 2 (Fall 2008): 10.

57. *Vista*, 14.

58. *Vista*, 15. Original quote: "En el sentido de que sean negros, ausencia de colores—o personas que nosotros en Puerto Rico clasificamos como 'indio'; o sea persona que es de color, de tez negra pero que tiene el pelo lacio, o persona que consideramos mulato—que hay una variación, desde la persona que tiene características negroides, pero puede ser blanco de color. Pero incluye el pelo, los labios y las demás características negroides. Y cuando me refiero a 'indio' me refiero a la persona de pelo lacio, completo. La persona 'mulata', cualquier persona que no fuera clasificada 'blanca' en el sentido de una característica exterior es de tipo negroide en el sentido usual de las palabras."

59. *Vista*, 50.

60. *Vista*, 53.

61. *El Mundo*, classified advertisement section, January 1938.

62. *El Mundo*, January 27, 1938, 18.

63. Omi and Winant, *Racial Formation*, 60.

64. Omi and Winant, *Racial Formation*, 50.

65. *Vista*, 56.

66. Zaire Dinzey-Flores, "Temporary Housing, Permanent Communities: Public Housing Policy and Design in Puerto Rico," *Journal of Urban History* 33, no. 3 (March 2007): 468–493.

67. Dinzey-Flores, "Temporary Housing," 480.

68. Dinzey-Flores, "Temporary Housing," 480.

69. Roy Simón Bryce-Laporte, "Urban Relocation and Family Adaptation in Puerto Rico: A Case in Urban Ethnography," in *Peasants in Cities: Readings in Anthropology of Urbanization*, ed. William Mangin (Boston: Houghton Mifflin Co., 1970), 86.

70. See the study by Helen I. Safa, *The Urban Poor of Puerto Rico: A Study in Development and Inequality* (New York: Holt, Rinehart and Winston, Inc., 1974), 68–69.

71. Safa, *The Urban Poor*, 482–485. Dinzey-Flores suggested that this is one of the reasons why many families were forced to stay in the limited housing option they were given and the dream of becoming a homeowner dissipated.

72. Safa, *The Urban Poor*, 485.

73. The difficulties and negative labels associated with living in the *caserío* are captured in the novel *Laguna negra* by Luis Lassén (New York: Editorial Mirta, 2011).

74. *Vista*, 52. Original quote: "me parece a mí que obedece al complejo ése, y segundo es que como los bancos, en los años anteriores, no tomaban empleados negros, o también puede ser que porque no acudían a solicitar."

75. *Vista*, 54. Original quote: "Bueno, mi sugerencia es que yo creo que se debiera de hacer una campaña mucho mayor . . . bueno, una campaña, porque actualmente no existe, en eliminarle el complejo ese que tienen."

76. Omi and Winant, *Racial Formation*, 60.

77. Omi and Winant, *Racial Formation*, 60.

78. Jeannette Ramos de Sánchez Vilella, "Estudio para determinar el alcance y ramificaciones de la discriminación por razón de color, sexo y origen nacional en la empresa privada en Puerto Rico" (Master's thesis, University of Puerto Rico, San Juan, 1975), 120–123, 127.

79. Ramos de Sánchez Vilella, "Estudio para determinar," 120–123, 127.

80. Ramos de Sánchez Vilella, 123, 285.

81. Ramos de Sánchez Vilella, 123, 285.

Bibliography

Archival Materials

Arturo Schomburg Collection. Manuscripts, Archives, and Rare Books Division, Schomburg Center for Research in Black Culture, New York Public Library.

Booker T. Washington Papers. Tuskegee Records. Library of Congress, Manuscript Division, Washington, DC.

Cecilia Orta Allende. Archivo y Centro de Investigación Histórica de Carolina, Plaza de Recreo, Centro Urbano, Carolina, PR.

Estado Libre Asociado de Puerto Rico. *Diario de la Convención Constituyente.* Orford, NH: Equity Publishing Corporation, 1961. www.oslpr.org/v2/PDFS/DiarioConvencionConstituyente.pdf

Estado Libre Asociado de Puerto Rico. *Informe de la Comisión de los Derechos Civiles del Estado Libre Asociado de Puerto Rico.* Tomo I (años 1959–1968). Orford, NH: Equity Publishing Company, 1973.

———. Oficina del Gobernador. Consejo Asesor de Gobernador sobre política Laboral. *Discrimen en el empleo por razón de color: Derechos y protección legal.* San Juan, Diciembre 1980.

———. Cámara de Representantes. *Transcripción de las declaraciones prestadas en la Vista Pública celebrada por la Comisión Especial de la Cámara de Representantes para investigar si el sistema de selección de empleados en los bancos de Puerto Rico discrimina por razones de color, raza, condición social.* July 22–23, 1963.

———. Cámara de Representantes. *Transcripción de las declaraciones prestadas en la Vista celebrada por la Comisión Especial de la Cámara de Representantes para escuchar testimonios en relación con la R. de la C.-109, sobre discrimen racial en las fraternidades y sororidades.* September 7, 1965.

———. Puerto Rico Reconstruction Administration. *Censo de Puerto Rico: 1935,* Washington, DC: United States Government Printing Office, 1937.

Fondo Departamento de Estado, Archivo General de Puerto Rico (AGPR), San Juan, Puerto Rico.

Fondo Oficina del Gobernador. Archivo General de Puerto Rico (AGPR), San Juan, Puerto Rico. Franklin Delano Roosevelt Papers. Documents pertaining to Puerto Rico. Center for Puerto Rican Studies, Hunter College-CUNY, New York.

The Harry S. Truman Presidential Library. www.trumanlibrary.org/hstpaper/psf.htm

José A. Martí Photographic Collection. Center for Puerto Rican Studies, Hunter College-CUNY, New York.

Luis Muñoz Marín. Particular Correspondence. Series V. Fundación Luis Muñoz Marín and Archives, Trujillo Alto, Puerto Rico.

The Martin Luther King, Jr. Research and Education Institute. https://kinginstitute. stanford.edu

Records of the Division of Territorial, Insular, and Foreign Statistics. Bureau of the Census. United States National Archives I (NARA), Washington, DC.

Records of the Bureau of the Census. Classified File for the 16th Decennial Census. United States National Archives I (NARA), Washington, DC.

Records of the Bureau of the Census. Scrapbooks Relating to Territorial Decennial Censuses, 1920–1940. United States National Archives I (NARA), Washington, DC.

Report of Commissioner of Education for Porto Rico to the Secretary of Interior. Washington DC: Government Printing Office, 1906.

Selected Documents Concerning Puerto Rico from the Papers of Franklin D. Roosevelt, Eleanor Roosevelt, Rexford G. Tugwell, Harry L. Hopkins, Charles W. Taussing, and Adolf A. Berle, from the Franklin D. Roosevelt Library. Center for Puerto Rican Studies, Hunter College-CUNY, New York.

United States Bureau of the Census. *A Report of the Seventeenth Decennial Census of the United States. Population: 1950.* Washington, DC: United States Government Printing Office, 1953.

United States Department of Commerce. Puerto Rican Relief Emergency Administration, *1935 Census.* Washington, DC: Government Printing Office, 1937.

United States Department of the Interior. *Official Register of the United States, containing a list of the Officers and employees in the Civil, Military, and Naval Service together with a list of vessels belonging to the United States.* Washington, DC: Government Printing Office, 1903.

United States Government. *Official Register of the United States.* Washington, DC: U.S. Government Printing Office, 1909.

United States Civil Service Commission. *Official Register of the United Sates, 1936.* Washington, DC: United States Government Printing Office, 1936.

———. *Official Register of the United Sates, 1937.* Washington, DC: United States Government Printing Office, 1937.

———. *Official Register of the United Sates, 1938.* Washington, DC: United States Government Printing Office, 1938.

————. *Official Register of the United Sates, 1951*. Washington, DC: United States Government Printing Office, 1951.

————. *Official Register of the United States, 1952*. Washington, DC: United States Government Printing Office, 1952.

Secondary Sources

Abbad y Lasierra, Fray Iñigo. *Historia geográfica, civil y natural de la isla de San Juan Bautista de Puerto Rico*. Estudio preliminar de Isabel Gutiérrez del Arroyo. Río Piedras: Editorial Universitaria, 1970.

Acosta-Belén, Edna, ed. *The Puerto Rican Woman: Perspectives on Culture, History, and Society*. New York: Praeger, 1986.

Alegría, Ciro. "Algunas anotaciones mas acerca del prejuicio racial en la isla." *El Mundo*, June, 18, 1950, 1.

————. "Considero puede aumentar el prejuicio en la isla." *El Mundo*, June 25, 1950, 15.

————. "Mas opiniones en el debate sobre el prejuicio racial." *El Mundo*, July 2, 1950, 10.

————. "El problema racial en la isla es a base de blancos y negros." *El Mundo*, August 13, 1950, 11.

Allende-Goitía, Noel. *De Margarita a El Cumbanchero. Vida musical, imaginación racial y discurso histórico en la sociedad puertorriqueña (1898–1940)*. San Juan: Ediciones Puerto, 2010.

Alleyne, Mervyn C. *The Construction and Representation of Race and Identity in the Caribbean and the World*. Kingston: University of West Indies Press, 2002.

Alvarado, Josie. "Clemente Walker, Roberto." In *Dictionary of Caribbean and Afro-Latin American Biography*, vol. 2. Franklin W. Knight and Henry Louis Gates Jr., eds. New York: Oxford University Press, 2016, 171–172.

Álvarez Curbelo, Silvia. *Un país del porvenir: el afán de modernidad en Puerto Rico (siglo XIX)*. San Juan: Ediciones, 2004.

Álvarez-Curbelo, Silvia, and María Elena Rodríguez Castro, eds. *Del nacionalismo al populismo: cultura y política en Puerto Rico*. Río Piedras: Ediciones Huracán, 1993.

Álvarez-Curbelo, Silvia. "La conflictividad en el discurso político de Luis Muñoz Marín: 1926–1936." In *Del nacionalismo al populismo: cultura y política en Puerto Rico*. Silvia Álvarez-Curbelo and María Elena Rodríguez Castro, eds. Río Piedras: Ediciones Huracán, 1993, 13–35.

Álvarez Nazario, Manuel. *El elemento afronegroide en el español de Puerto Rico*. San Juan: Instituto de Cultura Puertorriqueña, 1974.

Anazagasty Rodríguez, José, and Mario R. Cancel, eds. *"We the People." La representación americana de los puertorriqueños, 1898–1926*. UPR-Mayagüez: Fundación Puertorriqueña de la Humanidades, 2008.

Anderson, Benedict. *Imagined Communities: Reflections on the Origin and Spread of Nationalism*. New York: Verso, 1983.

Anderson, Thomas, and Marisel Moreno. *Art at the Service of the People. Posters and Books from Puerto Rico's Division of Community Education (DIVEDCO)*. Catalog of Exhibition at Site Museum of Art. Notre Dame, Indiana, January 22–March 11, 2012.

Aponte Vázquez, Pedro. *¡Yo Acuso! tortura y asesinato de don Pedro Albizu Campos*. Río Piedras: Publicaciones René, 1991.

———. *Pedro Albizu Campos: su persecusión por el F.B.I*. San Juan: Publicaciones René, 1975.

Appelbaum, Nancy P., Anne S. McPherson, and Karin Alejandra Rosemblatt, eds. *Race and Nation in Modern Latin America*. Chapel Hill: University of North Carolina, 2003.

Armstrong, Robert G. "Inter-Group Relations in Puerto Rico." *Phylon* (September 1949): 220–224.

Armstrong, Tenisha, ed. *Save the Soul of America. The Papers of Martin Luther King, Jr.*, vol. 8. Clayborne Carson, senior editor. Oakland: University of California Press, 2014.

Ashley, Wendy. "The Angry Black Woman: The Impact of Pejorative Stereotypes on Psychotherapy with Black Women." *Social Work in Public Health* 29, no. 1 (2014): 27–34.

Ayala, César J. *American Sugar Kingdom. The Plantation Economy of the Spanish Caribbean 1898–1934*. Chapel Hill: University of North Carolina Press, 1999.

Ayala, César J., and Rafael Bernabe. *Puerto Rico in the American Century. A History since 1898*. Chapel Hill: University of North Carolina Press, 2007.

Azize, Yamila. *La mujer en la lucha*. Río Piedras: Editorial Cultural, 1985.

Baerga, María del Carmen, ed. *Género y trabajo: La industria de la aguja en Puerto Rico y el Caribe Hispánico*. Río Piedras: Editorial de la Universidad de Puerto Rico, 1995.

———. "Women and the Right to (Needle) Work in Puerto Rico." In *Work, Protest and Identity in Twentieth-Century Latin America*. Vincent Peloso, ed. Delaware: Scholarly Resources, Inc., 2003.

Baptiste, Fitzroy A. *War, Cooperation, and Conflict: The European Possessions in the Caribbean, 1939–1945*. Westport, CT: Greenwood Press, 1988.

Baralt, Guillermo. *Tradición de futuro: el primer siglo del Banco Popular de Puerto Rico, 1893–1993*. San Juan: Ediciones Carimar, 1993.

———. *Esclavos rebeldes. conspiraciones de esclavos en Puerto Rico (1795–1873)*. Río Piedras: Ediciones Huracán, 1981.

Barbosa, Belén, "La mujer negra." *Revista de Estudios Generales* 8, no. 8 (June 1993): 353–367.

Barbosa. José C. *Problemas de Razas. La obra de José Celso Barbosa*. Vol. III. Pilar Barbosa, ed. San Juan: Model Offset Printing, Inc., 1984.

Barreto, Amílcar A. *The Politics of Language in Puerto Rico*. Gainesville: University Press of Florida, 2001.

———. *Language, Elites, and the State: Nationalism in Puerto Rico and Quebec*. Westport, CT: Praeger, 1998.

Bauer, Sherrie L. *The Political Economy of Colonialism. The Sate, and Industrialization in Puerto Rico*. Westport, CT: Praeger, 1993.

Bayron-Toro, Fernando. *Catálogo de Gobernadores y legisladores de Puerto Rico*. Mayagüez: Editorial Isla, Inc., 1995.

Belaval, Emilio. *Problemas de la cultura puertorriqueña*. Río Piedras: Editorial Cultural, Inc., 1971.

Berenguer, Jerónimo. "Sin prejuicios raciales. Aconsejan maestros que visitaran la isla." *El Mundo*, July 5, 1963, 4.

Betances, Samuel. "The Prejudice of Having no Prejudice in Puerto Rico." *The Rican: A Journal of Contemporary Puerto Rican Thought*, no. 2 (Winter 1972): 41–54.

———. "The Prejudice of Having No Prejudice in Puerto Rico: Part II." *The Rican: A Journal of Contemporary Puerto Rican Thought*, no. 3 (Spring 1973): 22–37.

Blanco, Tomás. *El prejuicio racial en Puerto Rico*. Con estudio preliminar de Arcadio Díaz Quiñones. 3ra edición. Río Piedras: Ediciones Huracán, 1985.

———. *Prontuario histórico de Puerto Rico*. Prólogo por Margot Arce Vázquez. Río Piedras: Ediciones Huracán, 1981.

———. "El substantivo jíbaro." *Revista del Instituto del Cultura Puertorriqueña* 3, no. 8 (July–September 1960):1–5.

———. "El mito del jíbaro." *Revista del Instituto del Cultura Puertorriqueña* 2, no. 5 (October–December, 1959): 5–10.

Bolland, O. Nigel. *Struggle for Freedom: Essays on Slavery, Colonialism, and Culture in the Caribbean and Central America*. Kingston, Jamaica: Ian Randle Publishers, 1997.

Bonilla-Silva, Eduardo. "Rethinking Racism: Toward a Structural Interpretation." *American Sociological Review* 62 (June 1996): 465–480.

———. *White Supremacy and Racism in the Post-Civil Rights Era*. Boulder, CO: Lynne Rienner Publishers, 2001.

Brau, Slavador. *Historia de Puerto Rico*. Río Piedras: Editorial Edil, 2000.

Briggs, Laura. *Reproducing Empire. Race, Sex, Science, and United States Imperialism in Puerto Rico*. Berkeley: University of California Press, 2002.

Bryce-Laporte, Roy Simón. "Urban Relocation and Family Adaptation in Puerto Rico: A Case in Urban Ethnography." In *Peasants in Cities: Readings in Anthropology of Urbanization*. William Mangin, ed. Boston: Houghton Mifflin Co., 1970.

Burnett, Christina Duffy, and Burke Marshall, eds. *Foreign in a Domestic Sense. Puerto Rico, American Expansion and the Constitution*. Durham, NC: Duke University Press, 2001.

Cabán, Pedro A. *Constructing Colonial people: Puerto Rico and the United States, 1898–1932.* Boulder, CO: Westview Press, 1999.

Caplow, Theodore, Stryker Sheldon, and Samuel E. Wallace. *The Urban Ambivalence. A Study of San Juan, Puerto Rico.* New York: The Bedminster Press, 1964.

Carlo, Darío. "Líder Político Africano se siente feliz porque aquí no existe discrimen racial." *El Mundo,* July 15, 1963, 7.

Carrasquillo, Rosa E. *Our Landless Patria: Marginal Citizenship and Race in Caguas, Puerto Rico, 1880–1910.* Lincoln: University of Nebraska Press, 2008.

Carrión, Juan Manuel, Teresa C. Garcia Ruiz, and Carlos Rodríguez Fraticelli, eds. *La nación puertorriqueña: ensayos en torno a Pedro Albizu Campos.* Río Piedras: Editorial de la Universidad de Puerto Rico, 1993.

Carroll, Henry K. *Report of the Island of Porto Rico; its Population, Civil Government, Commerce, Industries, Productions, Roads, Tariff, and Currency.* Washington, DC: Government Printing Office, 1899.

Castro-Arroyo, María de los Angeles, María Dolores Luque de Sánchez, and Gervasio Luis García Rodríguez. *Los primeros pasos: una bibliografía para empezar a investigar la historia de Puerto Rico.* Río Piedras: Ediciones Huracán, 1994.

Centro de Estudios Puertorriqueños. *Manos a la Obra. The Story behind Operation Bootstrap.* New York: Center for Puerto Rican Studies, 1986.

Centro de Investigaciones Históricas. *El proceso abolicionista en Puerto Rico: Documentos para su estudio 1866–1896.* 2 vols. San Juan: Instituto de Cultura Puertorriqueña, 1978.

Chinea, Jorge. *Race and Labor in the Hispanic Caribbean: The West Indian Immigrant Worker Experience in Puerto Rico, 1800–1850.* Gainesville: University of Florida Press, 2005.

Cifre de Loubriel, Estela. *La formación del pueblo puertorriqueño. La contribución de los vascongados, navarros y aragoneses.* San Juan: Instituto de Cultura Puertorriqueña, 1986.

———. *La formación del pueblo puertorriqueño. La contribución de los catalanes, balearicos y valencianos.* San Juan: Instituto de Cultura Puertorriqueña, 1975.

Clark, Truman R. *Puerto Rico and the United Sates, 1917–1933.* Pittsburgh: University of Pittsburgh Press, 1975.

Clark, Victor S. *Porto Rico and Its Problems: The Puerto Rican Experience.* New York: The Brookings Institute, 1930.

Colombán Rosario, José, and Justina Carrión. *El negro: Haití-Estados Unidos-Puerto Rico.* San Juan: Negociado de Materiales, Imprenta y Transporte, 1940.

Coll y Toste, Cayetano, ed. *Boletín Histórico de Puerto Rico.* 14 vols. San Juan: Tipografía Cantero Fernández, 1914.

Combas Guerra, Eliseo. "En torno a la Fortaleza." *El Mundo,* April 7, 1960, 6.

Combas Guerra, Eliseo. *En torno a la Fortaleza.* San Juan: Biblioteca de Autores Puertorriqueños, 1950.

Comisión de Derechos Civiles de Puerto Rico. *¿Somos racistas?* 2nda edición. Puerto Rico: Talleres de Gráfica Metropolitana, 1998.

Commissioner of Education of Puerto Rico. "Letter to Booker T. Washington, November 14, 1911. The Booker T. Washington Papers. Library of Congress Manuscript Division. Correspondence.

Conniff, Michael, ed. *Populism in Latin America.* Tuscaloosa: University of Alabama Press, 1999.

Córdova, Nathaniel I. "In His Image and Likeness: The Puerto Rican jíbaro as Political Icon." *Centro: Journal of the Center of Puerto Rican Studies* 25, no. 2 (2005): 170–195.

Corretjer, Juan Antonio. *Albizu Campos y las huelgas en los años '30.* Guaynabo, PR: Private Publisher, 1969.

Cortés-Zavala, María. "Barbosa, José Celso." In *Dictionary of Caribbean Afro-Latin American Biography*, vol. 1. Franklin W. Knight and Henry Louis Gates Jr., eds. New York: Oxford University Press, 2016, 215–217.

Cruz-Janzen, Marta I. "Out of the Closet: Racial Amnesia, Avoidance, and Denial—Racism among Puerto Ricans." *Race, Gender and Class* 10, no. 3. (2003): 64–81. www.jstor.org/stable/41675088

Curet Cuevas, Eliezer. *El desarrollo económico de Puerto Rico: 1940 a 1972.* Hato Rey: Management Aid Center, 1976.

Da Costa, Emilia Viotti. *The Brazilian Empire. Myths and Histories.* Revised edition. Chapel Hill: University of North Carolina Press, 2000.

Dávila, Arlene M. *Sponsored Identities: Cultural Politics in Puerto Rico.* Philadelphia: Temple University Press, 1997.

Dávila-Santiago, Rubén. "El pensamiento social obrero a comienzos del siglo XX en Puerto Rico." *Revista de Historia* 1, no. 2 (July–December 1985): 149–167.

De la Cadena, Marisol. "Reconstructing Race, Racism, Culture and Mestizaje in Latin America." *NACLA Report on the Americas* 34, no. 6 (May–June 2001): 16–23.

De la Fuente, Alejandro. "Myths of Racial Democracy in Cuba, 1900–1912." *Latin American Research Review* 34, no. 3 (1999): 39–53.

Del Moral, Solsiree. *Negotiating Empire. The Cultural Politics of Schools in Puerto Rico, 1898–1952.* Madison: University of Wisconsin Press, 2013.

De Oliveras, José *Our Islands and Their People as Seen with Camera and Pencil: Embracing Perfect Photographic and Descriptive Representations of the People and the Islands Hawaii & the Philippines.* With an Introduction by Major-General Joseph Wheeler. Vol. 1. St. Louis/Chicago/New York/Atlanta: ND Thompson Publishers, 1899.

Denis-Rosario, Milagros. "Intersecciones de raza, clase y género: la vida de Cecilia Orta "la pintora del pueblo." *Hispanófila. Ensayos de literature*, no. 189 (June 2020): 17–32.

————. "Deciphering the Notion of a Raceless Nation: Racial Harmony and Discrimination in Puerto Rican Society." *Latino Studies* 18, no. 1 (Spring 2020): 45–65.

Department of Education. *The Porto Rico School Review/Revista Escolar de Puerto Rico* 7, no. 2 (April 1922): 30. www.google.com/books/edition/The_Porto_Rico_school_review/PI8QAAAAYAAJ?hl=en&gbpv=1&bsq=Andres%20Tirado%20Sanchez%20

Díaz Quiñones, Arcadio. "Tomás Blanco: Racismo, historia y esclavitud." In *El prejuicio racial en Puerto Rico*. Tomás Blanco, ed. Río Piedras: Ediciones Huracán, 1985, 13–91.

Díaz Soler, Luis M. *Historia de la esclavitud negra en Puerto Rico*. Río Piedras: Editorial de la Universidad de Puerto Rico, 2000.

————. "Relaciones raciales en Puerto Rico." *Revista/Review Interamericana* 3, no. 1 (Spring 1973): 61–72.

Dietz, James L. *Economic History of Puerto Rico. Institutional Change and Capitalist Development*. Princeton, NJ: Princeton University Press, 1986.

————. *Puerto Rico. Negotiating Development and Change*. London: Lynne Reinner Publishers, 2003.

Dinzey-Flores, Zaire. "Temporary Housing, Permanent Communities: Public Housing Policy and Design in Puerto Rico." *Journal of Urban History* 33, no. 3 (March 2007): 468–493.

Domínguez, Jorge I., ed. *Race and Ethnicity in Latin America*. New York: Garland Publications, 1994.

Dorvillier, William. "Afirman que hay discrimen racial en la isla." *El Mundo*, October 30, 1947, 1–2.

Duany, Jorge. *The Puerto Rican Nation on the Move. Identities on the Island and in the United States*. Chapel Hill: University of North Carolina Press, 2002.

Edelman, Murray. *From Arts to Politics*. Chicago: University of Chicago Press, 1995.

Editorial. "Imputan Dos Clubs de San Juan negar entrada a gente de color." *El Mundo*, September 19, 1949, 5.

Editorial. "Sugiere llevar maestros Boricuas al Continente." *El Mundo*, January 19, 1947, 3.

Editorial. "La Raza' de color." *El Diario de Puerto Rico*. July 9, 1951, 4.

Editorial. "Falú Zarzuela pide Villaronga y Moscoso le muestren 'hechos.'" *El Mundo*, July 25, 1951, 7.

Editorial. "Declaran plantearán problemas de color sin eufemismos." *El Mundo*, July 14, 1951, 23.

Editorial. "Protesta sobre discrimen, va ante Justicia." *El Mundo*, October 15, 1960, 40.

Erman, Sam. *Almost Citizens: Puerto Rico, the U.S. Constitution, and the Empire*. Cambridge: Cambridge University Press, 2019.

Estades Font, María Eugenia. *La presencia militar de Estados Unidos en Puerto Rico, 1898–1918. Intereses estratégicos y dominación colonial.* San Juan: Ediciones Huracán, 1999.

Falú, Georgina. "Falú Zarzuela, Juan 'Juanín.'" In *Dictionary of Caribbean and Afro-Latin American Biography*, vol. 2. Franklin W. Knight and Henry Louis Gates Jr., eds. New York: Oxford University Press, 2016, 492–493.

Faragher, John M., Mary Jo Buhle, Daniel Czitrom, and Susan H. Armitage. *Out of Many: A History of American People.* 4th edition. New Jersey: Prentice Hall, 2004.

Fernández Méndez, Eugenio, ed. *Crónicas de Puerto Rico desde la conquista hasta nuestros dias (1493–1955).* Río Piedras: Editorial Universitaria, 1981.

Fernández Méndez, Eugenio. *Historia cultural de Puerto Rico.* San Juan: Ediciones Cemí, 1970.

Ferrante, Joan, and Prince Brown Jr., eds. *The Racial Construction of Race and Ethnicity in the United States.* Upper Saddle River, NJ: Prentice Hall, 2001.

Ferrao, Luis Angel. *Pedro Albizu Campos y el nacionalismo puertorriqueño.* San Juan: Editorial Cultural, 1990.

Figueroa, Loida. *Breve historia de Puerto Rico.* 2 vols. Río Piedras: Editorial Edil, 1979.

Figueroa, Luis A. *Sugar, Slavery and Freedom in Nineteenth Century Puerto Rico.* Chapel Hill: University of North Carolina Press, 2005.

Fiol-Matta, Licia. *The Great Woman Singer: Gender and Voice in Puerto Rican Music.* Durham, NC: Duke University Press, 2017.

Fitzpatrick, Joseph P. "Attitudes of Puerto Ricans towards Color." *American Catholic Sociological Review* 20, no. 3 (1959): 219–233.

Fleagle, Fred K. *Social Problems in Porto Rico.* New York: Arno Press, 1975.

Flinter, George. *Examen del estado actual de los esclavos de la isla de Puerto Rico,* 2nd edition. Río Piedras: Editorial Coquí, 1976.

Flores, Juan. "The Puerto Rico that Jose Luis González Built." *Latin American Perspectives* 11, no. 3 (1984): 173–184.

———. *Insularismo e ideología burguesa nueva lectura de Antonio S. Pedreira.* Río Piedras: Ediciones Huracán, 1979.

Foner, Philip S. *The Spanish–Cuban–American War and the Birth of American Imperialism.* New York: Monthly Review Press, 1972.

Forbes, Jack D. *Africans and Native Americans: The Language of Race and the Evolution of Red-Black Peoples.* 2nd edition. Chicago: University of Illinois Press, 1993.

Frazier, Franklin E., and Eric Williams, eds. "Eric Williams and the Anglo-American Caribbean Commission, 1942–1944." In *The Economic Future of the Caribbean.* New preface by Erica Williams Connell; new introduction by Tony Martin. Dover, MA: The Majority Press, 2004.

Fundación de la Humanidades. *Enciclopedia de Puerto Rico On line*. www.enci-clopediapr.org/esp/article.cfm?ref=08050501&page=2&highlight=+Guanica

Garcia, Gervasio L., and A.G. Quintero. *Desafío y solidadridad: breve historia del movimiento obrero puertorriqueño*. Río Piedras: Ediciones Huracán, 1982.

Garver, Simon Earl, and Ernest B. Fincher. *Puerto Rico: Unsolved Problem*. Elgin, IL: Elgin Press, 1945.

Gatzambide-Arrillaga, Carlos. *Historia de Puerto Rico cronológica e illustrada, sus hombres y mujeres (1492-1989)*. San Juan: Ramallo Bros. Printing, 1989.

Gaztambide, Antonio, and Silvia Álvarez Curbelo, eds. *Historias vivas; historiografía puertorriqueña contemporánea*. San Juan: Postdata, 1996.

Geggus, David P. *Haitian Revolution Studies*. Bloomington: Indiana University Press, 2002.

Giusti-Cordero, Juan. "Afro-Puerto Rican Cultural Studies: Beyond the *cultura negroide* and *antillanismo*." *Journal of the Center of Puerto Rican Studies* 8, no. 1-2 (1996): 114-121.

Glasser, Ruth. *My Music is My Flag: Puerto Rican Musicians and Their New York Communities, 1917-1940*. Berkeley, CA: University of California Press, 1997.

Go, Julian, and Anne L. Foster. *The American Colonial State in the Philippines*. Durham, NC: Duke University Press, 2003.

Godes, Roy. "Martin Luther King elogia la fraternidad racial de Puerto Rico." *El Mundo*, February 19, 1962, 5.

Godreau, Isar P. *Scripts of Blackness: Race, Cultural Nationalism, and U.S. Colonialism in Puerto Rico*. Chicago: University of Illinois Press, 2015.

———. "Slippery Semantics: Race Talk and Everyday Uses of Racial Terminology in Puerto Rico." *Centro: Journal of the Center of Puerto Rican Studies* 20, no. 2 (Fall 2008): 4-33.

Godreau Isar, Mariolga Reyes Cruz, Mariluz Franco, and Sherry Cuadrado. "The Lessons of Slavery: Discourse of Slavery, *mestizaje* and *blanqueamiento* in an Elementary School in Puerto Rico." *American Ethnologist* 35, no. 1 (February 2008): 115-135.

González, José Luis. *El pais de cuatro pisos y otros ensayos*. Río Piedras: Ediciones Huracán, 1980.

González, José Luis. *Puerto Rico: The Four-Storeyed Country: The Question of an Afro-Mestizo Culture*. Translated by Gerald Guinness. Princeton, NJ: Markus Wiener Publishing, Inc. 1993.

González, Lydia Milagros, and Angel G. Quintero. *La otra cara de la historia. La historia de Puerto Rico desde su cara obrera, 1800-1925*. Río Piedras: CEREP, 2000.

———. "Este silencio. Reflexiones sobre la historia del hombre y la mujer negros en Puerto Rico." *Cultura* 7, no. 6 (1998).

González Vales, Luis E. "La puertorriqueñidad: una visión histórica." *Boletín de la Academia Puertorriqueña de la Historia* 17, no. 54 (1997).

Gordon, Maxine W. "Race Patterns and Prejudice in Puerto Rico." *America Socio-logical Review* 14, no. 2 (1949): 294–301.

———. "Cultural Aspects of Puerto Rico's Race Problem." *American Sociological Review* 15 (1950): 382–392.

Graham, Richard, ed. *The Idea of Race in Latin America, 1870–1940.* Austin: University of Texas Press, 1990.

Grupo Editorial EPRL. "Antonio Salvador Pedreira." *Enciclopedia de Puerto Rico online.* https://enciclopediapr.org/content/antonio-pedreira

Guerra, Lilliam. *Popular Expression and National Identity in Puerto Rico.* Gainesville: University Press of Florida, 1998.

———. "The Promise and Disillusion of Americanization." *Centro: Journal of the Center of Puerto Rican Studies* 11, no. 1 (Fall 1999): 8–31.

Guridy, Frank A. *Forging Diaspora: Afro-Cubans and African Americans in a World of Empire and Jim Crow (Envisioning Cuba).* Chapel Hill: University of North Carolina Press, 2010.

Hall, Stuart. "What is the 'Black' in Black Popular Culture?" In *Black Popular Culture.* Michele Wallace and Gina Dent, eds. Baltimore: The New Press, 1992,

Hanchard, Michael, ed. *Racial Politics in Contemporary Brazil.* Durham, NC: Duke University Press, 1999.

Harlan, Louis, ed. *The Booker T. Washington Papers (1895–1898).* 14 vols. Chicago: University of Illinois Press, 1975.

Haslip-Viera, Gabriel, ed. *Taino Revival: Critical Perspectives on Puerto Rican Identity and Cultural Politics.* New York: Centro de Estudios Puertorriqueños, 1999.

Hayward, Beresford. "Martin Luther King ¿Qué significa su visita a Puerto Rico? *El Mundo,* February 24, 1962, 6.

Hernández, Tanya K. "Multiracial Matrix: The Role of Race Ideology in the Enforcement of Antidiscrimination Laws, a United States-Latin America Comparison." *Cornell Law Review* 87, no. 5 (July 2002): 1093–1176.

Hernández Cruz, Juan *La invasión de Puerto Rico: consideraciones histórico-Sociológicas.* San Germán: Editorial Xaguey, 1992.

Hochschild, J.L., and B.M. Powell. "Racial Reorganization and the United States Census 1850–1930: Mulattoes, Half-Breeds, Mixed Parentage, Hindoos, and the Mexican Race." *Studies in American Political Development* 22, no. 1 (2008): 59–96.

Hoetink, H. "Race and Color in the Caribbean." In *Caribbean Contours.* Sidney Mintz and Sally Price, eds. Baltimore: Johns Hopkins University Press, 1985.

Hofstadter, Richard. *Social Darwinism in American Thought.* With an Introduction by Eric Foner. Boston: Beacon Press, 1992.

Hollister, Frederick J. "Skin Color and Life Chances in Puerto Ricans." *Caribbean Studies* 9, no. 3 (1969): 87–94.

Hooker, Juliet. "Negotiating Blackness within the Multicultural State: Creole Politics and Identity in Nicaragua." In *Comparative Perspectives in Afro-Latin America*. Kwame Dixon and John Burdick, eds. Gainesville: University Press of Florida, 2012, 262–281.

James, Winston. *Holding Aloft the Banner of Ethiopia. Caribbean Radicalism in Early Twentieth-Century America*. Brooklyn: Verso, 1998.

Jiménez de Wagenheim, Olga. *Puerto Rico. An Interpretative History from Pre-Columbian Times to 1900*. Princeton, NJ: Markus Wiener Publishers, 1998.

Jiménez-Román, Miriam. "Un hombre (negro) del pueblo: José Celso Barbosa and the Puerto Rican '"Race' towards Whiteness." *Centro: Journal of the Center of Puerto Rican Studies* 8, no. 1–2 (1996): 8–29.

Johnston, Joseph Forney. "Letter from Joseph Forney Johnston to Booker T. Washington, June 28, 1899." *The Booker T. Washington Papers (1898–1898)*. 14 vols. Louis Harlan et al., eds. Chicago: University of Illinois Press, 1975, vol. 5, 140.

Kennedy, Philip W. "Race an American Expansion in Cuba and Puerto Rico, 1895–1905." *Journal of Black Studies* 1, no. 3 (1971): 306–316.

Kennerly, Catherine Marsh. *Negociaciones culturales. Los intelectuales y el proyecto pedagógico del estado muñocista*. San Juan: Ediciones Callejón, 2009.

King, Martin Luther, Jr. "Strides towards Freedom" and "The Future of Integration." Transcripts of speeches during visit to Puerto Rico February 1962. Latino rebels.com. www.scribd.com/document/200921486/Martin-Luther-King-Jr-Speeches-in-Puerto-Rico-1962

Kinsbruner, Jay. *Not of Pure Blood: The Free People of Color and Racial Prejudice in Nineteenth Century Puerto Rico*. Durham, NC: Duke University Press, 1996.

Knight, Franklin W. *The Caribbean. The Genesis of a Fragmented Nationalism*. 2nd edition. New York: Oxford University Press, 1990.

Knight, Franklin W., and Colin A. Palmer, eds. *The Modern Caribbean*. Chapel Hill: University of North Carolina Press, 1989.

Knight, Franklin W., and Henry Louis Gates Jr., eds. *Dictionary of Caribbean Afro-Latin American Biography*. 6 vols. New York: Oxford University Press, 2016.

Laguerre, Enrique. "El problema racial de la isla no es a base de blancos y negros." *El Mundo*, August 13, 1950, 11.

Larrain, Jorge. *Modernity and Identity*. Cambridge: Polity Press, 2001.

Lassén, Luis. *Laguna negra*. New York: Editorial Mirta, 2011.

Lauria-Perricelli, Antonio. "Images and Contradictions. DIVEDCO's Portrayal of Puerto Rican Life." *Centro: Journal of the Center for Puerto Rican Studies* 3, no. 1 (Winter 1990–1991): 92–96.

Lawrence, Keith, and Terry Keleher. "Structural Racism." Proceedings from the Race and Public Policy Conference. Aspen Institute, 2004. www.intergroupre-sources.com/rc/Definitions%20of%20Racism.pdf

Levis, José Elías, "La raza de color y Mariano Abril." In *Literatura puertorriqueña negra del siglo XIX escrita por negros. Obras encontradas de Eleuterio Der-*

kes, *Manuel Alonso Pizarro y José Ramos y Brans.* Roberto Ramos-Perea, ed. Estudio preliminar, recopilación y notas de Roberto Ramos-Perea. Segunda edición corregida y aumentada. San Juan: Publicaciones Gaviota, 2011, 461–462.

Lewis, Gordon K. *Puerto Rico: Freedom and Power in the Caribbean.* New York: Monthly Review, 1974.

Lewis, Oscar. *La Vida: A Puerto Rican Family in the Culture of Poverty—San Juan and New York.* New York: Random House, 1965.

Library of Congress. "The World of 1898: The Spanish–American War." www.loc. gov/rr/hispanic/1898/miles.html

Lloréns, Hilda. *Imagining the Great Puerto Rican Family. Framing Nation, Race, and Gender during the American Century.* Lanham, MD: Lexington Books, 2014.

Lluch Vélez, Amalia. *Luis Muñoz Marín: poesía, periodismo y revolución, (1915–1930).* Caguas: Universidad del Sagrado Corazón/Fundación LMM, 1999.

López-Baralt, Mercedes, ed. *Sobre Insulas extrañas: el clásico de Pedreira.* Anotado por Tomás Blanco. San Juan: Editorial de la Universidad de Puerto Rico, 2001.

———. "La tercera salida de 'Tuntún de Pasa y grifería.'" In *Tuntún de Pasa y grifería.* Luis Palés Matos, ed. Edición de Mercedes López-Baralt. San Juan, PR: Instituto de Cultura Puertorriqueña/Universidad de Puerto Rico, 1993, 9–68.

López Ortíz, Miguel. "Amílcar Tirado." Fundación Nacional para la Cultura Popular, San Juan, Puerto Rico. https://prpop.org/biografias/amilcar-tirado

López Sierra, Héctor E. "Un acercamiento desde la sociología de la religión a la relación de raza, política y religión en Puerto Rico: del 1929 al 1930: una hipótesis de trabajo." *Revista/Review Interamericana* 24, no. 1–4 (1994): 68–78.

Loveman, Mara, and Jerónimo O. Muñiz "How Puerto Rico Became White: Boundary Dynamics and Intercensus Racial Reclassification." *American Sociological Review* 72 (December 2007): 915–939.

Maeztu, Ramiro de. *Defensa de la hispanidad.* Edición autorizada por la señora viuda del autor para America y Filipinas. Buenos Aires: Editorial Poblet, 1941.

Malcomson, Scott L. *One Drop of Blood. The American Misadventure of Race.* New York: Farrar Straus Giroux, 2000.

Maldonado, A.W. *Teodoro Moscoso and Puerto Rico's Operation Bootstraps.* Gainesville: University of Florida Press, 1997.

Maldonado-Denis, Manuel. *Hacia una historia marxista de la historia de Puerto Rico y otros ensayos.* Río Piedras: Editorial Antillana, 1977.

———. *Puerto Rico y Estado Unidos: emigración y colonialismo.* Mexico: Editorial Siglo 21, 1976.

Mangin, William, ed. *Peasants in Cities: Readings in Anthropology of Urbanization.* Boston: Houghton Mifflin Co., 1970.

Manuel, Peter, Kenneth Bilby, and Michael Largey, eds. *Caribbean Currents: Caribbean Music from Rumba to Reggae.* Revised and expanded edition. Philadelphia: Temple University Press, 2006.

Maraniss, David. *Clemente. The Passion and Grace of Baseball's Last Hero.* New York: Simon & Schuster, 2006.

Martín Berrio, Raúl. "1898: Intervencionismo militar de los EE.UU. sobre Puerto Rico y Cuba." *Quinto Centenario,* no. 16 (1990): 253–269.

Marx, Anthony W. *Making Race and Nation: A Comparison of the United States, South Africa, and Brazil.* Cambridge: Cambridge University Press, 1998.

Mathews, Thomas. *Puerto Rican Politics and the New Deal.* Gainesville: University of Florida Press, 1960.

Mathews, Thomas G. "The Question of Color in Puerto Rico." In *Slavery and Race Relations in Latin America.* Robert Brent Toplin, ed. Westport, CT: Greenwood Press, 1974.

Matos-Rodríguez, Félix V. "The Invasion of Puerto Rico: Writings by Journalists and Other Observers from the United States, 1898." *Centro: Journal of the Center of Puerto Rican Studies* 10, no. 1–2 (Fall 1998): 96–122.

McFerson, Hazel. *The Racial Dimensions of American Overseas Colonial Policy.* Westport, CT: Greenwood Press, 1997.

Megenney, William W. "The Black Puerto Rican: An Analysis of Racial Attitudes." *Phylon* 35 no. 1 (1974): 83–93.

Memmi, Albert. *Dominated Man: Notes towards a Portrait.* New York: Orion Press, 1968.

Meneses de Albizu Campos, Laura. *Dr. Albizu Campos y la independencia de Puerto Rico.* San Juan: Partido Nacionalista de Puerto Rico, 1961.

Meneses Albizu Campos, Cristina, and Silvia Lora Gamarra. *Una vida de amor y sacrificio: Laura Meneses de Albizu Campos: una vida dedicada a la lucha.* Dorado: Taller Gráfico Gongolí, 1997.

Merino Falú, Aixa. *Cecilia Orta. Allende. La pintora del pueblo.* Carolina: Imprenta, 2006.

———. *Raza, género y clase social. El discrimen contra la mujeres afropuertor-riqueñas.* San Juan: Oficina de la Procuradora de las Mujeres, 2004.

———. *Maía Libertad Gómez Garriga. Una mujer con voluntad de acero.* San Juan: Oficina Procuradora de las Mujeres, 2004.

———. "El gremio de las lavanderas de Puerta de Tierra." In *Historias vivas: historiografía puertorriqueña contemporánea.* Antonio Gaztambide and Silvia Álvarez-Curbelo, eds. San Juan: Asociación Puertorriqueña de Historiadores/Postdata, 1996, 74–79.

———. "El discurso de la armonía-social en Puerto Rico: siglos XVIII–XX." Proceedings from conference *Carolina: Humanismo y tecnología.* Universidad de Puerto Rico en Carolina. Año 5 no. 1. UPR-Carolina, March 26–29, 2001, 115–125.

Miller, Marilyn. "Plena and the Negotiation of 'National' Identity in Puerto Rico." *Centro: Journal of the Center for Puerto Rican Studies* 16, no. 1 (Spring 2004): 36–59.

Montañez, Ligia. *El racismo oculto en una sociedad no racista.* Caracas: Fondo Editorial Tropykos, 1993.

Montano, Agnes J. "Falta de datos dificulta medir el efecto del racismo." *El Nuevo Día,* March 24, 2002.

Morales Carrión, Arturo, ed. *Puerto Rico. A Political and Cultural History.* New York: W.W. Norton and Company, Inc., 1983.

———. "The Hope and the Trauma." In *Puerto Rico: A Political and Cultural History.* Arturo Morales Carrión, ed. New York: W.W. Norton and Company, Inc., 1983, 129–151.

———. "The PPD Democratic Hegemony (1944–1969)." In *Puerto Rico: A Political and Cultural History.* Arturo Morales Carrión, ed. New York: W.W. Norton & Company, Inc., 1983, 256–307.

———. "El reflujo en Puerto Rico de la crisis Dominico-Haitana, 1791–1805." *Revista Eme y Eme: Estudios Dominicanos* 5, no. 27 (1976): 19–40.

Morales Otero, Pablo. *Nuestros Problemas.* San Juan: Biblioteca de autores puertorriqueños, 1947.

Morner, Magnus, ed. *Race and Class in Latin America.* New York: Columbia University Press, 1970.

Movimiento Pro-Independencia. *Tesis política a la hora de la independencia.* San Juan: Movimiento Pro Independencia, 1973.

Muñoz Marín, Luis. *Historia del Partido Popular Democrático.* San Juan: Editorial El Batey, 1984.

Negrón de Montilla, Aida. *La Americanización de Puerto Rico y el Sistema de Instrucción Pública.* 2nda edición. Río Piedras: Editorial de la Universidad de Puerto Rico, 1990.

Nash, Gary B., Julie R. Jeffrey, John R. Howe, Peter J. Frederick, Alleen F. Davis, and Allan M. Winkler. *The American People: Creating a Nation and Society.* 3rd edition. New York: Longman, 2000.

Navarro, José Manuel. *Creating Tropical Yankees: Social Science Textbooks and the United States Ideological Control in Puerto Rico, 1898–1908.* New York: Routledge, 2002.

Negrón Portillo, Mariano. *Las turbas republicanas, 1900–1904.* Río Piedras: Ediciones Huracán, 1990.

Negrón Portillo, Mariano, and Raúl Mayo Santana. *La esclavitud menor: la esclavitud en los municipios del interior de Puerto Rico siglo XIX: Estudio del Registro de Esclavos de 1872: segunda parte.* Río Piedras: Centro de Investigaciones Sociales/Universidad de Puerto Rico, 2007.

Nieves-Rivera, M. "El juez Bennazar decidió caso de Zero Club distinto al Esquife." *El Mundo,* September 24, 1949, 7.

———. "Teodoro Moscoso niega haya prejuicio racial en empresas apoya Fomento." *El Mundo,* April 11, 1960, 12.

Ober, Ralph. "Párroco destaca ausencias barreras raciales en isla." *El Mundo*, January 29, 1963, 24.

Omi, Miachael, and Howard Winant. *Racial Formation in the United States*. New York & London: Routledge, 1996.

Orta Allende, Cecilia. "Letter to Luis Muñoz Marín." June 28, 1964. Luis Muñoz Marín Foundation and Archives. Correspondence.

––––––. "Letter to Luis Muñoz Marín, August 2, 1964. Luis Muñoz Marín Foundation and Archives. Correspondence.

Osuna, Juan José. *A History of Education in Puerto Rico*. 2nd edition. Río Piedras: Editorial de la Universidad de Puerto Rico, 1949.

Padilla, Víctor M. "Hará pesquisa sobre posible discrimen." *El Mundo*, March 23, 1962, 32.

––––––. "Hoy iniciarán investigación por discrimen." *El Mundo*, July 18, 1962, 11.

––––––. "En empleos, Nombran asesor en pesquisa, alegado discrimen bancos." *El Mundo*, July 21, 1962, 1.

Padró-Rivera, Lino. "Letter from Lino Padrón-Rivera to Dr. Washington." December 10, 1910. The Booker T. Washington Papers. Library of Congress, Manuscript Division. Students' files, A–K 1910.

Pagán, Bolívar S. *Historia de los partidos políticos puertorriqueños*. 2 vols. San Juan: Librería Campos, 1972.

Palés Matos, Luis. *Tuntún de pasa y grifería*. Río Piedras: Editorial de la Universidad de Puerto Rico, 1993.

Pedreira, Antonio S. *Insularismo*. Río Piedras: Editorial Edil, 1972.

––––––. *Un hombre del pueblo: José Celso Barbosa. La obra de José Celso Barbosa*. Vol. I. Pilar Barbosa, ed. San Juan: Model Offset Printing, Inc., 1990.

Perea, Juan F. "Fulfilling Manifest Destiny: Conquest, Race, and the Insular Cases." In *Foreign in a Domestic Sense Puerto Rico, American Expansion and the Constitution*. Christina Burnett and Marshall, eds. Durham, NC: Duke University Press, 2001, 140–166.

Pérez, Marvette. "La negra de Ponce: una entrevista con Ruth Fernández (el alma de Puerto Rico hecha canción). *Centro: Journal of the Center for Puerto Rican Studies* 16, no. 1 (Spring 2004): 61–67.

Picó, Fernando. *Los gallos peleados*. 3ra edición. Río Piedras: Ediciones Huracán, 2003.

––––––. "Los chivos expiatorios. Los tortolos en Puerto Rico, 1898–1899." *Revista Mexicana del Caribe* 3, no. 6 (1998): 100–115.

––––––. *Al filo del poder: subalternos y dominantes en Puerto Rico*. Río Piedras: Editorial de la Universidad de Puerto Rico, 1993.

––––––. *Historia general de Puerto Rico*. Río Piedras: Ediciones Huracán,1988.

––––––. *La guerra después de la guerra*. Río Piedras: Ediciones Huracán, 1987.

––––––. *San Fernando de la Carolina: identidades y representaciones*. Carolina: Municipio Autónomo de Carolina, 2003.

Picón Salas, Mariano. *Apología de la pequeña nación. Discurso pronunciado en la cuadragésima segunda colación de grados de la Universidad de Puerto Rico.* Río Piedras: Imprenta Venezuela, 1946.

President Harry S. Truman Civil Rights Commission Report. *To Secure These Rights* Washington, DC: Government Printing Office, 1947.

Quiñones Calderón, A. "Ante Comisión Especial abogado alega hubo discriminación en solicitud empleo hizo en banco." *El Mundo*, July 24, 1963, 1.

Quiñones Rivera, Maritza. "From Trigueñita to Afro-Puerto Rican. Intersections of the Racialized, Gendered and Sexualized Body in Puerto Rico and in the U.S. Mainland." *Meridians: feminism, race, transnationalism* 7, no. 1 (2006): 169–182.

Quintero Rivera, Ángel G. "La ideología populista y la institucionalización universitaria de las Ciencias Sociales." In *Del nacionalismo al populismo: cultura y política en Puerto Rico.* Silvia Álvarez-Curbelo and María Elena Rodríguez Castro, eds., Río Piedras: Ediciones Huracán, 1993, 107–145.

———. "Socialista y Tabaquero: La proletarización de los artesanos." *Sin Nombre* 8, no. 4 (1987): 101–137.

———. *Conflictos de clase y política en Puerto Rico.* Río Piedras: Ediciones Huracán, 1986.

———. *Puerto Rico: identidad nacional y clases sociales.* Río Piedras: Ediciones Huracán, 1979.

———. *Workers' Struggle in Puerto Rico: A Documentary History.* New York: Review Press, 1976.

———. "La ideología populista y la institucionalización universitaria de las ciencias sociales." In *Del nacionalismo al populismo: cultura y política en Puerto Rico.* Silvia Álvarez-Curbelo and María Elena Rodríguez Castro, eds. Río Piedras: Ediciones Huracán, 1993, 107–177.

Ramos. Josean. "Ruth Fernández." Fundación Nacional para la Cultura Popular. http://prpop.org/biografias/ruth-fernández

Ramos-Perea, Roberto. *Literatura puertorriqueña negra del siglo XIX escrita por negros. Obras encontradas de Eleuterio Derkes, Manuel Alonso Pizarro y José Ramos y Brans.* Estudio preliminar, recopilación y notas de Roberto Ramos-Perea. Segunda edición corregida y aumentada. San Juan: Publicaciones Gaviota, 2011.

Ribes-Tobar, Federico. *100 puertorriqueños ilustres.* New York: Plus Ultra Educational Publishers, 1973.

Rivera, M. "El Juez Bennazar decidió Caso de Zero Club distinto al Esquife." *El Mundo* September 24, 1949, 7.

Rivera Ortíz, Lcdo Marcos A. *Justicia negra. Casos y cosas.* Hato Rey: Ediciones Situm, 2001.

Rivera-Ramos, Efrén. *The Legal Construction of Identity. The Judicial and Social Legacy of American Colonialism in Puerto Rico.* Washington, DC: American Psychological Association, 2001.

Rivera-Rideau, Petra R. "From Carolina to Loíza: Race, Place and Puerto Rican Racial Democracy." *Identities* 20, no. 5 (2013): 616–632.

Rivero, Angel. *Crónica de la Guerra Hispanoamericana en Puerto Rico.* New York: Plus Ultra Educational Publishers, Inc., 1975.

Rodríguez, Jorge. "En busca de la pintora del pueblo." *Escenario* (June 3, 2006): 6–7.

Rodríguez-Beruff, Jorge. *Política militar y dominación en el contexto Latinoamericano.* Río Piedras: Ediciones Huracán 1988.

Rodríguez Castro, María E. "Foro de 1940: las pasiones e intereses se dan de la mano." In *Del nacionalismo al populismo: cultura y política en Puerto Rico.* Silvia Álvarez-Curbelo and María Elena Rodríguez Castro, eds. Río Piedras: Ediciones Huracán, 1993, 61–105.

Rodríguez Cruz, Juan. "Las relaciones raciales en Puerto Rico." *Revista de Ciencias Sociales* 9, no. 4 (1965): 373–386.

Rodríguez Ramos, Reniel. *Rethinking Puerto Rican Precolonial History.* Tuscaloosa: University of Alabama Press, 2010.

Rodríguez-Silva, Ileana. *Silencing Race: Disentangling Blackness, Colonialism, and National Identities in Puerto Rico.* New York: Palgrave-Macmillan, 2012.

Rodríguez Vázquez, José J. *El sueño que no cesa: la nación deseada en el debate intelectual político puertorriqueño, 1920–1940.* San Juan: Ediciones Callejón, 2004.

Román, Reinaldo L. "Scandalous Race: Garveyism, the Bomba, and the Discourses of Blackness in 1920s Puerto Rico." *Caribbean Studies* 31, no. 1. (January–June 2003): 213–259.

Romero, María Soledad. "Fernández Cortada, Ruth Noemí." In *Dictionary of Caribbean and Afro-Latin American Biography,* vol. 3. Franklin W. Knight and Henry Luis Gates Jr., eds. New York: Oxford University Press, 2016, 5–7.

Romero-Rosa, Ramón. "A los negros puertorriqueños." In *Source for Study of Puerto Rican Migration, 1879–1930.* History Task Force. New York: Centro de Estudios Puertorriqueños, 1982, 30–33.

Root, Elihu. *The Military and Colonial Policy of the United States.* Collected and edited by Robert Bacon and James Brown Scott. New York: AMS Press, 1970.

Rosa, Richard. "Business as Pleasure: Culture, Tourism, and Nation in Puerto Rico in the 1930s." *Nepantla: Views from South* 2, no. 3 (2001): 449–488.

Rosado, Marisa. *Las llamas de la aurora: acercamiento a una biografía de Pedro Albizu Campos.* San Juan/Santo Domingo: Editora Corripio, 1992.

Rosario Natal, Carmelo, ed. *Albizu Campos: preso en Atlanta, historia del reo # 51298-A: correspondencia.* San Juan: Producciones Históricas, 2001.

———. *Los pobres del '98 puertorriqueño. Lo que le pasó a la gente.* San Juan: Producciones Históricas, 1998.

Roy-Fequiere, Magali. *When Gender Meets Race: Women, Creole Identity, and the Intellectual Life in Early Twentieth-Century Puerto Rico.* Philadelphia: Temple University Press, 1999.

Safa, Helen I. *The Urban Poor of Puerto Rico. A Study in Development and Inequality.* New York: Holt, Rinehart and Winston, Inc., 1974.

Safa, Helen I., ed. "Introduction." *Latin American Perspectives* 25, no. 3 (May 1998): 3–20.

Sagrera, Martin. *Racismo y política en Puerto Rico.* Río Piedras: Editorial Edil, 1973.

Salas Herrero, Miguel. "Un interesante experimento en Puerto Rico." *Bohemia Libre Puertorriqueña* (January 1962): 3–5.

Sánchez Cappa, Luis. "Nueva agencia Federal procesará información y datos censo 1960." *El Mundo*, August, 11, 1960, 24.

Santana Rabell, Leonardo. *Planificación y política durante la administración de Luis Muñoz Marín: un análisis crítico.* 1ra edición. Santurce: Revista de Planificación, 1984.

Santiago, Josefa. "Los obreros de Puerta de Tierra y la guerra, 1917–1918." In *Historias vivas: historiografía puertorriqueña contemporánea.* Antonio Gaztambide and Silvia Álvarez Curbelo, eds., San Juan: Asociación Puertorriqueña de Historiadores/Postdata, 1996, 80–84.

Santiago-Valle, Kelvin. "Our Race Today (Is) the Only Hope for the World: An African Spaniard as Chieftain of the Struggle against 'Sugar Slavery' in Puerto Rico (1926–1934)." *Caribbean Studies* 35, no. 1 (2007): 107–140.

———. " 'Still Longing for the Plantation': The Visual Parodies and Racial National Imaginary of United States Overseas Expansionism, 1898–1903." *American Studies International* 37, no. 3 (October 1999): 18–43.

———. *"Subject People" and Colonial Discourses: Economic Transformation and Social Disorder in Puerto Rico.* Albany, NY: SUNY Press, 1994.

Scarano, Francisco. "The Jíbaro Masquerade and the Subaltern Politics of Creole Identity Formation in Puerto Rico, 1745–1823." *American Historical Review* 101, no. 5 (December 1996): 1398–1431.

Seda-Bonilla, Eduardo. *Requiem para una cultura: ensayo sobre la socialización del puertorriqueño en su cultura y en el ámbito del poder.* Río Piedras: Editorial Edil, 1970.

———. "Who Is a Puerto Rican: Problems of Social/Cultural Identity in Puerto Rico." *Caribbean Studies* 17, no. 1–2 (1977): 105–121.

———. *Los derechos civiles en la cultura puertorriqueña.* Río Piedras: Editorial Universitaria, 1963.

———. "Social Structure and Race Relations." *Social Forces* 40, no. 2 (December, 1961): 141–148.

Seijo Bruno, Miñi. *La insurección nacionalista de Puerto Rico, 1950.* Río Piedras: Editorial Edil, 1989.

Sepúlveda, Aníbal. *San Juan: historia ilustrada de su desarrollo urbano, 1508–1898.* San Juan: Carimar, 1989.

Sepúlveda, Aníbal, and Jorge Carbonell. *Cangrejos-Santurce: historia ilustrada de su desarrollo urbano (1519–1950)*. San Juan: Centro de Investigaciones Carimar/Oficina Estatal de Preservación Histórica, 1988.

Silva-Gotay, Samuel. *Protestantismo y política en Puerto Rico 1898–1930*. 2nd edition. Río Piedras: Editorial de la Universidad de Puerto Rico,1998.

Silvestrini, Blanca. *Violencia y criminalidad en Puerto Rico, 1865–1973: Apuntes para un estudio de historia social*. Río Piedras: Editorial Universitaria, 1980.

———. *Los trabajadores puertorriqueños y el Partido Socialista,1932–1940*. Río Piedras: Editorial Universitaria, 1979.

Silvestrini, Blanca G., and Maria Dolores Luque. *Historia de Puerto Rico: Trayectoria de un pueblo*. San Juan: Ediciones Cultural Panamericana, 1991.

Sociedad Histórica de Puerto Rico. *Puerto Rico: 1897–1917 y un apéndice*. San Juan: Sociedad Histórica de Puerto Rico, 1998.

Stepan, Nancy Leys. *The Hour of Eugenics: Race, Gender, and Nation in Latin America*. Ithaca, NY: Cornell University Press, 1991.

Stevens Arroyo, Antonio M. *Catholicism as Civilization: Contemporary Reflections on the Political Philosophy of Pedro Albizu Campos*. San Germán: Inter-American University, 1992.

Steward, Julian et al., eds. *The People of Puerto Rico: A Study of Social Anthropology*. Chicago: University of Illinois Press, 1956.

Suárez-Findlay, Eileen J. *Imposing Decency: The Politics of Sexuality and Race in Puerto Rico, 1870–1920*. Durham, N.C. & London: Duke University Press, 1999.

Sued Badillo, Jalil, and Ángel López Cantos. *Puerto Rico Negro*. Río Piedras: Editorial Cultural, 1986.

Sweet, James H. "The Iberian Roots of American Racist Thought." *The Mary and William Quarterly* (3rd Series) 54, no. 1 (January 1997): 143–166.

Taller de Formación Política. *La cuestión nacional: El partido nacionalista y el movimiento obrero puertorriqueño*. Río Piedras: Ediciones Huracán, 1982.

———. *No estamos pidiendo el cielo, la huelga portuaria de 1938*. Río Piedras: Ediciones Huracán, 1982.

Tapia y Rivera, Alejandro, ed. *Biblioteca Histórica de Puerto Rico*. San Juan: Imprenta Marquéz, 1854.

Taylor, Charles M. *Modern Social Imaginaries*. Durham, NC: Duke University Press, 2004.

Teletipo. "Senior señaló en Nueva York caso de Albizu." *El Mundo*, December 5, 1950, 3.

Thomas, Evan. *The War Lovers: Roosevelt, Lodge, Hearst, and the Rush to Empire, 1898*. New York: Back Bay Books, 2010.

Thompson, Lanny. *Nuestra isla y su gente. La construcción del "otro" puertorriqueño en "Our Islands and Their People"*. San Juan: Centro de Investigaciones Sociales, 1995.

Tirado, Amilcar, Jr. Interviewed in person by Milagros Denis-Rosario. July 2014.

Tirado Avilés, Amílcar. "Ramón Romero Rosa. Su participación en la luchas obreras." *Revista* Caribe 2, no. 2–3 (1980–1981): 3–15.

Torres, Arlene. "La Gran Familia Puertorriqueña 'ej prieta de beldá'" (The Great Puerto Rican Family "Is Really Black"). In *Blackness in Latin America and the Caribbean*, vol. 2. Arlene Torres and Normann E. Whitten Jr., eds. Bloomington: Indiana University Press, 1998, 285–306.

Torres, J. Benjamín. *Pedro Albizu campos: obras escogidas*. 4 vols. Río Piedras: Editorial Jelofe, 1982.

Trask, David. *The War with Spain in 1898*. New York: McMillan Publishing, Co., 1981.

Trias Monge, José. *Historia Constitucional de Puerto Rico*. 5 vols. Río Piedras: Editorial Universitaria, 1984.

Tribunal Supremo, Puerto Rico. *Muriel v. Suazo 72 DPR 370* (1951).

Tumin, Melvin. "Social Class and Skin Color in Puerto Rico." In *Comparative Perspectives on Race Relations*. Melvin Tumin, ed. Boston: Little Brown Company, 1969.

United States Bureau of the Census. *Guánica, Puerto Rico. Block Map. 2000.* www2.census.gov/geo/maps/blk2000/st72_PuertoRico_sp/Place/7231189_Guanica/CBP7231189_002_sp.pdf

———. "The Hispanic Population: 2010," *Census Briefs*, 2. www.census.gov/prod/cen2010/briefs/c2010br-03.pdf

U.S. Naval Institute. *Log of the U.S. Gunboat Gloucester. Commanded by Lt. Richard Wainwright and the Official Reports of the Principal Events of Her Cruise during the Late War with Spain.* Annapolis: The Navy Department, 1898. www.google.com/books/edition/Log_of_the_U_S_Gunboat_Gloucester/obxCAAAAYAAJ?hl=en&gbpv=1&dq=Lieutenant+H.+P.+House+of+the+-Gloucester&pg=PA90-IA3&printsec=frontcover

Valdés, Vanessa K. *Diasporic Blackness: The Life and Times of Arturo Alfonso Schomburg*. Albany, NY: SUNY Press, 2017.

Vaquero, María. *Tesoro Lexicográfico del español de Puerto Rico*. Primera edición. San Juan: Editorial Plaza Mayor, 2005.

Vargas, Patricia. "Negra ¿y qué? *El Nuevo Día*, October 12, 2000.

Vargas-Ramos, Carlos C. "Black, Trigueño, White . . . ? Shifting Racial Identification among Puerto Ricans." *Du Bois Review: Social Science Research on Race* 2, no. 2 (2005): 1–19.

Vargas, Patricia, ed. *Race, Front and Center: Perspectives on Race Among Puerto Ricans*. New York: Centro Press, 2017.

Vasconcelos, José. *La Raza Cósmica*. A bilingual edition. Translated and annotated by Didier T. Jaén. Afterword by Josefa Gabilondo. Baltimore: Johns Hopkins University Press, 1997.

———. *Indología. Una interpretación de la cultura Ibero-Americana*. Barcelona: Agencia Mundial de Librería, 1927.

Wade, Peter. *Blackness and Race Mixture: The Dynamics of Racial Identity in Colombia*. Baltimore: Johns Hopkins University Press, 1993.

Wells, Henry. *The Modernization of Puerto Rico: A Political Study of Changing Values and Institutions*. Cambridge, MA: Harvard University Press, 1969.

Weston, Rubin F. *Racism in United States Imperialism: The Influence of Racial Assumptions on American Foreign Policy, 1893-1946*. Columbia: University of South Carolina Press, 1972.

Whitten, Norman, and Rachel Corr. "Contesting the Images of Oppression. Indigenous Views of Blackness in the Americas." *NACLA Report on the Americas* 34, no. 6 (May/June 2001): 24-28.

Williams, Eric E. "Race Relations in Puerto Rico and the Virgin Islands." *Foreign Affairs* 23 (January 1945): 309-317.

Wingfield, Aida Harvey. "The Modern Mamie and the Angry Black Man: African-American Professionals' Experiences with Gendered Racism in the Workplace." *Race, Gender and Class* 14, no. 1-2 (2007): 196-212.

Wright, Winthrop R. *Café con leche: Race, Class and National Image in Venezuela*. Austin: University of Texas Press, 1990.

Zelinsky, Wilbur. "The Historical Geography of the Negro Population of Latin America." *The Journal of Negro History* 34, no. 2 (April 1949): 153-221.

Zenón Cruz, Isabelo. *Narciso descubre su trasero: el negro en la cultura puertorriqueña*. 2 vols. Humacao: Editorial Furidi, 1974.

Master's and Doctoral Theses

Alemañy-Álvarez, Vivian. "La independencia en la balanza: crisis colonial y el liberalismo puertorriqueño." MA thesis, University of Puerto Rico, San Juan, 1992.

Baldrich, Juan José. "Class and the States: The Origins of Populism in Puerto Rico, 1934-1952." PhD dissertation, Yale University, New Haven, Connecticut, 1981.

Carbonell Ojeda, Sonia. "Blanton Winship y el Partido Nacionalista, 1934-1939." MA thesis, University of Puerto Rico, San Juan, 1984.

Collazo, José. "Guerra y educación: la militarización y americacion de las escuelas públicas de Puerto Rico durante la Segunda guerra Mundial, 1939-1945." PhD dissertation, University of Puerto Rico, San Juan, 1997.

Colón Pizarro, Mariam. "Poetic Pragmatism: The Puerto Rican Division of Community Education (DIVEDCO) and the Politics of Cultural Production, 1949-1968." PhD dissertation, University of Michigan, Ann Arbor, Michigan, 2011.

Del Moral, Solsiree. "Race, Science, and Nation: The Cultural Politics of Schools in Colonial Puerto Rico, 1917-1938." PhD dissertation, University of Wisconsin-Madison, Madison, Wisconsin, 2006.

Denis, Watson. "Miradas de mutua desconfianza entre dos Repúblicas americanas: el expansionismo marítimo de Estados Unidos frente a la francofilia haitiana (1888–1898)." PhD dissertation, University of Puerto Rico, San Juan, 2004.

Giusti-Cordero, Juan. "Labor, Ecology and History in a Caribbean Sugar Region: Piñones (Loíza), Puerto Rico 1770–1950." PhD dissertation, State University of New York at Binghamton, Binghamton, New York, 1995.

Ramos de Sánchez Vilella, Jeannette. "Estudio para determinar el alcance y ramificaciones de la discriminación por razón de color, sexo y origen nacional en la empresa privada en Puerto Rico." MA thesis, University of Puerto Rico, San Juan, 1975.

Rodríguez-Berrios, Luis Guillermo. "Nationalism, Socialism, and Modernization in Puerto Rico during the Muñoz Era, 1898–1980." PhD dissertation, New School for Social Research, New York, 1982.

Thompson, Michael O. "Puerto Rican Nationalism and the United Sates Decolonization, 1898–1953." PhD dissertation, Howard University, Washington, DC, 1976.

Venator Santiago, Charles R. "The Other Nationalists: Marcus Garvey and Pedro Albizu Campos." MA thesis, University of Massachusetts at Amherst, Amherst, Massachusetts, 1996.

War years, 1945–1953." PhD dissertation, University of Pennsylvania, Philadelphia, Pennsylvania, 1986.

Zapata Oliveras, Carlos R. "United States-Puerto Rico Relations in the Early Cold War years, 1945–1953." PhD dissertation, University of Pennsylvania, Philadelphia, Pennsylvania, 1986.

Index

Abbad y Lasierra, Fray Iñigo, 6
Afro-Boricuas, 9
  Artists (Cecilia Orta), 109 (Ruth
    Fernández), 100
  Exclusion (from nation-building
    and modernity), 2, 128 (from
    teaching in higher education), 96
  In clerical positions, 145
  In the arts, 77, 148
  Musical performance (Ruth
    Fernández), 100, 102, 109, 148
  Organizations, 63 (La Liga)
Afro-Puerto Ricans, 3, 14, 38, 48
  bomba (musical genre), 100, 104,
    119, 210
  plena (musical genre), 100, 105, 182
Alegría, Ricardo (Institute for Puerto
  Rican Culture), 109
Albizu Campos, Pedro, "drop of
  nationalism," 65, 173–174, 184,
  188, 196, 198–199, 201, 220, 206,
  210, 212–213, 215
  American Civil Liberties Union
    (investigation on racial
    discrimination), 130–131
  Civil Rights Commission
    (investigation about), 130–132
  Concept of race (*raza*
    iberoamericana), 70
  Hispanic-centered, 70

  International League of the Rights
    of Men (investigation on racial
    discrimination), 130, 131
  La Nación (Nationalist Party
    newspaper), 67
  latinidad, 67
  Laura Meneses del Carpio (wife
    of), 66
  Nationalist Party leadership, 65–67
  Nationalist's insurrections, 128–131
  Persecution of nationalists, 129,
    131
  Puerto Rican culture and racial
    views 67–70
  Release from prison (1947), 128
  Santiago-Valles, Kelvin (on Albizu's
    racial narrative), 69–70
  Subjected to Racialization (by
    Americans), 66–67 (Robert
    Gore), 131 (Clarence Senior)
Allen, Charles H. (Governor of
  Puerto Rico), 34
American invasion (of Puerto Rico),
  17, 27, 38 (ideological meaning),
  American soldiers, 19, racist
  attitudes, 22
American (U.S) citizenship
  Commissioner Carroll, 51
  Commissioner Luis Muñoz Rivera
    (proponent), 54

American (U.S) citizenship *(continued)*
Discussion (about), 29, 31–32, 54, 55, 83, 163, 165 (Mexicans)
Dr. Barbosa (proponent), 48, 50
Education (Americanization), 40
Native Americans, 51
Americanization, 26, 39, 51, 162, 166, 203
Anglo-Saxon Protestant (notions), 29, 39, 68, 70
Definition (political project), 27–29
English language, 20, 29, 57
(elimination of), 67
Educational system (part of), 40
Racialization, 13

Barbosa, José Celso (Dr.), "drop of advocacy," 46
Contradictions (apparent), 50–51
Creoles, 26
El País and *El Tiempo*, 49
First Black Puerto Rican surgeon, 47
Meeting with Commissioner Henry K. Carroll, 28
Meeting with President William McKinley, 48
Partido Ortodoxo (member of), 47
Race and racism (views on), 48
Republican Party of Puerto Rico (founder of), 46
"un hombre del pueblo," 46
Barbosa, Pilar (Dr.), 50
Betances, Samuel, 10, 49, 169, 197
Black Puerto Ricans 9, 13, 14, 34–38
Advocacy, 49, 111, 119, 126, 148
Arturo Alfonso Schomburg, 62
Enrique Lefebre, 62
Exclusion, 4, 13
Juan Falú Zarzuela, 62–65, 126, 127, 140, 173
Manuel Gaetán Barbosa, 62

National identity, 14
Stigma of slavery, 3, 7
Blanco, Tomás (denial of racism), 61, 85, 157, 158, 179, 187, 200
Blanqueamiento (whitening), 157, 202
Buena apariencia (good appearance), 120, 141
Bulerín, Ramón (artist), book cover, xi, xii
Brooke, John R. General (Governor of Puerto Rico), 24

Cádiz Constitution (Spanish citizenship), 6, 7, 158, 163
Canóvanas, xi, xii
Carroll, Henry K. Commissioner (United States Census 1899), 13, 29, 30, 51, 151, 164, 165, 170
Americanization (and Education), 27–30
Meeting with Dr. José C. Barbosa, 48
Color-blind (society), 92
Latin American Liberals, 122
Puerto Rico promoted, 135–136
Color (race), 5, 41
Abbad y Lasierra (description of), 6
Black (synonym), 7
Color data in Puerto Rican census (absence of), 134
De color (of color), 13, 35, 187
Definition (Puerto Rican context), 139, 140, 143–144, 157, 164, 166, 190
Discrimination based on skin color, 11, 191
People of color/*persona de color*, 128, 138–139
PPD and registration forms, 77–79
Raza de color (Barbosa), 149, 27, 170
Self-identification, 137
Slavery, 8

Clemente Walker, Roberto, 123
Clemente, Vera (widow of Roberto
    Clemente), 123
Creole (s), 6, 7, 26 (class), 61, 109
Cuba (Spanish American War), 15,
    23–24, 31, 33, 160
    Afro-Cubans (at Tuskegee), 46, 74
    (music), 102
    Hispanic definition (part of), 175
    negritude movement 56, 159, *batey*
    74, national identity and racial
    democracy, 84
    nineteenth-century insurgents, 64
    Puerto Rico (Spanish Cortes), 135
    Revolución Cubana Chapter of
    Puerto Rico 162
    segregation (of Cubans and Puerto
    Ricans), 44

Davis, George W. General (Governor
    of Puerto Rico), 26
Del Moral, Solsiree (historian),
    system of education and
    Americanization, 41
Department of Instruction, 106
Díaz Quiñones, Arcadio, 3, 6, 157,
    172, 179, 197
División de Educación a la
    Comunidad (DIVEDCO), 89,
    106, 183, 196

Falú, Georgina, 62, 172, 187
Falú Zarzuela, Juan, "drop of
    organization" 62
    Commonwealth of Puerto Rico
    supporter (affiliated with PPD),
    64
    Constitutional Assembly (*Asamblea
    Constituyente*), 128
    Dr. Barbosa (political ally of),
    62, Republican Party County
    Executive of Santurce, 173

*Liga para Promover el Progreso de
    los Negros en Puerto Rico* (League
    to Promote the Advancement of
    Blacks in Puerto Rico), 62–65
    Uncovering racism and racial
    discrimination 126, 127, 1137,
    140, 172, 173, 187, 200, 201
Fernández, Ruth, "drops of ingenuity,"
    100
    "El alma de Puerto Rico hecha
    canción" (the soul of Puerto Rico
    made song), 102–103
    Colorism, 103, 104
    Commonwealth of Puerto Rico,
    102
    Fiol-Matta, Licia (analysis of),
    102–103
    Fortunato Vizcarrondo, 102
    Intersections of gender, class and
    race, 103
    Patriarchal society, 101
    Performances, 102, 104
    Ponce, 100, 104
    Popularized Afro-Puerto Rican
    music, 103–104
    Racial discrimination (experiences
    with), 103, 104
    Stigma (of Black women), 103
    Teatro Hispano (New York City),
    102
Folklorization, 3
Folkloric imaginary, 9
Fomento (Industrial Development
    Company), 88, tourist industry
    and racial discrimination, 90, 99
Foraker Act 1900, 28, 29–30, 51–52,
    164, 165
Forum of 1940 (UPR), 86–87

Gaetán Barbosa, Manuel, Judge San
    Juan District and Republican
    Party (candidate), 62, 172

Generación del treinta (Hispanicization), 57–59, 60, 62, 86, Antonio S. Pedreira, 58–59
Godreau, Isar (slippery semantics), 8, 139
Gómez Garriga, María Libertad, Constitutional Assembly (*Asamblea Constitucional*), 128
González, José Luis, national identity essentially African and Indian, 72
Gore, Robert (Governor of Puerto Rico), 66 (pragmatic view of race) 67
Guánica, 15, 161–165
    Bay of Guánica (Landing of Americans), 162, 213
    July 25th 1898, 15
    Map downtown (Appendix A), 151
    Simón Mejil, 18–19, 68, street name after, 19, 152
Gran familia puertorriqueña (great Puerto Rican family), 9, 136, 147, 213

Haiti (Hayti), 36
Haitian Revolution, 6, 158, 166, 202
Henna, Julio H., 22
Henry, Guy V. (Governor of Puerto Rico), 25
Hernández, Rafael "drop of nostalgia," 80
    El jibarito, 80
    Hispanicization, 81–82
    "Preciosa," 80–82
    Ruth Fernández (performed songs), 102

Iberian Peninsula, 5
Intellectual elite (s), 23, 37, 70, 84, 86, 89, 115, 117, 122
Inter-American University (history of), 120 (Dr. King visit), 120–123, 144, 186

Institute of Puerto Rican Culture, 109, revival of Taino-Indian culture 110

Jíbaro (white peasant), 58, 61, 72, 84 (comparison with southern Americans and Appalachians) (as the other), 73
    Creoles nineteenth-century, 5–6, 26, 27 (jíbaros), 109 (Carolina)
    Partido Popular Democrático (PPD) campaign, 73, *pava* icon
Jiménez-Román, Miriam (discussion on Barbosa), 47, 169, 204
Jones Act, 29

King, Martin Luther, Jr. (Puerto Rico chapter of the Fellowship of Reconciliation), 120
    Inter-American University (San Germán campus), 120
    Puerto Rico model of "social ease," 122
    Visit to Puerto Rico, 120

Laguerre, Enrique, 88 (works)
    Argument with Ciro Alegría, 125
    Comparison of racial democracy in Puerto Rico to Brazil, 126
Larrain, Jorge, 2, modernity process in Latin America, 59, industrialization of Latin American countries, 86, 98
Liga para Promover el Progreso de los Negros en Puerto Rico (League to Promote the Advancement of Blacks in Puerto Rico), 13–14, 62–65, 125–127, 173
Lefebre, Enrique (Black's advocate), 62
Levis Bernard, José Elías, "drop of participation," 37
    Afro-Puerto Rican intellectuals, *El País,* 38

Loíza, xi–xii, 72, 107–108, 181, 210, 215

Maldonado, Antonio "Tony," (artist), 109
Marín Muñoz, Luis (Governor of Puerto Rico and stateman), 13
Commonwealth of Puerto Rico (Estado Libre Asociado de Puerto Rico), 97, 102, 132–134 189
Culebra (PPD registration forms and racial narrative), 76–79
El Batey (PPD newspaper), 74
Idealization of the jíbaro (white rural man), 73–76
La pava (icon of PPD), 73, 76, 79
Latin American political and intellectual elites, 85
Popular Democratic Party (Partido Popular Democrático), 13, populism 75
Puerto Rican national identity (Anglo-Saxon-Hispanic), 71
Mejía, Francisco (mayor of Yauco), 20
Mejil López, Simón, "drop of authority," 17
"Maestro Simón," 16
María Cabó Bertú (2nd wife of), 18
Parents, 17
Social order, 18
Merino Falú, Aixa (historian) 106
Carolina (history), 109–111, 113–114, 119, 159, 161
Cecilia Orta Allende, 106–107, 1930 Census, 107
Mexico, 31 (conquest of)
Indigenismo, 110
Rafael Hernández, 80
San Carlos Academy (Cecilia Orta, Tony Maidonado, and Tufiño studied (in), 109
U.S.-Puerto Rico-Mexico, 109

Miles, Nelson A. (General), 19
Miranda-Pratts, José, "drops of experience," 137
Racial classifications, 138–140, buena apariencia (good appearance), 140–141
Spatial discrimination (public housing), 141–144
Testimony (Puerto Rican House of Representatives racial discrimination investigation), 131–139
Modernity, 4, 23
Puerto Rican project, 83, 86, 88, 90, 98, 108 (Carolina), 124
Modernization (industrialization of economy), 4, 44 (under PPD), 87, 97–99, 125, 127–128, 181–182, 197
Morel Campos, Ramón (Revista Obrera), 37
Morel Campos, Juan (music composer), 100
Moscoso, Teodoro (see Fomento), 88, 98 (Falú Zarzuela), 90
Muñoz Rivera, Luis, 25 (La Democracia), 38, U.S. citizenship (proponent) 53–55
Muriel, Rafael Lieutenant, "drop of justice," 90
Discrimination based on skin color, 200
Muriel vs. Suazo, 91–93, 180
Racial discrimination in social clubs, 90

National identity (and Puerto Rican politics), 57
Negrón de Montilla, Aida, 27 (definition of Americanization), 39
Nation-based paradigm (Omi and Winant), 4

Nation-building, 2, 4, 59, 78, 97, 99, 100, 138, 175
Nationalist Party, 13, 65, 97, 129, 131
  Elimination of the English language, 67
  Pedro Albizu Campos, 13

Oliveras, José de (perception of the other), 20
Omi, Michael (and Howard Winant), 4 (nation-based paradigm) 3, 5, 83, 91, 122, 157, 172–174, 186
Operation Bootstraps (industrialization), 106
Osuna, Juan José (Commissioner of Education), 40
Orta Allende, Cecilia, "drop of creation," 106
  Art and education (eradicate poverty), 106, 112, 114–115
  Art exhibitions, 113, 114
  Black Puerto Rican women and teaching profession, 109
  Commonwealth of Puerto Rico (activism), 112, 116, 118
  Department of Instruction (conflicts with), 109, 112, 115, 119
  Educational projects, 111, 114–115
  Intersections of gender, class and race, 113, 118–119
  "La pintora del pueblo," 119
  Municipality of Carolina, 107–108 (history), modernization, 108, Black families, 108
  Muñoz Marín (correspondence with), 112, 113, 116
  Project of modernity (collaboration with), 112, 115–116, 118
  Public housing, 114–115
  Racialization (subjected to), 113, 116–119
  San Carlos Academy (studied in), 109, 115

Spanish culture and identity, 110
University of Puerto Rico (studied in), 109
U.S. Census of 1930 (Carolina), 107

Padró-Rivera, Lino (labor leader and Senator) Booker T. Washington, 45
Palés Matos, Luis (folklorization of Afro-Puerto Rican culture), 59–61
Partido Popular Democrático (PPD) and modernization, 85
Perea, Juan F. United States Manifest Destiny and racism, 31
Pedreira, Antonio S. (see Barbosa), 47
Political elite(s), 9, 11, 79, 88, 134
Prim, Juan de (Spanish Governor), Bando contra la raza africana, 6
Protestant (see Protestantism/o), Carroll and education, 27, Osuna 39
Puerto Rican Planning Board (1960 Census and elimination of race question), 134–135
Puerto Rican society
  Machista, 104
  Patriarchal, 101
  Racial exclusion, 2–4, 9, 59, 63, 76, 81–82 105, 143, 146–147, 173
  Racial paradise 95, 124, 147
  Racial tolerance (example of), 9, 95, 121 (Dr. King visits)
  Pureza de sangre (purity of blood), 5, 17, 33

Quiñones-Rivera, Maritza (salsa and racialization), 105

Racial discrimination (Puerto Rico) Based on skin color 191, 200

Civil Rights violations, 93–95
Denial (of), 8–9, 36, 43, 59, 90–93,
  122, 136, 140, 147, 180, 199
Dr. Matin Luther King, Jr. (racial
  discrimination as social disease),
  123
Eric Williams 94, 169, 180, 201
House of Representatives (Puerto
  Rico), investigations, 85, 129,
  137–139, 189,
In financial institutions (banks),
  137, 139, 143, 145
Judicial cases, 93
"Report to the Honorable
  Governor," 131
Tourist industry (in), 90
University of Puerto Rico (in),
  86–87, 96
University of Puerto Rico, 125, 127
Racial exclusion (of Black Puerto
  Ricans), 2, 4, 76, 81, 105, 124, 127
Racial classifications, 8, 134, 136,
  138–140, 167
Racial democracy, 71
  Comparison with Brazil, 126
  In Puerto Rican society, 136,
    178–179, 181, 199, 210
  In Cuba, 84
  Myth (of), 95
Racial codes, 104
Racial inclusivity, 1
Racial intolerance, 5, 95
Racial harmony, 1, 10, 13–14 (myth),
  83, 86 (and modernization) 86,
  94–96, 105, 121–122, 124, 147
Racial hierarchies, 1, 8, 13, 17,
  41, 107 (in Spanish colonial
  Carolina), 135–136, 147–148
Racial formation, 2, 8, 91, 122, 178
Racial narrative, 3, 102
Racialization, 3 (and slavery), 4, 8
  (definition of)
  New American possessions, 31

Process, 144, 173
Puerto Ricans (of), 13, 21, 45–46,
  67, 70 (of Iberian peoples), 85
Spatial (redlining), 141–144
Racism, 8, 9, 11, 13–14, 31–32, 35,
  36, 47, 48
  Allegations (of), 64, 90–91
  Anti-Black, 8, 33, 49, 50
  Cruz-Jansen, Marta (denial among
    Black Puerto Ricans), 92
  Dr. Barbosa, 50–51
  Dr. Martin Luther King, Jr., 120
  Negotiated (Black Puerto Ricans),
    147
  Solution (to), 143–144
  Structural racism (patterns of), 92
  Systematic, 124
  Tomás Blanco, 61 (denial)
  University of Puerto Rico (in
    fraternities), 123
  US-brand (of), 126
  Zenón Cruz, Isabelo (literary
    critic), 36, 96
Ramos de Sánchez Vilella, Jeannette
  (assessing racial discrimination in
  banks), 144–146
Ramos-Perea, Roberto, 37–38
Rios, Palmira Dr., Civil Rights
  Commission, 134
Rivera-Osorio Manuel, "drops of
  experience," 137
  Racial classifications, 138–140,
    buena apariencia (good
    appearance), 140–141
  Spatial discrimination (public
    housing), 141–144
  Testimony (Puerto Rican House
    of Representatives racial
    discrimination investigation), 138
Rivero, Angel (Captain), 16–18,
  160–161, 210
Romero Rosa, Ramón, "drop of
  leadership," 33

borinqueño discourse, 35–36
Federación Libre de Trabajadores
 (FLT), 35
La Miseria (labor union
 newspaper), 33
labor leader anti-racist struggle 34–36

Santurce (San Mateo de Cangrejos),
 62, 77, 112, 115, 172, 184
Schomburg, Arturo Alfonso, 62
Spain 5, 7, 13 (Spanish-American War),
 19, 21, 23, 25, 37, 40, 50, 51, 58,
 64, 71, 81 (Rafael Hernández),
 160, 160, 161, 163, 213
Spanish-American War, 13, 21, 30, 205
 American narrative of the "other,"
 20–22
Spanish citizenship, 7

Tirado Sánchez, Andrés, "drop of
 education," 41–44
 Amílcar Tirado Santiago (son), 167,
 205
 Asociación de Maestros de Puerto Rico
 (Coamo chapter president), 43
 Coamo, Census 1910, 41 and 45,
 census 1920, 42
 Librada Santiago (wife), 42
 Puerto Rican Republican Party (Dr.
 Barbosa), 43
 Puerto Rico Reconstruction
 Administration (PRRA), 43–44
 Report of the Commissioner of
 Education (appears in), 42
 San Juan (moved to), 44
 Teaching as social mobility, 42, 44
 Tuskegee Normal and Industrial
 Institute, 42
Todd, Roberto H., 22, 23
Tufiño, Rafael (artist), 109
Tugwell, Rexford G. (Governor of
 Puerto Rico, 98, 108

U.S Census of Puerto Rico Selected
 Figures (Table I.1), 12
United States Censuses (in Puerto Rico)
 Race and US citizenship (early
 discussions), 31–33
 1910, education/school ages, 40, 44,
 demographics, 41
 1920 (whitening), 42, 167
 1930, 107
 1960 (elimination of the race
 questions), 134–135
 "Report of Porto Rico 1899," 30
 (*see* H.K. Carroll)
University of Puerto Rico (UPR), 86,
 89
 Dr. Martin Luther King, Jr. (speech),
 122
 Forum of 1940, 86–87
 modernization and national
 identity/ Hispanicization, 85–87
 Picón-Salas, Mariano (Venezuela),
 Hispanicization, 87–89, 179
 Racial discrimination, 96, 125, 127

Vizcarrondo, Fortunato, 102

Washington, Booker T. (Tuskegee),
 42, 45, 167, 199, 203–204, 210
Winant, Howard (and Michael Omi),
 3, 5, 83, 91, 122, 157, 172–174,
 186
Whitening (in census of Puerto Rico),
 11, 33 (promotion of), 42, 136

Yauco (municipality), 16
 marriage of Simón Mejil, 18

Zenón Cruz, Isabelo (literary critic)
 Palés Matos's work (critique of),
 60–61
 Racism in fraternities, 96
 U.S. brand or racism, 36

CPSIA information can be obtained
at www.ICGtesting.com
Printed in the USA
BVHW031138271222
654958BV00028B/362